COLLABORATIVE
R&D

National Association of Manufacturers Series

Published titles in this series are:

Pathways to Agility: Mass Customization in Action
by John D. Oleson

Time Out: Using Visible Pull Systems to Drive Process Improvement
by Wayne Smith

COLLABORATIVE R&D

Manufacturing's New Tool

GENE ALLEN
RICK JARMAN

JOHN WILEY & SONS, INC.
New York • Chichester • Weinheim • Brisbane • Singapore • Toronto

This book is printed on acid-free paper. ∞

Copyright © 1999 by Gene Allen and Rick Jarman. All rights reserved.

Published by John Wiley & Sons, Inc.
Published simultaneously in Canada.

This publication is designed to provide accurate and authoritative information in regard
to the subject matter covered. It is sold with the understanding that the publisher is not
engaged in rendering legal, accounting, or other professional services. If legal advice or
other expert assistance is required, the services of a competent professional person
should be sought.

Library of Congress Cataloging-in-Publication Data:
Allen, Gene, 1956–
     Collaborative R&D : manufacturing's new tool / Gene Allen, Rick
Jarman.
          p.   cm.—(National Association of Manufacturers series)
     ISBN 0-471-31994-5 (cloth : alk. paper)
     1. Research, Industrial.   2. Research and development partnership.
I. Jarman, Rick, 1951–   . II. Title. III. Series.
T175.A45   1999
658.5'7—dc21   98-53560
                                                                          CIP

Printed in the United States of America.

10 9 8 7 6 5 4 3 2 1

Contents

Part VI

Appendixes

Acknowledgments

As you read this book, you will see that a collaborators' network of people plays a most important role in the successful outcome of every collaborative project. It is from within these networked resources that the ingredients of knowledge, creativity, influence, and perseverance are brought together for a better result. We've had the good fortune to be able to collaborate with many exceptional individuals, and it's to their credit that we've been able to write this book. All members of a collaborative team bring with them the power and strength of their own network and experience. Within our business and personal networks there are those who are special and most important, those who are the sources of energy, enthusiastic support, and motivation. This book is possible only with these key individuals in our networks, to whom we offer our sincere thanks.

From Gene Allen

Very special thanks go to my loving wife, Kathy, for her understanding, encouragement, and support in the writing of this book and her effort in taking care of our young daughters, Katherine and Rebecca, to enable the book to be written. Ed Stanton of the MacNeal-Schwendler Corporation has been a superb mentor, providing counsel and support, as well as meticulous reviews of the manuscript. It is hard to imagine a more supportive individual as a supervisor. I particularly want to thank my coauthor, Rick

Jarman, whose initiative and interest prompted the writing of this book, and whose perspective has made it that much richer.

From Rick Jarman

My deepest appreciation goes to my family, and most especially my wife Alicia, who keeps my life together with love, support, and sharing of thoughts that enable me to reach out for my goals and dreams. Before partnering and alliances were a part of many business vocabularies, David R. Smith of Eastman Kodak Company understood how collaboration would add to, and not detract from, the value of core competencies. I will always be grateful for his vision and support that have empowered me to make all of this work. My initial efforts to convince Gene Allen to solely author this book only proved once again why he is the true champion of collaboration. Only with his knowledge and experience, which he generously shares could this have been possible.

From Gene and Rick

Lessons learned and generously passed along to shorten the learning cycle are one of the true success measures of collaboration. The following friends and fellow collaborators have been there to contribute those lessons to us and so to this book, and we will always appreciate their support. We hope this book helps in passing on to a greater audience the knowledge they so freely shared with us. Bill Waddell of the National Center for Manufacturing Sciences provided valuable guidance, advice, and input during the drafting of the manuscript, for which we are thankful. Frank Pijar of United Technologies–Pratt & Whitney and Steve Babcock of Boeing-Rocketdyne provided detailed comments in their reviews of the manuscript, which have been incorporated. Their exceptional efforts in review demonstrated their commitment and belief in collaboration. Others who have reviewed and provided beneficial input to sections include Pat Ziarnik of the National Center for Manufacturing Sciences; Bob Carman, Gene Jackson, and Glenn Havskjold of Boeing-Rocketdyne; Pete Sferro and Howard Crabb of Ford Motor Company; Ray Amador and Larry Johnson of the MacNeal-Schwendler Corporation; Larry MacArthur of Accent Logic; Allan Hrncir and John Richardson of Texas Instruments/Raytheon. George Drakeley and Cynthia Gonsalves of the Department of Defense provided an unsolicited review of the chapter on government. Kathy Allen and Richard Cox also provided valuable review.

Introduction

In this book, empirical data and lessons learned in establishing and managing collaborative research and development (R&D) programs have been organized into an easy-to-follow, how-to style. This is to allow you, the reader, the manager, the technology officer, and the student to realize the value and means of collaboration described in this book. However, like other books that provide the secrets of reengineering, or golf or tennis, or the recipes for a perfect sauce, the ultimate return can only be realized by putting these lessons to use in your own applications. As the old story goes: "How do you get to Carnegie Hall?" The answer is, "Practice." You and your technical staff can gain real confidence and efficiency in collaboration only by adopting and applying these techniques in your actual environment. This will likely take some innovation on your part, as there are no fundamental laws for collaboration.

We have, however, provided a map for collaboration, taken from our collective years of experience in creating, promoting, and managing many successful collaborative R&D initiatives over the past decade. It is valuable reading for any business that plans to thrive in a new global economy where all available financial and human assets will need to be leveraged for the greatest return with minimal risk.

Thomas Jefferson continuously reiterated the need to expand the franchise as much as society would allow, while leaving open the possibility for future generations to expand it further. Inscribed in the wall of the Jefferson Memorial: "As the human mind becomes more developed, more enlightened, as new discoveries are made, new truths discovered and manners and opinions change, with the change of circumstances, institutions must advance also to keep pace with the times."

With the advent of the telecommunications and information infrastructure realized in the 1990s, we have come to one of those times in history where we can further expand the franchise to include every human being. The realization of this business expansion requires broader acceptance of collaboration as the preferred means to conduct business.

The ability to collaborate, particularly in new manufacturing technology development, may likely become the corporate competence that could determine which companies survive in next decade. With the existence of an infrastructure that can effectively support collaboration, companies that can effectively collaborate to get new technologies applied sooner have a better chance to prosper.

Understanding how collaboration fits into the Big Picture of our culture can provide the underlying foundation for making decisions that result in successful collaboration. The following is a short explanation of the underlying rationale for collaborative research and development in manufacturing relative to society, as well as the answer to the fundamental philosophical question—"Why collaborate?"

Most of us like to have at least some understanding about why we do what we do—at least how we expect our work to contribute to our own well-being. Most of us are also interested in seeing that our efforts contribute to the well-being of some larger entity or just the common good. In this century we have seen the rise and fall of many cultures built around powerful governments, companies, and social groups that have had at their core the control of information and knowledge. Those of us who have witnessed firsthand the collapse or deterioration of these cultures know how fragile human culture actually is. From this we have gleaned a particular interest in seeing our actions provide some positive results that will produce a better world, and hopefully one with a higher quality of life for future generations. History has tended to repeat itself because people have tended to forget the lessons of past generations over time, and have had to relearn them through experience.

Twentieth-century advancements in information and communication technologies continue to enable more of us to be better informed, effectively share our thoughts, be aware of our collective history, and watch changes in the world in real time. These advancements enable us to reduce the risk of failure and increase the chances of success in our ventures. Our society will continue to be challenged, with our responding actions defining our future civilization. Central to our future existence will be the free flow and sharing of information, ideas, and knowledge. This exchange, once rooted, will put real distributed strength in a world culture that will be long lasting and greater than the sum of its parts.

The ability of any of us to make a significant contribution in today's world requires that we be able to effectively work with other people—to collaborate. Contributing means taking actions that add value to the total. Actions that have the desired positive impact require knowledge about the rationale for and consequences of those actions. Our society today is evolving so quickly and is so complex that no one person has all the knowledge needed to ensure that the best decisions and actions are taken. Indeed, there is often no ultimate best decision or action in many, if not most, situations. In today's information society, we have the ability to at least make informed decisions. Through collaboration with other people who have complementary experience to our own we can make better and more knowledgeable decisions. A major reason to collaborate is to enable us to make the best decisions and take the best actions possible in a given situation.

Warren Bennis and Patricia Ward Biederman in their book *Organizing Genius: The Secrets of Creative Collaboration* (Addison-Wesley, 1997) conducted case studies of six collaborative development efforts that have taken place this century. These efforts included the Manhattan Project's development of the atomic bomb, Walt Disney's development of animation, the Xerox Palo Alto Research Center's development of the personal computer, and the Lockheed Skunk Works' development of high-performance aircraft. The book identifies a number of lessons in common with these collaborative efforts. Among these lessons are the focus and leadership a collaborating group needs to have toward an objective, and the dedication to that focus by all involved. The following rationale represents this type of "religious" commitment some people have to pursuing collaborative development efforts in manufacturing research and development (R&D) and commercialization.

Religious Rationale for Collaborative R&D in Manufacturing

A culture will be stable only if it provides freedom and economic opportunity for its people to have a quality of life acceptable to them. Society breaks down if a large portion of a population lacks opportunity and has unmet needs. The ability to provide economic opportunity to a population has to have as a foundation the ability to generate wealth—to add value through providing a desired product or service. This has been a valuable lesson learned by 20th-century mankind through the experiences of two World Wars and the Cold War—a lesson that has historically always been evident.

Prior to the industrial revolution, the world depended on agriculture as the primary means of generating wealth. The vast majority of mankind was involved in occupations related to agriculture in order to feed the world's population. While everyone still needs to eat, the number of people working in agriculture is less than 2 percent of the population of modern nations. The dawn of the industrial world provided a new means of generating wealth through providing products—products which all of us now supposedly need. The wealth generated through industrial manufacturing of goods and supporting related services is the foundation that enables our society to provide economic opportunity to today's population. If dollar volume of sales is used as a measure of wealth generation, Table I.1 shows the influence the automotive industry has, with the U.S. Big Three auto producers and two oil companies that provide gas for autos making up five of the top ten companies. Wal-Mart is a retailer of manufactured products. General Electric is primarily a producer of manufactured goods. IBM and AT&T are both major manufacturers of information and communications hardware. Only Philip Morris is associated with the agricultural sector that dominated wealth generation in past ages.

The wealth generated by these companies has come from the commercialization of technological innovations generating products such as

TABLE I.1 Top 10 Companies of 1997 by Sales in Billions of Dollars

Company	Sales
1. General Motors	$178
2. Ford	154
3. Exxon	122
4. Wal-Mart	119
5. General Electric	90
6. IBM	79
7. Chrysler	61
8. Mobil	60
9. Philip Morris	56
10. AT&T	53

automobiles, washing machines, telephones, and computers; processes such as the assembly line and improved design-manufacturing processes; and infrastructures that support transportation and communications. The ability to get technology developed and commercialized continues to be a major factor in being able to generate wealth. Our capacity to produce goods is directly determined by the quantity and quality of our human and economic capital. The constantly changing nature of these variables in today's global economy reinforces the importance of strategic alliances and partners, cycle time, and flexible asset utilization.

Collaboration is proving to be a very effective tool in reducing the technology development-commercialization cycle and making the best use of all resources.

It can be argued that:

1. Freedom and economic opportunity are needed to ensure we have a stable society.
2. The generation of wealth is needed to ensure economic opportunity is available to everyone.
3. The ability to generate wealth is determined by the quantity and quality of capital and labor.
4. The variables in our global economy constantly change and drive the need to be flexible with short cycle times and to maintain strategic alliances.

5. Collaborative research and development that leads to the most efficient commercialization of products ensures that society will continue to be able to generate wealth.

These principles are the basis for the conviction held by believers in the process of collaborative development in manufacturing R&D that we are adding value to a system that will help to sustain and ensure the stability and progression of the economic engines that provide the foundation for improving society.

PART I

Collaboration

Collaboration—working together toward a common goal—has led to some of the most productive and successful outcomes in history. When historians look back at the 20th century they are likely to take particular notice of a time period filled with numerous military conflicts, including two World Wars. They will probably conclude that these wars produced significant alliances and collaborative efforts that enabled the allies to push back aggressive political leaders bent on geographical domination. They may also note that many of these relationships did not end with the conflicts which gave them life, but continued in the form of large collaborative organizations where many members could discuss economic, security, and environmental concerns, as well as their respective potential actions.

While the actual successes of these organizations remain inconclusive and are still debated, it can be said that at the very least they have provided the world forums for sharing thoughts through discussion and nonviolent debate. As a result, a world culture of sharing and working together at critical times has contributed to some degree of trust and collaboration. Many other partnerships and alliances both informal and formal have demonstrated significant outcomes and success. The *keiretsus* in Japan are notable, as are many European government-led consortia, as well as numerous product marketing relationships.

Yet, it often remains very difficult to make collaboration work, and get the expected results we want, especially in the business world. A major reason for this lies with the competing priorities we face in making decisions. Competitive instincts, reward systems, antitrust-type laws, and asset valuation standards are just a few of the barriers we encounter when attempting to implement a favorable collaborative business strategy. These barriers can be so ominous that if making collaboration work is not an underlying foundation for the decisions that need to be made, then a collaborative effort will most likely fail. Understanding how collaboration fits into the Big Picture of a culture can provide the underlying foundation for making decisions that result in successful collaboration. The emergence of worldwide collaboration may be the most significant sociological development of the 20th century.

United States Business Perspective

Throughout the 1950s and 1960s the United States enjoyed a superior business climate. While the rest of the world rebuilt its factories and infrastructure from another World War, products from U.S. businesses enjoyed unparalleled success. During this time reinvestment of profits to research and development and infrastructure improvement were easily applied. More than half of all the industrial innovation and growth in the United States can be linked to investments in science and technology since World War II.[1] However, the rest of the world did rebuild, and in many cases used collaborative industrial partnerships and consortia of industry, government, and academia to focus on niches, specific products, industries, and infrastructure capabilities to regain competitiveness.

By the 1970s businesses and industries in the United States were facing competitive pressure from other parts of the world. This pressure reduced product revenues and research and development dollars in these areas at a time when more investment was needed to ensure new quality

---

[1]Coalition for Technology Partnerships, *R&D Is an Investment*, February 25, 1998.

products and more efficient processes. The need for the benefits of collaborative alliances and consortia in the United States became more apparent.

Because a culture existed where it was against the law for businesses
to share strategic information, and fears of antitrust liability were always
present, it took some time for U.S. companies to adopt collaborative
strategies. In 1984 the U.S. government passed the National Cooperative Research Act, which allowed businesses to do joint precompetitive
or preproduct research and development. In addition to the change in
law the government also budgeted R&D dollars to be spent in consortia
where U.S. industry had been hardest hit. Some of these dealing with
manufacturing R&D included:

Organization	Industry
SEMATECH	Advanced semiconductor methods, tools, and materials
National Center for Manufacturing Sciences	Better machine tools, manufacturing processes, and materials
Microelectronics and Computer Technology Corporation	Advanced computers, software, semiconductor packaging

Since that time hundreds of consortia have been formed that have
thousands of member companies. The benefits and successes of some of
these groups have led to other government initiatives such as the Department of Commerce's Advanced Technology Program (ATP), and the
United States Council for Automotive Research (USCAR).

Manufacturing Business Perspective

The totality of knowledge involved in the businesses of making today's
products is beyond the comprehension of the most knowledgeable businesspeople, scientists, and engineers. Still, the generation of wealth con-

tinues to be determined by the application of new manufacturing processes and information technology. Managing this complexity is becoming one of the preeminent manufacturing business problems of the next decade.

From a business perspective, collaboration is proving to be an effective way to reduce the risk of developing and commercializing new technology. Advances in communications and easy access to air travel are part of the infrastructure for business. Collaboration as a means to more quickly realize the business objectives driving manufacturing research and development is a very effective use of this infrastructure.

Benefits

A number of successful collaborative development programs have been established in the 1990s. These programs are, in many ways, predecessors to the way business will likely be conducted in the next decade. The communications and information infrastructure that facilitates collaboration is increasingly more available. Those corporate cultures that take advantage of this technology infrastructure to collaborate will have a significant tool to help them flourish.

Collaboration in manufacturing research and development generates a range of benefits. These include:

- Reducing the risk and cost involved in emerging technology investments.
- Reducing time needed to apply new technologies.
- Gaining exposure to new ideas.
- Gaining recognition and employee satisfaction.
- Developing collaborative team business relationships.
- Creating new businesses and business opportunities.
- Accelerating technology adoption.
- Leveraging collaborative research and development costs.

CHAPTER I

The Manufacturing Business Perspective

The application of emerging technology to manufacturing businesses is, and will continue to be, the principal driver of economic growth. Economists have found that investments in manufacturing technology yield high rates of return to private R&D investment, averaging 20 to 30 percent annual return on investment to firms, and approximately 50 percent to society overall. For some specific products, rates of return have been remarkably high. One study of information technology (IT) found returns are estimated to have exceeded 80 percent per year.[1] These technology advances are in areas that include:

- Computer hardware and software
- Communications
- New materials
- Microelectromechanical technology
- Sensors
- "Bio-everything"

---

[1]National Science Foundation, *NSF FYI-Backgrounder on Economic Impact of R&D*, February 6, 1997.

A challenge to all manufacturing businesses is how to maintain the critical levels of investment needed to effectively develop and adopt constantly evolving technologies. A company's future depends on how it conducts and/or acquires and applies new technology. Effective technology adoption often requires organization and culture changes; this adds to the challenge.

Manufacturing Research and Development

Manufacturing companies conduct research and development to improve:

- **Products.** Physical goods or services the company provides to the market may be revolutionary to the marketplace, or may be incremental improvements to established products. Competitiveness is being increasingly driven by a company's ability to meet, on schedule, customer demands for specific products. Products are expected to be of high quality, safe, and available when desired at low cost. The technologies being developed and applied by manufacturing businesses focus on improving the ability of the company to provide products and related services that meet these expectations.
- **Processes.** Business, manufacturing, design, administrative, contracting, purchasing, and legal processes (enterprise processes) may be modified to more cost-effectively provide product to market. This may involve the establishment of new, revolutionary processes, or incremental improvements to processes in place. For process changes to be considered improvements, they need to improve the productivity of the total enterprise.

The primary objective in conducting research and development is to get the new technologies into practice in a way that a competitive advantage can be provided.

Technology as a Business Base

Many companies have been formed around one fundamental technological breakthrough. In some cases, the company continues to leverage this breakthrough into a viable business for decades or longer. Most companies that have been successful over the long term, however, follow a derivative of the premise set forth by Lou Platt, chief executive officer (CEO) of Hewlett-Packard: A growth company should derive over half of its revenue from products less than two years old. In either case it's the application of new technology that provides the basis for the company.

Several different mechanisms can be used to generate revenue from a company's technology. These mechanisms include:

- Patents and other legal mechanisms, where technology can generate royalties through licenses.
- Secrecy, where technology describing how a product works is kept confidential.
- Complementary sales and services, where technology results in products and/or services.
- Complementary manufacturing facilities and know-how, where technology manifests itself in the manufacturing processes used to make products.
- Lead time to market, where technology application reduces the time to get products to market.

Collaboration in research and development benefits all of these mechanisms, with the obvious exception of secrecy. Secrecy is an effective means for companies to get the most out of a particular technological innovation, but is very limiting in efforts to try to grow and evolve a concept. While collaboration can benefit in providing the technical innovation needed for patents (the Printed Wiring Board program filed four patent disclosures and one patent application), the filing of patents is not a principal objective driving collaboration. The other identified revenue-producing mechanisms for technology—complementary sales, services, facilities, know-how, and lead time to market—are drivers encouraging companies to collaborate in technology research, development, and application.

Many people have believed that the compromise of a company's base technology would jeopardize the existence of the company. In actuality, it is generally the competence of the personnel and processes in place to effectively use the technology that comprise the fundamental corporate competence. The ability of the company's personnel and processes to develop product and process technologies that complement and/or evolve the foundation technology will ensure the company stays in business.

Intangible assets, including intellectual property (IP), account for approximately 74 percent of the $4.6 trillion value of the S&P 500 index corporations.[2] This reveals the impact of IP and other intangible assets in publicly traded companies. As the world's economic growth is largely technology-based, this condition places immense pressure on the protection of IP and corporate security practices. Downsizing and virtual workplace accommodations for the knowledge worker have stimulated the need to access and protect "knowledge contributions." Legal and contracts experts in large manufacturing companies have been well educated and trained in the discipline of protecting their companies' intellectual property, and if to err, to err more on the side of too much protection than not quite enough. To do this, they have built fortresses of fire walls and layers of protection around products and processes and people that come in contact with intellectual property deemed key to the existence of the business. This has been further complicated by the 1996 Economic Espionage Act, which clearly defines trade secrets for the first time as part of U.S. federal law for both domestic and foreign protection as meaning:

> all forms and types of financial, business scientific, technical, economic, or engineering information, including patterns, plans, prototypes, methods, techniques, processes, programs, or codes, whether tangible or intangible, and whether or how stored, compiled, or memorized physically, electronically, graphically, photographically, or in writing which:
>
> 1. A business has taken reasonable efforts to keep secret,
> 2. Derives its value from being secret,
> 3. Is not easily developed by the public, or
> 4. Is not protected by patents or copyrights.

---

[2]Coopers & Lybrand, *Maximizing the Value of Intellectual Property*, 1998.

Market opportunities make it imperative to organize, access, and apply knowledge to new initiatives quickly. This condition makes the ability to team with individuals and other knowledge groups an essential competitive competency. While companies must continue to protect and defend their knowledge based assets that have competitive value, they must also find ways to determine which information is core and not critical, so that value adding operations can be performed. Corporations must understand that intellectual property management includes the creation, protection, valuation, and commercial application of new technology. Only the most forward thinking corporations have begun to consider IP management a part of their business strategy. IP is typically not considered a responsibility of the technology or business worker. It is preemptively and increasingly a legal function, thereby excluding intellectual property rights (IPR) from the creative & innovative processes in large corporations. Complex business strategies which include collaborative relationships will demand that business, technical, and legal personnel be more closely aligned in order to meet the demands of shorter times to market, and greater return on intellectual property assets.

Much of the wealth created in the information age will be intellectual property, not capital, created, manipulated, and managed by knowledge workers. The knowledge-intensive enterprise can find opportunities for competitive advantage in the process of converting information to knowledge. Market opportunities make it imperative to organize, access, and apply knowledge to new initiatives quickly. This condition makes the ability to team with individuals and other knowledge groups an essential competitive competency.

The Collaboration Challenge

Collaboration in the conduct of research and development in manufacturing technology is a means for reducing risk and ensuring that the business succeeds. There have been many examples of successful collaboration through informal and formal partnerships and alliances, such as the *keiretsus* in Japan and numerous product marketing relationships.

However, most of the incentive systems in society and the workplace fail to encourage collaboration. Rewards, recognition, and compensation are provided for individual achievement, which often discourages collaboration. In a recent interview for the *Wall Street Journal*, Christopher Galvin, chief executive of Motorola, Inc., concluded that "Motorola traditionally has been unable to collaborate successfully inside or outside of the company." He went on to attribute his comments to an "arrogant and dogmatic" attitude and to point to a culture of "warring tribes"—the teams sectors that have traditionally fought each other for funding and support from the corporation. The article went on to say that this approach once had been very effective for selecting the best places to invest resources but now had become counterproductive. These tribes often repeated each other's mistakes and impeded the ability to work with outside partners and collaborators. He decreed an end to the warring tribes in the middle of 1997.

These comments could have honestly been repeated by many CEOs in companies both large and small, successful or not, well-recognized firms and those yet to have their day. Mr. Galvin deserves a lot of credit for recognizing these cultural problems in his company, which has previously frustrated potential collaborators who might have made contributions to Motorola. His leadership and commitment from the top is vital to any chance for changing attitudes and culture. However, if this thinking is not embedded into a process that the whole infrastructure recognizes, it will remain frustrating for the believers, and will ultimately legitimize certain "tribes" destined to look only inward.

During the past 40 years it has been documented that U.S. manufacturing companies have spent approximately 80 percent of R&D dollars on product development and 20 percent on process improvement. In other parts of the world where collaboration appears to come somewhat easier the picture is different. In Japan these percentages were just about the opposite and in Europe the percentages have been closer to 50/50.

It seems fair to conclude that the manufacturing engineers in the United States who find collaboration so hard to accept are in fact very threatened by the thought of trying it. In the internal fight for resources, product wins and process gets less almost every time. Yet the direction of markets is toward mass customization, which is accomplished by process improvement, versus the traditional product focus resulting from mass production processes. Process people rarely get feedback from the final customer, so much of their self-worth is tied to their technical achievement and hopefully the recognition by senior management of the value of their work. When we are faced with new metrics for continuous improvement in cycle time and the leverage of all resources for the greatest return on assets, we ask these process improvement engineers with more at risk to share their valuable expertise with others. The companies that make this work are those where senior management demonstrates an ongoing appreciation as to the value of the manufacturing processes to the company.

The Technology Development Process

Improving the way a company adopts new technology requires an understanding of the Technology Development Process. Figure 1.1 shows a generalized view of the technology research, development, and commer-

BASIC RESEARCH	DEVELOPMENT	COMMERCIALIZATION		
		CHASM	NICHE	GENERAL MARKET
THEORIES CONCEIVED, VALIDATED, EVOLVED	PRACTICAL APPLICATIONS OF THEORIES DEMONSTRATED	MARKET EXISTENCE?	CUSTOM APPLICATIONS	GENERAL APPLICATIONS

FIGURE 1.1   The Technology Development Process

cialization process. This process is referred to in the rest of this book as the Technology Development Process.

The Basic Research stage consists of establishing an understanding of how nature works through theories, and then validating those theories through observation or experimentation.

The Development stage consists of envisioning how applications of validated theories might provide benefit and developing a prototype or demonstration to realize the vision.

The Commercialization process starts with the Chasm stage of market evaluation. Culture, public perception, and infrastructure support all impact the determination as to whether a market exists or can be created for prototyped technology applications. The chasm has not only been identified by Geoffrey Moore,[3] but David Cauffman has stated that "we have a serious problem in that there is a funding gap between ideas once they have been invented, but before they can be demonstrated. This is sometimes called the 'valley of death' by people seeking funding."[4]

The Niche stage often helps get products over the chasm through providing customized applications of technology to a select group of customers.

The General Market stage is reached when a significant portion of the population use technology products.

Barton Krawetz, director of Idaho National Engineering and Environmental Laboratory (INEEL), has said, "The connection between research and development and the quality of human life has to be described better to the public. We talk about radar and computer games and robots, but we don't talk about the intellectual excitement that preceded them."[5] It takes decades for new technologies to result in commercial products that provide value in society, as shown in Table 1.1. The Technology Development Process is complex, influenced by culture,

---

[3]Geoffrey Moore, *Crossing the Chasm*, HarperBusiness, 1995.

[4]David Cauffman, INEEL, Basic Research White Paper, *Defining Our Path to the Future*, *R&D* Magazine, 1997.

[5]Barton Krawetz, INEEL, Basic Research White Paper, *Defining Our Path to the Future*, *R&D* Magazine, 1997.

TABLE 1.1 Technology Commercialization Time

Product	Invention First Demonstrated	General Commercial Use*
Air-conditioning	1902	1955
Airplane	1903	1954
Automobile	1876	1924
Camera	1840	1920
Computer	1946	1984
Copier	1938	1978
Fax	1843	1987
Penicillin	1928	1944
Plastic	1907	1935
Radio	1895	1925
Telephone	1888	1937
Television	1907	1956
Vacuum cleaner	1907	1923

*Approximate date that the technology was readily accessible to the average person.

knowledge, and infrastructure. Yet, the ability to get new technology to market fast is a prime factor in ensuring success, and even survival, in companies today, whether it is in integrating technology into a company's products or incorporating technology into a company's processes to better produce products. The Technology Development Process takes time, requires a lot of financial and human resources, and has unpredictable risk.

Neal Lane, director of the National Science Foundation, points out:

> The words basic and applied really span a whole continuum—from the most exploratory kinds of research to focused direct research where you are trying to make a process slightly better, or make a circuit work faster."[6]

[6]Neal Lane, National Science Foundation, Basic Research White Paper, *Defining Our Path to the Future*, R&D Magazine, 1997.

New Technology Risk

There is considerable corporate risk involved with a company's technology strategy. A company's future is determined by where and how it invests in research and development. There is no certainty that the development of a particular technology will work. We don't know what we don't know. Dr. Glenn Havskjold of Boeing-Rocketdyne indicates that 70 percent of the problems fixed on the Space Shuttle main engine were failure modes unknown at the time of initial design (i.e., unknown unknowns). The only way we can find out if a technology will benefit a company is to select a research path and pursue it. As much as this path diverts some of the best talent in the company in a direction that does not generate a high payback for the company, the company is at risk. It should also be recognized that a plan not to conduct research and development or acquire and apply technology is the highest-risk plan for a business.

Companies have a limited amount of resources consisting of (1) personnel with varying types of expertise, (2) finances, and (3) established infrastructure consisting of facilities and process machinery. How well a company deploys its key personnel and finances with respect to its established infrastructure determines its success. Some percentage of the company's resources needs to be focused on the Technology Development Process as the application of new technology is needed for a company's survival. The Timing as to how and where a company's personnel and financial resources are applied to the Technology Development Process fixes a company's corporate strategy and determines its future. Significant risk is involved in these decisions.

Companies need to decide what technologies are in their best interest to buy, and what they should develop. In companies that have the capability to do technology development, the development conducted drives the future of the company. If the personnel resources developing future products, and more importantly processes, are directed toward technologies which are not adopted by the market or do not work, the consequences can be disastrous. In the mid-1980s IBM made huge investments in mainframe computer architectures and operating systems. The market preferred to adopt personal computers and their operating systems; between 20,000 and 30,000 jobs were lost as a result. General

Motors attempted to automate the company by using robots in the early 1980s. The failure to effectively adopt this technology nearly destroyed the U.S. robotics industry. The effective adoption of robotic automation by Japanese automotive companies during the same period provided the Japanese with a competitive advantage. Resources in smaller companies are more limited, making technology investment decisions even more critical. Once it has been determined what technologies the company will pursue with its own research and development, the company needs to ensure it gets a future return from the R&D it conducts.

One aspect of timing is whether the necessary technology support infrastructure is in place to operate, maintain, and support new technology products. Roads had to be improved and a gas and service station network had to be established to support broad use of automobiles. Airports had to be created and radar developed before safe commercial flight was established. Power lines had to be run before we were able to provide electricity to everyone. Technologies lacking an infrastructure include the dirigible, nuclear power (waste disposal), and space access. This does not mean that we will not see these infrastructures develop in the next century. (Nuclear fission is environmentally safer than burning carbon and can be designed to be fail-safe. The utilization of nuclear fusion, if it can be developed, is even more promising as a safe, clean, and inexhaustible power source. Commercial interest in space is beginning to take off with hundreds of commercial low earth-orbit satellite launches planned.) The time lag in the adoption of these technologies shows the importance of infrastructure support in technology commercialization. In addition, it was not that long ago that people did not buy or use products that they could not understand and, if they had to, fix themselves. This was because the supporting infrastructures were not sufficient to provide the services needed. Now we depend on the supporting infrastructure.

Another aspect of timing is market acceptance. Companies that are ahead of their time have a hard time getting enough of a market to stay in business. Eastman Kodak introduced the Super 8 video recorder tape format during the period when VHS and Beta were competing for the home video market. Super 8 sales did not grow enough for Kodak to continue supporting the product. After VHS won the market for home videos, it came out with the VHS-C format for video recorder tapes, which was essentially the same as Kodak's Super 8. VHS-C sales took off. Kodak may have been ahead of the market with the Super 8 technology.

Companies that become complacent with their market share can see it drop quickly when another company is able to apply technology to produce a better product and often provide it more cost-effectively. This was the case with Bucyrus Erie, the dominant manufacturer of power shovels in the 1960s. Bucyrus's view of the market was that the market wanted ever bigger shovels that could hold more dirt per scoop. Komatsu recognized that the market really wanted reliable fast, flexible earth-moving shovels—it was the rate of earth moving, not the amount per shovel that was important—and quickly stole the market by applying new technology to design and build shovels the market preferred. Bucyrus Erie closed its Erie plant in 1983.

The cost of commercializing new technologies is generally between 10 and 100 times the cost of developing and demonstrating the technology. The process for making aluminum was so costly that the first aluminum sold at more than the equivalent amount that platinum costs today. When the market demand for aluminum grew to the point of being able to offset the cost of establishing the infrastructure for making it, the price went down. Product development needs to be complete enough to ensure that products are sufficiently robust to endure all kinds of potential use scenarios they might encounter in all kinds of use and misuse. This has historically been accomplished through testing designs until they fail, modifying the design, and testing it again. The more test-failure-fix cycles the product goes through before it reaches the market, the more expensive the product has to be to cover its development costs. Figure 1.2 shows the cost of a rocket engine from initial design to commercial availability. Costs are in billions of dollars and the time is in years. New car models follow a similar commercialization cost profile.

The Figure 1.2 development costs represent only incremental technology improvements to products that have an already established support infrastructure. New technologies such as additive product fabrication processes, where material is formed into the final desired product as the material is processed, do not have the supporting infrastructures available. These technologies include free-form fabrication techniques and laser metal deposition. While these processes may ultimately be more cost-effective as they are more environmentally benign, their present costs are prohibitive because, like the first aluminum, they do not have a supporting infrastructure in place.

The ability to reduce the timing risk and costs of commercializing

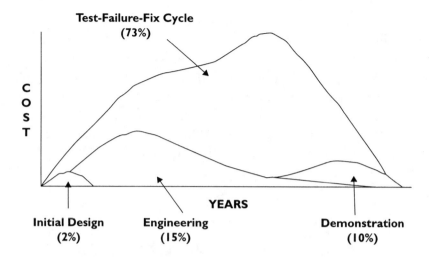

FIGURE 1.2 Development Cost to Get to First Production

new technologies, as well as assure some level of supporting infrastructure, becomes the key characteristic in determining a company's ability to produce goods in this very competitive global economy. More and more, this Technology Development Process requires collaboration, either formal or informal. Shortening the Technology Development Process will result in competitive advantage.

Efficient, formal collaboration in the Technology Development Process has evolved as the most effective means (outside of massive government subsidies directed in wartime economies) to reduce both the risk and cost associated with researching and developing next-generation technologies that will ensure future markets. Efficient, formal collaboration is accomplished by integrating representatives of the different stages of the Technology Development Process (academia or research institutes for research, companies in the business of developing and providing technology, and end users of technology) into a collaborative development effort, and establishing collaborative processes that reduce the Technology Development Process cycle time and reduce risk.

The structure of collaborative development programs should provide a natural commercialization path for the technology being developed. Technology user companies frequently establish business relationships with the technology developer/supplier companies involved with them in collaborative development programs. This benefits the user company, providing a commercialization path that reduces the cost of maintaining and supporting the technology once developed. Most large companies have focused down to their core competencies, and would prefer to buy the technologies they use from a third party that has the business of maintaining and supporting the technology, keeping them current with the rapidly evolving telecommunications and computing infrastructures.

The Evolving (or Exploding) Information Infrastructure

Informal collaboration has always been needed in the Technology Development Process, and has taken place through people talking to one another and sharing ideas and experiences. Informal collaboration can be defined as the collaboration that takes place without a formal agreement or contract between individuals or companies. The recent dramatic changes in information and communications technologies enable much more informal collaboration. One could argue that it was this informal collaboration, fueled by evermore readily available information on how the rest of the world worked, that resulted in the fall of the Soviet Bloc in Eastern Europe. While informal collaboration is a natural outcome of the world's information infrastructure, today it is generally not efficient enough to foster meeting business objectives through collaboration. In the future, the use of informal collaboration to meet business objectives may become more readily accepted as business cultures evolve. Rocketdyne and Fiat have informally collaborated to their mutual benefit on the development of laser and machining technologies. This resulted from the mutual respect each organization had for the other, the reputation of their respective work (Fiat in lasers and Rocketdyne in particular machining applications used for rocket engines), and companies pursuing markets that are noncompetitive.

Formal collaboration efforts are established to try to improve the efficiency of collaboration; they have often been difficult to establish due to differences in culture and understanding among various participants. Formal collaboration requires a high degree of trust among participants to work. Francis Fukuyama in his book *Trust: The New Foundations of Global Prosperity* (Free Press, 1995) identifies trust as the principal difference between societies and their ability to progress to an improved quality of life.

A society's industry has to remain globally competitive to establish or maintain a high quality of life. To be competitive, corporations need to become flexible enough to rapidly design and manufacture products around the world to meet varying regional market demands. At the same time, corporations are not able to maintain full, vertically integrated product development and production capabilities while reducing the cost of their products. The emergence of more capable information and communication technologies available through the Internet is enabling the development of enterprise-wide technologies that can be used to improve the design and manufacture of products.

Today's information infrastructure is enabling formal collaboration among individuals representing all aspects of the Technology Development Process from all around the world. Formal collaboration is being facilitated by the continually progressing information infrastructure and new efficient and accessible tools. As formal collaboration efforts continue to demonstrate their effectiveness in getting new technologies commercialized, the information age is making formal collaboration the process of choice.

CHAPTER 2

Benefits of
Collaboration

Collaboration in manufacturing research and development generates a range of benefits. These include:

- Reducing the financial exposure and risk that the technology the company is committing to will not work or directly benefit the company.
- Reducing the time it takes to get new technologies applied in a company's processes.
- Exposing company personnel to new ideas and cultures.
- Broadening the recognition an individual or organization gets for good work.
- Providing a means for developing constructive business relationships.
- Providing a means for creating new businesses.
- Accelerating the adoption of technology in society.
- Ultimately generating revenue.
- Cost sharing/leverage.

Benefits are usually obtained in a shorter period of time if the participating organizations choose to collaborate in areas that are closely aligned to work they have in progress, or have planned. Individually, each participant needs to be selfish in ensuring that collaboration meets its needs, as opposed to working on projects that while interesting and highly leveraged are not aligned with its plans and do not have a defined commercialization path.

Reducing Risk

As described in Chapter 1, a company's research and development plan has some amount of risk. Collaboration is an effective means of reducing this risk in the Technology Development Process—in making the way over the chasm sometimes referred to as the valley of death. Having a number of companies working on the development of a common technology reduces the financial risk involved in getting cost-effective, commercially available technology products. Collaboration will more likely lead to the larger commercial acceptance of a technology with supporting infrastructure, leading to reduced costs.[1]

A company with good, world-class internal direction for its research and development portfolio may get 85 percent of its technology development commitments generating useful applications for the company. It should be recognized that technology decisions will be made that do not lead to the desired result. Business decisions need to be made to terminate or refocus research that is not heading toward desired results, with lessons learned from the research well understood and applied to complementary efforts. This can be difficult as people become attached to their efforts.

Collaboration enables more experts to be involved in research and development from a number of different company and organization perspectives. This provides more information when establishing a program and can raise the percentage of research and development generating improvements in company processes and products to 95 percent or better. Simply stated, by being able to start with more information, a re-

---

[1]Dr. Bob Carman, October 1, 1998, dinner with authors.

search program can be established that will have a higher probability of success. Similarly, when conducting a research program, it is much more valuable to have input from a number of different knowledgeable perspectives as the program progresses. As foreign competitors have been able to speed up the commercialization process, and survive and grow in an era of shorter product, process, and service life cycles, industry-university-government partnerships have become critically important. These partnerships provide a way to speed up the research commercialization process in the United States, and help ensure that more of the output of U.S. universities can be commercialized.[2]

A good example in which a collaborative research and development program reduced the risk involved in selecting what technology to develop was in the Printed Wiring Board (PWB) program sponsored by the National Institute of Standards and Technology (NIST) Advanced Technology Program (ATP) and coordinated through the National Center for Manufacturing Sciences (NCMS). The PWB program is described in Appendix A. In this program Texas Instruments, AT&T, Digital Equipment Corporation, Hamilton Standard, Allied Signal, Hughes Electronics, IBM, and Sandia National Laboratories focused their research on developing the capability to enable them to mount the next generation semiconductor chips they produced into the electronic components they sold to their customers. By focusing their development efforts through collaboration in four general areas (materials, surface finish, imaging, and product), the PWB program has been credited with saving the PWB industry in the United States.[3] The equal participation by all of the parties enabled the team to focus development on facts and experience based on empirical evidence rather than corporate biases stemming from past company background. This resulted in redirecting one of the main research focus areas initially proposed in the program after the team recognized that the research topic would have low impact relative to improving PWBs. The group was able to collectively reprioritize its development efforts. As one member of the Steering Committee established to manage the program stated: "There is better synergy when

---

[2]Office of Science and Technology Policy, *International Plans, Policies, and Investments in Science and Technology*, April 1997, p. 2.
[3]John Decaire, president of NCMS, annual Technical Conference, May 12, 1997.

a management team directs the research rather than one company taking the lead. Members of the Steering Committee vote on membership changes, capital expenditures, licensing issues, patent disclosures, and the like. As a result of this type of involvement, there are high-level champions in all member companies rather than in only one."[4]

In addition to reducing technology risk, collaboration also reduces the market risk connected with commercializing the results of research and development programs. Having companies involved from a number of different industries that will be end users of the technology being developed ensures that there is a generic market input into the program development. This helps assure a receptive market for the technologies emerging from the program within the end-user companies. Technology development companies benefit in getting feedback from users on next product generation development needs, reducing risk and helping them get the technology to the market faster. In addition, the end users participating in collaborative development generally have more resources to bring to bear in the development effort.

The Rapid Response Manufacturing (RRM) program Analysis Advisor Project is a good example of the ability of a company that develops and supplies technology products to the market to work with end users to reduce market risk involved in development. The RRM program is described in Appendix B. The MacNeal-Schwendler Corporation (MSC) was the "technology supplier" company in the project. MSC is a provider of software used by engineers to assist them in analyzing product designs represented through a computer. The "end users" in the project were two divisions of General Motors Delphi, Eastman Kodak, and Pratt & Whitney. The objective of the Analysis Advisor Project was to develop a software package to assist the casual user of analysis software tools in performing first-order engineering analysis. The project was successfully completed with the MSC developers working closely with the end users in defining the development project, and in conducting the development (described in Chapters 16 and 17). The results have been a project that extends the use of technology across more personnel at end-user sites, and a commercial MSC product that is generating revenue.

---

[4]Albert N. Link, *Advanced Technology Program Case Study: Early Stage Impacts of the Printed Wiring Board Research Joint Venture, Assessed at Project End*, November 1997.

Technology Application Lead Time

Collaboration can reduce the time it takes to get developing and recently developed technologies into a company's production environment. It provides a broader and quicker validation of the technology.[5] This is the principal objective companies have for conducting research, and a major reason original equipment manufacturer (OEM) production centers should be involved in collaborative research and development programs. The production centers not only establish desired technology objectives, but their involvement in conducting the technology development enables them to better integrate the technology into their processes and benefit from their investment.

The RRM Fan Exit Guide Vane Project provides a good example of how the lead time needed to integrate a new technology into a production application can be reduced. Pratt & Whitney established an RRM project based on requirements from its Rocky Hill, Connecticut, production facility. This plant made composite parts for commercial jet engines, and was competing with other engine designs that had parts made out of metal. The cost of the composite parts and the time needed to develop new designs were competitive barriers faced by the Rocky Hill facility.

The fan exit guide vane, a composite blade in the engine that guided exhaust gases leaving the jet engine, was one of the key parts in the engine production process. The fan exit guide vane was identified as a bottleneck in the product design-manufacture process when a new engine design was needed to meet Boeing's new production schedule for its 777. A new fan exit guide vane was needed in two months.

The traditional time needed just to design and build the tooling

[5]Dr. Bob Carman, October 1, 1998, dinner with authors.

needed for the fan exit guide vane was 15 weeks. (The tooling is the metal forms used to mold and cure the composite materials.) The process being used was a manual process done by a third party. The process not only took a significant amount of time, but part quality varied from one toolmaker to another. Pratt & Whitney was at risk that it might not be able to meet the Boeing production schedule.

One of the technology suppliers brought into the RRM program by General Motors was ICAD. ICAD software provides a means to capture the knowledge behind a product design. (The company later changed its name to Concentra, and in 1998 spun off Knowledge Technology International to provide ICAD software to the market.) An RRM project was established to see if the knowledge behind the design rationale used in the design-manufacture process for the fan exit guide vane tooling could be captured. It was hoped that the ability to capture and use this design knowledge could reduce the time needed to design and make the tooling. The project demonstrated that ICAD could be used to capture the design rationale for the fan exit guide vane. The knowledge captured in the ICAD software enabled use of a compression molding process which was able to remove the variability in product quality. The tooling could be machined right from the computer model. Personnel working on the design process were able to react to engineering changes as they came up, as opposed to avoiding them. With the new tooling design process, Pratt & Whitney was able to design and build the tooling in 10 days. The reduction in the design-manufacture time for the composite fan exit guide vane assembly tooling enabled the Boeing 777 engine production requirement to be met. Plant production personnel relayed to the RRM Steering Committee in a meeting at the plant that the application of the results of this project had prevented United Technologies from closing the Rocky Hill production plant at that time.

The results of this RRM project were relayed within Pratt & Whitney to other fan exit guide vane designs on other engines and to the other RRM consortia members. Ford leveraged the process in another RRM project (involving air conditioner hose design), which was so successful that Ford initiated an internal program to see if knowledge could be captured, stored, and used to design and build a full automobile.

Information Exchange

The collaborative working environment provides exposure to alternative ideas and business cultures. The exchange of information promoted in this environment provides significant value to the participating companies. Experts from different user companies and technology development companies have the opportunity to exchange views from different, but highly respected, experience bases. It provides a mechanism for conducting self-benchmarking of your company against others. A company can better rank its efforts with respect to industry. If three other companies independently came to the same decision relative to a particular technology, there must be some good reason.[6]

One example is in generic research conducted by one company being readily shared among the other participants. Once one company breaks the ice, the other companies on the team follow its lead. This prevents other companies from needing to duplicate similar research. In the Printed Wiring Board (PWB) program, Digital Equipment Corporation readily shared information it had developed involving PWB chemical coating processes with the rest of the participants, Texas Instruments shared its background information on flexible PWB manufacturing processes, AT&T shared its experience in mass production while touring the team through its facilities, and the list goes on. The decision of what technologies a company needs to develop versus what technologies a company would be better off buying is complex. Simple sharing of experiences between companies reduces the duplication of the effort needed to evaluate new technologies. Research savings realized by the PWB joint venture through sharing information and avoiding duplication of effort amounted to an estimated 156 work years, worth about $24.7 million.[7]

More significant than exchanging information on common research topics is the synergy that can be obtained in changing the company's business culture. At present Ford Motor Company is pursuing such an evolution in its business through the application of Direct Engineer-

---

[6]Ibid.
[7]Link, *Advanced Technology Program Case Study*, p. 23.

ing[SM].[8] Direct Engineering[SM] is an initiative to create and capture knowledge and then establish the ability to use that knowledge through a "knowledge management organization." The vision is to have "a single engineer who develops a completely defined product," which can be done by using knowledge bases. Building the structure to integrate Direct Engineering[SM] into Ford's product development work flow requires changes in individual attitudes, changes in the Ford culture (through training), continuous technology development, and, most importantly, implementation. Other companies are pursuing technology development initiatives that are similar to and complementary with Direct Engineering[SM]. Direct Engineering[SM] is used as a description to encompass the inclusion of these efforts outside Ford as well as the Ford Direct Engineering[SM] initiative.

Several projects completed in the Rapid Response Manufacturing program (Appendix B) validated the benefits available through Direct Engineering[SM], which were shared with the rest of the Rapid Response Manufacturing program participants. The success of the RRM project applying ICAD software to the air conditioner hose design (previously mentioned) was a significant factor in the establishment of Ford's present Direct Engineering[SM] initiative. The initiative is testing Direct Engineering[SM] to determine if this process can scale within the company and be applied to meet the Ford Product Development System goal of reducing the car development cycle from 60 months to 24 months.

The Technologies for Enterprise Wide-Engineering (TEWE) program (Appendix C) proposed to extend Direct Engineering through working with companies that represent the first-tier supply bases of Ford (as well as Boeing, General Motors, and Kodak), and through technology development focused on establishing a generic, interactive knowledge base accessible through the Internet.

Ford's collaboration with Boeing, General Motors, and Kodak provides a group of credible corporations sufficient enough to impact the business culture in society. As the benefits of Direct Engineering[SM] are demonstrated through technology development pilot projects, this will provide the energy needed to drive change in the corporate business culture. At some point a sufficient number of Direct Engineering[SM] benefits

---

[8]Direct Engineering[SM] is a Service Mark of Ford Motor Co. All rights reserved.

will be demonstrated that the momentum they generate will drive the business cultures of the partners to change. The rest of the world's business base will most likely follow, as Direct Engineering[SM] has the potential to impact manufacturing to the same extent as the assembly line did. The information exchange among a collection of companies can drive cultural change.

Participation in a collaborative development program is also a much more effective means for benchmarking than the traditional method of contracting to an outside consultant. The key people in the company can find out where they are relative to other companies through firsthand discussions, rather than having to read a report. This can provide valuable insight on where the company needs to invest in technology development and application to ensure that it stays competitive.

Recognition

Everyone and every organization likes to be associated with success. Recognition is not only beneficial to the companies that participate in a successful collaborative development effort, but is a principal value to a government agency, university, or facilitator. To a government agency, collaboration means the government is cost sharing the program through an agreement that is something other than a contract or grant.

The recognition for a government agency, in being able to initiate and leverage government funds through a successful collaborative development program, shows that the agency is doing a good job investing the taxpayers' money. This helps ensure future funding for the agency. The Defense Advanced Research Projects Agency (DARPA) has a highly regarded reputation for conducting research, having a long and successful track record of successful research and development; the Internet and Saturn V rocket are just two of the many successes in DARPA's history. DARPA's most significant collaborative development program has been SEMATECH, a program in which DARPA worked with the U.S. semiconductor industry to ensure that the United States maintained a capability to fabricate the chips needed to process information in computers.

The threatened loss of this capability would have jeopardized the leading capability in the Department of Defense to process information. SEMATECH is largely credited with saving the U.S semiconductor industry through its focus on developing the machine tools needed to fabricate silicon chips.

DARPA is a mission-driven agency coordinating research needed to ensure that the U.S. Department of Defense maintains the most advanced defense capabilities in the world. Most government agencies are driven toward a mission mandated by Congress. The National Aeronautics and Space Administration (NASA) and the Department of Energy (DOE) are mission-driven in their research, as is the Department of Defense (DOD). The Advanced Technology Program (ATP) at the National Institute of Standards and Technology (NIST), however, is mandated to "assist U.S. businesses to improve their competitive position and promote U.S. economic growth by accelerating the development of a variety of pre-competitive generic technologies by means of grants and cooperative agreements."[9] The ATP has benefited from the success of the PWB, RRM, and numerous other programs it has selected for cofunding.

Recognition for an organization that facilitates collaboration demonstrates the capability that the organization can establish and manage successful collaborative development programs. The National Center for Manufacturing Sciences (NCMS) and Consortium for Advanced Manufacturing—International (CAM-I) are organizations that depend on their ability to successfully establish collaborative research and development programs for their member companies. The recognition that results from the success of those programs attracts companies interested in future collaborative development efforts and assists in getting those efforts funded from industry and/or government.

University participation with industry in collaborative research and development enhances the institution's reputation. This, in turn, attracts students and faculty with interest in the subject area being recognized. Funding from industry or government can also be directed toward those institutions. The Massachusetts Institute of Technology's Leaders for Manufacturing program is one example of industry working with academia.

---

[9]Federal Register, July 24, 1990.

Recognition is also valuable for the internal research and development organizations within large manufacturing companies. Internal recognition for getting research applied to production processes or integrated into a product helps ensure future corporate funding for a company's Research and Development Center.

Teams also gain recognition across companies for their roles in collaborative development programs. A team led by Dave Bremmer of the MacNeal-Schwendler Corporation was recognized by customers in Boeing for their work on the Agile Infrastructure for Manufactured Systems program Simple Low-Cost Innovative Engine Project (Appendix D) and by customers at General Motors, Pratt & Whitney, and Eastman Kodak for their work on the Rapid Response Manufacturing program Analysis Advisor Project.

Business Relationships

Collaboration in research and development efforts leads to relationships that promote additional business between participants. These relationships are established between individuals responsible for managing and/or conducting development. This type of business relationship is generally difficult to establish through a company's sales and marketing force. Individuals in those organizations have incentives and time frames that are not always compatible with collaborative development programs.

There are a number of mutually beneficial relationships that can evolve from collaborative development programs. These include relationships between:

- The various technology user companies and technology developer/ supplier companies.
- Private sector companies and government agencies.
- Private sector companies and academia.
- Private sector companies and industry consortia.
- Industry consortia and government agencies.

The business relationships that can develop between the partners in a collaborative development program become based on the credibility and trust established between the individuals working together toward common goals. Once established, these relationships lead to an assortment of benefits among the participating companies. The benefits stemming from these relationships can lead to additional business ventures between companies, product sales between companies, and even strategic partnerships.

A few examples of the many benefits that have resulted from the business relationships established through collaborative development programs include:

- Establishment of the Robust Design Computational System program between Ford, Rocketdyne, and the MacNeal-Schwendler Corporation (Appendix E).
- ICAD, a principal provider of knowledge-based engineering software, expanded its number of customers from General Motors and Pratt & Whitney to all of the end user companies involved in the Rapid Response Manufacturing program.
- The MacNeal-Schwendler Corporation enhanced its relationships with Lockheed Martin and Boeing as a result of their participation and execution in International Standards Organization (ISO) Standard for the Exchange of Product Model Data (STEP) pilot projects sponsored by PDES, Inc. (Appendix F).
- Private business relationships between Eastman Kodak and Texas Instruments.

Collaborative development programs, once established and effectively operating, provide a neutral environment in which relationships can be established among the participating individuals—relationships that drive business. More on this in Chapter 12.

Business Creation

Successful collaboration can result in the formation of new companies. As new technologies are developed, businesses are established to support and maintain those technologies. Some examples of businesses resulting from collaborative development programs include:

- Conductor Analysis Technologies Inc. is a company spun off out of the Printed Wiring Board program.
- Nexprise is a company spun off from the Lockheed Martin Corporation to commercialize development from the Agile Infrastructure for Manufactured Systems program.
- MacNeal-Schwendler Corporation (MSC), the world's largest mechanical computer-aided engineering software company, developed its flagship product on a NASA-funded collaborative development of the NASTRAN structural analysis code involving Computer Sciences Corporation, the Martin Company, and MSC in 1969.

Technology Commercialization

The most significant benefit of collaborative R&D programs is their ability to more efficiently focus R&D to rapidly get the new technology applied in industry—reducing the time and cost of the Technology Development Process. The following collaborative R&D commercialization strategy has evolved over the past seven years. Two efforts that exemplify the implimentation of this strategy are:

- The experience in commercializing the standards for software data exchange from Product Data Management (PDM) systems resulting from work done through the Rapid Response Manufacturing program's Interoperability Services Working Group.
- The commercialization of new robust design capabilities coming from the Robust Design Computational System program.

COMMERCIALIZATION STRATEGY

The strategy for moving technologies developed under collaborative R&D programs into commercial applications is captured through the composition of the companies participating in a program, technology end users working with technology suppliers. Commercialization of demonstrated technologies takes place through the technology suppliers, and market development takes place through conducting application pilots with the major end users in the program. Focusing development through enterprise applications that have real business drivers helps ensure that the technology developed is quickly evaluated and, if successful in showing business benefit, will have a higher probability of being commercialized by the participating technology suppliers.

The principal interest major end users of a technology have in participating is in seeing that any technology development showing benefit becomes commercialized. The business interests in these major companies is to produce better planes, cars, consumer goods, and so on, and not to maintain and support information technologies. While a particular technology development may hold the promise of providing enabling technologies that will improve an end user's competitiveness, they would much rather buy the technologies from companies that make a business of developing, maintaining, and supplying technologies. Assisting in the development of the technologies provides them the opportunity to influence development and to integrate the technologies into their corporate cultures faster than the competition.

The principal objective of technology supplier companies in participating in collaborative R&D programs is to be able to reduce the market risk involved in developing next-generation technologies. A collaborative R&D program provides the technology supplier companies the opportunity to work with a major representation of their markets in developing next-generation technologies. Demonstrating these technology developments through pilots in the enterprises of large end users enables the technology supplier companies to better focus the internal resources they have committed to commercialization. The pilots assist in identifying what further technology development needs to take place to provide a robust commercial product. Technology suppliers generally do not have the opportunity to work with multi-industry end users in identifying and piloting next-generation development. This is atypical when compared to the typical commercialization approach in industry.

Figure 2.1 depicts how a collaborative R&D program can realize the business objectives of the participating companies, and how the resulting technology can be commercialized. The objective for commercialization,

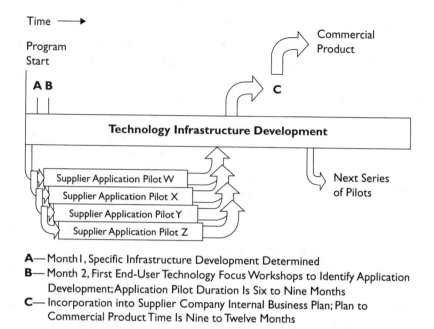

A— Month I, Specific Infrastructure Development Determined
B— Month 2, First End-User Technology Focus Workshops to Identify Application
Development; Application Pilot Duration Is Six to Nine Months
C— Incorporation into Supplier Company Internal Business Plan; Plan to
Commercial Product Time Is Nine to Twelve Months

FIGURE 2.1   Collaborative Process for Technology Commercialization—
Commercialization Milestones

and a metric for a collaborative R&D program, is the insertion of developed technologies into the internal product development plans of the technology suppliers.

The cost of technology commercialization is well over 10 times more than what is needed to demonstrate a capability. Technology needs to be tested to operate on all the different conditions and configurations that are likely to exist in the market. The technology suppliers are responsible for technology upgrades and validation and testing performed on all products released to the market. Technology suppliers can try to reduce commercialization costs by incorporating requirements into the pilot demonstrations that are robust enough not to require significant revision of the technology for any subsequent commercialization. Commercialization capital generally comes from the technology supplier's revenues. Technology suppliers may need to team with a major corporation to obtain commercialization funds.

The decision to make the investment to commercialize technologies lies with the technology suppliers, who make these decisions based on their expectations of the market. These decisions determine the success or failure of a company, and are what a company's CEO is accountable for to the company's board of directors. A principal element in commercializing resulting from a collaborative R&D program is the reduced market risk in these commercialization decisions for the technology suppliers. Risk reduction can be accomplished through the enterprise pilots, which enable the suppliers to work with the market. Early feedback on the technologies developed can be provided from the market through these pilots. Decisions can then be made on whether to modify, evolve, drop, or select alternative technology development approaches for follow-on pilots.

It is possible that some commercialization capital will come from venture capital, particularly if a spin-off company can grow out of a collaborative R&D program, but the same decisions and market forecasts will need to be made and defended to acquire venture capital.

PRODUCT DATA MANAGEMENT (PDM) INTEROPERABILITY

PDM systems have recently evolved as the data libraries large companies use to manage all of the product data they have on computers. The need to ensure interoperability among the PDM data library management tools is best relayed through the experience of Boeing St. Louis (previously McDonnell-Douglas) with building the C-17 military transport aircraft. Working through the Standard for the Exchange of Product Model Data (STEP), Boeing has reduced the time needed to exchange part model information between its design PDM system in St. Louis and its manufacture PDM system in Huntington Beach, California, from 2 to 10 weeks to overnight. Approximately 8000 part models are now being exchanged every night. The Rapid Response Manufacturing program's Interoperability Services Working Group has conducted work to extend PDM interoperability among all PDM systems, which has been adopted by the largest PDM systems as the standard approved by the Object Management Group (OMG). The promise of using computers to rapidly exchange, analyze, and use information is dependent on having interoperability standards such as these.

COMMERCIALIZATION OF ROBUST DESIGN CAPABILITIES

The Robust Design Computational System (RDCS) program (Appendix E) has demonstrated in its early release the ability to conduct hundreds of design analyses overnight. The use of computer-aided engineering tools has generally been restricted to postdesign validation due to the time it has taken to run analysis programs in the past (large models of an airplane have taken months to run on the fastest computers available). The RDCS capability developed by Boeing-Rocketdyne promises to be able to drive designs by conducting analysis on large numbers of design options to select the best design early in the design process. The MacNeal-Schwendler Corporation partnered with Boeing and Ford in this program, and is working closely with its partners toward developing a commercial product.

Cost Sharing Returns/ Leveraging Research and Development Expenditures

The generation of revenue is not a principal objective of collaborative development, but can be a direct benefit. This is particularly true for smaller technology developer/supplier companies, which do not generally have the resources needed to develop next-generation products. The revenue these companies generate from the sale of their technology-derived products generally covers the cost of maintaining their products and evolving them to keep current with the state of the art in telecommunications and computing.

All the organizations participating in a collaborative development program need to have an investment of people committed to the program to ensure that the program realizes its objectives. The smaller the company, the more difficult this gets. The company needs to have all of its key employees directed toward ensuring that revenue is generated. Personnel commitments from smaller companies represent a proportionally higher obligation of their company to a program than personnel commitments from large Fortune 500 manufacturers. As such, the ability to generate cash flow as an ability to offset costs is important for small companies. Cash is also needed for a collaborative R&D program to be able to hire any outside expertise the group may need.

The availability of matching funds from different government programs has provided a previously lacking incentive for establishing collaborative development programs, and particularly programs involving small companies. The most significant value provided by the availability of government funds is the deadline established for receipt of proposals for the funding. This deadline provides a forcing function to move people and organizations to action that may not otherwise exist.

Table 2.1 provides a summary of the amount of funding provided by government agencies for an example number of collaborative development programs. The significance of funding and identification of various government funding sources is further discussed in Chapter 6.

TABLE 2.1 Collaborative Development Program Funding in Millions of Dollars

Program	Total Program Cost	Government Funds
Printed Wiring Board (PWB)	$31.7	$12.9—ATP, $5.2—DOE[†]
Rapid Response Manufacturing (RRM)	65.3[*]	19.8—ATP, 4.5—DOE[†]
Agile Infrastructure for Manufactured Systems (AIMS)	16.0	8.0—DARPA
Robust Design Computational System (RDCS)	6.5	3.0—DARPA
Computational Aeroacoustics Analysis System (CAAS)	4.1	1.9—NASA

[*]Contract amount was for $50.3 million; however, the partners exceeded their committed in-kind by approximately $3 million per year.
[†]DOE funds covered participation of DOE laboratories only.

PART II

Ingredients of Collaboration

The following ingredients are needed to establish a workable collaborative development program:

- An end-user champion
- A vision
- A network of people
- Commitments
- Funding
- Organization with minimum overhead
- Timing

Collaborative R&D programs are referred to by some (such as the Advanced Technology Program at the National Institute of Standards and Technology) as joint ventures. In this context, collaborative R&D programs are informal joint ventures where there is no equity partnership between the participants. The partnership establishing a collaborative program is formalized through a project agreement addressing intellectual property, program scope, and management.

End-User Champion

An end user is a major manufacturer who will implement the technology being developed, and represents a market for that technology. The end-user champion is an individual employed by the major manufacturer who has a compelling vision to which the company is committing its personnel and funds. The company must also have a strong interest in leveraging the resources it is committing toward realizing the vision. End-user involvement is key to establishing successful collaborative development programs. A champion is needed from the end-user company who can proactively coordinate end-user involvement in the program.

Vision

The vision is an idea of how a technology can be developed and applied to improve a company's business. The vision has to be solid enough to be able to rally interest and commitment. It has to be a vision people believe they can achieve, yet be challenging. The vision forms the foundation for addressing decisions on technical development directions.

Network

Once an end-user champion has a vision he or she is willing to leverage through working with other companies, the next step is to identify companies with similar interests that can potentially work together. In most instances, these contacts are the result of personal relationships or referrals with other like-minded individuals at other companies. It is likely that several types of companies are needed to realize the commercial potential of a research vision. The network should be used to get other end users involved, as this will represent a broader market for the technologies developed. Technology development and technology supplier companies are needed. In many cases, these networks come through relationships established through organizations like the National Center for Manufacturing Sciences (NCMS) or the Consortium for Advanced Manufacturing—International (CAM-I).

Commitment

Once other companies with an interest in a common vision have been identified, the companies need to make individual commitments toward that vision. The best commitment is in the time of key personnel. The next best commitment is funding. An overview of issues and processes used in getting internal company commitment is provided in Chapter 10.

Funding

After a number of companies have identified a willingness to make commitments to realize a common vision, they need to ensure that there are sufficient resources to pursue the venture. Research is generally a long-term commitment measured in years. Businesses are generally measured on quarterly results. Research also has a degree of risk involved. External funding to minimize the risk involved is generally required for a company to justify committing key personnel to a long-term R&D program. In addition, the group of companies participating in the venture may not have all the necessary personnel with required capabilities to conduct all the development. These needs can only be met with funding.

Organization

It needs to be easy for people in a company to be able to collaborate with the people in other companies involved in the joint venture. There can not be any significant overhead burden involved in collaboration. Any large amounts of legal work involved in putting together the joint venture agreement, additional accounting or timekeeping requirements, or other administrative work must be minimized. Productively collaborating itself takes more time than a self-contained effort. Requiring additional overhead work from the personnel involved in collaboration can undermine the effort.

Timing

Timing is a major factor involved in being able to establish a collaborative development program. Timing can affect the ability of a company to provide a commitment, depending on where the company is in its internal budgeting process or business cycle. In addition, infrastructure technology, such as the hardware and software needed to support planned systems, must be mature enough to support development without breaking down. The maturity of the infrastructure and the availability of funding need to converge with a number of corporate commitments and the potential of a sufficient market to justify the additional investment needed for commercialization.

CHAPTER 3

The End-User Champion

The end user is defined as a Fortune 500 manufacturing company that is going to use the technology being developed in its manufacturing processes. A champion is a mid- to high-level manager within the end-user company who is committed to the development and application of the technology being pursued.

Our experience has shown that the key to successful collaboration is the proactive involvement of an end-user manufacturing firm. The goals of the collaborative development program have to be in the mainstream corporate business plan of the end user. Collaborative development programs that have been driven by political, economic development, and academic objectives have had goals focused more on recognition and getting additional government funding. These programs were not generally successful in transferring their R&D to usable processes for the market.

This chapter offers generic descriptions of the end-user company followed by a description of individuals who have been champions for collaborative development in their companies.

The End-User Company

The reason the end user is defined as a Fortune 500 company is that any single end user should be large enough to be a market for the technology being developed—a market that could be used as the base for a business. The active involvement of end-user companies is needed in collaborative manufacturing R&D programs to provide focus and direction. Without strong end-user involvement, there is a high probability that the development will produce a technological capability which, while it may be very interesting, can not be used by the market. As long as the objective of collaborative development is improved economic performance, end-user involvement is needed to reduce the commercialization risk associated with the development.

Fortune 500 manufacturing firms usually have a number of large production sites, often located around the world, that consist of their fabrication and assembly facilities. Most of these firms also have large R&D centers, such as the Bell Laboratories (formerly part of AT&T and now Lucent Technologies) and the General Motors corporate R&D centers. While one would assume that a close working relationship between a major company's R&D center and its production sites is fundamental to a successful business, in practice it isn't necessarily the reality. The business relationships between the corporate R&D centers and the companies' production sites vary from company to company, and are determined by a company's business culture.

End-user companies are recognizing that outside of a relatively few differentiating characteristics, the products they build and the processes they use are basically the same. They are coming to compete on corporate culture more than on product. It appears that it will be those corporate cultures that can best manage change that will be the winners in the next century. Collaboration in R&D is a tool that assists in managing the changes in technology that corporations will continue to experience.

THE END-USER COMPANY PRODUCTION SITES

The end-user production center represents the present manufacturing, information, and communication processes in use. What technologies to develop and when to insert them into a major production process are important business considerations. Any new technology being developed will need to be integrated into that environment, or be able to cost-justify the replacement of that environment. Collaborative development can help reduce the risk involved in these decisions by enabling companies to pilot new technologies prior to insertion into their production processes. This can be done together with other companies, which further reduces the cost to any one company.

End-user production sites are generally large facilities that have established processes and significant investment in the infrastructure supporting those processes. These include integrated systems, highly skilled and trained personnel to operate and maintain these systems, machine tools, and process environment controls.

The primary business driver for a production facility is to produce as efficiently as possible products that customers will buy. Production objectives are often set by a corporate business plan. Significant investment will have been made in the manufacturing, information, and communications processes in the production facility. The company gets its return on this investment through selling the products made in the facility. The higher the quantity of sold products made in the facility, the faster the facility pays for itself and the more profitable the company.

A number of characteristics impact the efficiency and productivity of a production center. The *ideal* manufacturing facility might be one which:

- Operates continuously, producing product 24 hours a day.
- Requires minimum maintenance and down time.
- Has every product it produces sold without going into inventory.
- Produces no waste.
- Is able to be quickly reconfigured to produce different products.
- Can monitor manufacturing product and process characteristics, providing digital feedback into controllers that compensate for variances to ensure quality production while alerting operators of the trends.

This description is an ideal for a factory manufacturing products for a mass market, like cars, cameras, or electronics. The characteristics, such as operations 24 hour per day, of this ideal manufacturing facility are different for medium- or low-rate production centers, such as those for jet engines or nuclear power plants. Flexibility to be able to accommodate a shift in volume or market demand for new products is becoming an important characteristic for almost all ideal manufacturing facilities. Product manufacturing flexibility will likely become even more important as the information age continues to mature.

The principal benefits an end-user production center can realize from participating in collaborative development are increased productivity, more robust production processes, and improved product quality. An additional benefit is a potentially enhanced supplier base. Productivity increases result from the application of technology developed to address end users' needs. Many times, improved processes and quality result from the sharing of insights among collaborators as to how a process might work better. Information sharing can also result in finding suppliers that may be more highly skilled in a particular area.

Role in the Technology Development Process

These end-user production sites represent the ultimate market for the manufacturing technology being developed. The implementation of technology in a product being manufactured or in the manufacturing process at a manufacturing production site is the final step in the Technology Development Process (described in Chapter 1). Getting a technology to this stage cost-effectively is the ultimate objective of collaborative manufacturing R&D programs. The market the end user represents for a particular technology product may be a niche applicable only to its particular application, or it may represent a general market applicable across many industries.

Role in Collaborative Development

The role of personnel from an end-user production site in a collaborative development program is to set the requirements for technology development. By representing the market, they provide scope and focus to collaborative development efforts. Additionally, end-user production sites can be sources of in-kind and financial support for collaborative development programs. End-user production sites are often more able than other parts of a company to get the resources they request from their corporation, as they are the source of the products the company sells (i.e., profit).

Particular opportunities for technology development and insertion exist if a company is building new factories or product and process design centers. In cases where rapid expansion and growth are not taking place, the integration of a new technology into the product or process will not likely take place for some time after the R&D work has been done. A company commitment to continuous improvement of its processes will reduce this time by getting production site personnel involved in a collaborative development program. Exposure to new thought processes and methods will bolster continuous improvement efforts.

However, getting production site personnel involved in development efforts is usually difficult (though in some large companies there are technology development divisions in place as part of the production organization). Production center personnel are responsible for producing the product the company depends on to stay in business. They are generally interested in what can be done to improve their work process today, or maybe next week. Production center personnel and resources need to be constantly focused on meeting daily production requirements.

An objective of production site management personnel is to improve the efficiency of production; they strive to obtain the ideal characteristics previously identified. With this need to continuously improve the efficiency of the production center, the insertion of new technology can raise concerns among production center operators and management. There are many unknowns relative to integrating a new technology into a process. One concern is that new technologies are not robust enough to withstand daily operations, and end up increasing system down time. There are many other potential concerns, usually reinforced from negative experiences in the past. As a result, production center personnel are conservative when it comes to integrating a new technology into their processes. New technology insertion is usually a low-priority task in a production center. New technology development is frequently not even considered.

While it is difficult to get production center personnel directly involved in a program, it is important to capture their views of what is needed to help them do a better job. People working in a collaborative development program need two key inputs from corporate production sites. These are an understanding of:

1. What processes are in place.
2. What productivity problems are being encountered.

The productivity problems encountered at production centers represent technology development challenges (or opportunities). These technology development challenges can often be addressed in collaborative efforts.

In an ideal collaborative development environment, a senior manager from a production site will be responsible for overseeing a collaborative development program, as the production center would be providing funding and market requirements. If production site personnel can not get directly involved, their interests should be represented through the end user's corporate R&D center.

THE CORPORATE RESEARCH AND DEVELOPMENT CENTER

Corporate technology centers are responsible for developing new technology for application within their company's products and processes. The terms "R&D center" and "technology center" are used to refer to all of the personnel in a corporation's R&D organization. Every company has a different, and generally changing, internal organizational structure for its R&D personnel. In most cases, a corporate R&D center consists of a number of geographically dispersed organizations with different types of research and/or development done at the various locations. There is generally one major location that provides central focus of the R&D for the company, even though the present tendency has R&D resources becoming more geographically distributed and connected through the Internet.

In-house R&D centers are under intense pressure to reduce cycle time and cut costs. These organizations are also being required to devote more of their resources to short-term or product programs. The principal benefit a corporate R&D center can realize from participating in collaborative development is the resource leverage and time compression leading to the adoption of its efforts by one of its company's production centers. Benefits are generally in the form of applying new process technology to improve productivity. The development of new products can also be a benefit that results from collaboration.

R&D's Role in the Corporation

The general role of corporate R&D organizations is in the development phase of the Technology Development Process described in Chapter 1. While some portion of the research staff in some corporations focuses on basic research, most are focused on developing and extending technology applications related to the company's business. In some cases, universities are funded to pursue more fundamental research.

The specific role of corporate R&D varies from company to company. In some companies the R&D organization is closely integrated with the production sites, while other companies segregate their R&D groups from their production organizations. When companies go through difficult times, some cut their R&D as it's considered an overhead luxury, while others augment their R&D to provide a means for recovery. Much of this is dependent on the experience and background of corporate management and the corporate culture. This establishes a corporate R&D environment that is characterized by:

1. How the R&D organization relates internally to the rest of the company.
2. How corporate R&D is funded.

Corporate R&D environments can vary from a company that keeps all information about its processes secret to a culture that promotes collaboration.

Internal R&D Relationships

Based on different corporate R&D environments, the relations between the corporate technology center and the company's production sites vary from company to company, and often between different sites within the same company. Generally those in corporate R&D want to see the results of their research implemented in the form of product or process improvements that contribute to their company. Internal corporate relationships between R&D centers and the production organizations will govern the effectiveness major companies have in getting new technologies integrated into their products. The better the relationships between R&D and production personnel, the more effective the R&D personnel are at getting technology to help the company. From a collaborative development perspective, it is best to work with companies that have good relationships between their R&D and production organizations.

Corporate R&D Funding

Another factor of the corporate R&D environment is how a company funds its R&D organization. R&D can be funded through a corporate shared resource budget, through the company's production organizations, or a combination of both. Some R&D centers are responsible for securing a portion of their own resources. The government is often the source of external R&D funds, as is the case with companies who service the defense and other government markets. Often a corporate R&D center must have support from one of the company's production divisions to pursue a development project. The more a corporate R&D center is dependent on its own efforts to obtain funding from other corporate divisions or external contracts, the more time it will need to devote to marketing its capabilities to other corporate divisions, and to preparing proposals for government funding.

R&D Center Technology Development

A corporate R&D center is generally not in business to commercialize developed technology. Its primary focus is on applying R&D to the corporate infrastructure that is in place at the company's production facilities. This focus is often on company-specific technology applications applicable only to the R&D center's own company. However, many end users independently develop similar process technologies from evolving research. These developments are ideal candidates for collaboration, as the objective of this research is often to provide a generic process capability that will later be accessible from the industrial infrastructure.

In many cases, R&D centers would like to see their developments picked up and commercialized by a third party, generally for two reasons:

1. To reduce the costs to the company in using the technology the R&D center developed by getting it into the general market.
2. To get back to doing more R&D. The responsibility for maintaining and updating the technology applications the R&D center has put in place is not the best use of the R&D staff's time and talent.

However, while the R&D staff may like to have their applied technology development taken over by a third party, there is generally a significant amount of further development needed to be able to make that technology applicable to the general market. A corporate R&D staff develops technology for internal production using the corporate infrastructure of facilities, equipment, computers, communications, and corporate processes. The general market does not have the same infrastructure and processes.

Value in Collaborative Development

Corporate R&D centers form the core of successful collaborative development programs. They are the source of personnel with some of the best capabilities to do collaborative R&D. Personnel from corporate R&D centers are some of the best technologists available, and they generally have a better understanding of their company's business than people from outside the company.

Involvement in collaborative development can help the R&D center by:

- Reducing the costs of application, maintenance, and support of technology after it's been developed.
- Providing access to additional sources of talent and knowledge, which is increasingly important to companies with diverse product technology competencies. This will help eliminate the "not invented here" problems fostered by past cultures.
- Improving internal company relationships.
- Sharing the cost of technology development. This enables a company to focus on certain technology areas while not losing sight of

related technology developments needed in complementary fields. (Many corporate development staffs go through periodic downsizing, but are still expected to produce results at the same or greater levels. Leveraging other organizations to conduct development becomes an effective means to get the job done.)

• Enabling the development of the standards in software and hardware that are needed for interoperability across the company's extended enterprise.

The early involvement of technology suppliers working with corporate R&D center personnel can help in ensuring that the technology being developed will be able to be more cost-effectively commercialized. This can be done by ensuring that the technology being developed can be supported in a generic infrastructure and with common processes. This enables a technology supplier, with a business interest in supporting the technology being developed, to be in a position to make the business decision that it can commercialize the technology after it has been piloted at a company's production site. Collaborative development programs provide the environment for this to happen. In most collaborative development programs, this is one of the intentions of the program. An example is how the MacNeal-Schwendler Corporation has worked with Boeing-Rocketdyne in commercializing the technology developed by Rocketdyne developers under the Robust Design Computational System program (Appendix E).

When other companies with recognized capabilities and products are working with a corporate R&D organization, it improves the stature of the R&D organization among the other sections of the company. This assists R&D center personnel in establishing the kinds of working relationships needed with production sites to the benefit of all involved.

The Individual

End-user champions form the core of a collaborative development program. They are the leaders. There should be more than one end-user champion involved in a program, ideally one from each end-user company involved. The end-user champion generally comes from the company's R&D center, though it's ideal to have a technologically knowledgeable champion from a production site and operational management. The champion has to be senior enough in the company to be able to get resources committed from the company. The champion should also have enough confidence in the personnel and in the concept being developed to be willing to take risks in attempting new business processes and procedures to initiate and implement the development of the concept. The champion has to believe that collaboration can help achieve the vision stated in the development concept. This belief in collaboration has to be strong enough to motivate the individual to be proactive in participating in the collaborative effort. A good relationship between managers and technical personnel will assist in getting the results of a project transferred to a product or process.

A good example of an end-user champion is Dr. Gene Jackson of Boeing-Rocketdyne. He is the champion of the Robust Design Computational System (RDCS) program (Appendix E). As a senior manager within Rocketdyne, he assembled a team working on probabilistic analysis in 1991. In 1993, Rocketdyne had the opportunity to work with Ford on a proposed DARPA program to integrate the ability to conduct structural, thermal, and fluid analysis on a product design using the latest supercomputers, the Compressing Integrated Product Engineering (CIPE) Using Massively Parallel Processing (MPP) program (Appendix G). Dr. Jackson committed his team, time, and resources to developing this program, meeting with Ford and DARPA. After being told in a meeting at DARPA that DARPA personnel had been looking for a program like this for the past two years, Dr. Jackson and his team were disappointed that the program wasn't funded. (DARPA had a funding reallocation shortly after providing this information which resulted in the program not getting funded.) It was recommended that the proposal be resubmitted under the Technology Reinvestment Project (TRP) later that year. Dr. Jackson followed through—with his cochampion from Ford, Dr. Howard Crabb—and resubmitted the program under the TRP. The CIPE program again failed to make the cut, and again was not funded.

While the original CIPE program never came into being, Dr. Jackson had enough confidence in the relationships established during the proposal effort to ask Ford and the MacNeal-Schwendler Corporation to continue to work with Rocketdyne in putting a proposal for a new computational analysis program together for cost-shared funding from NASA. The Robust Design Computational System (RDCS) program was proposed to NASA under NASA's Aerospace Industry Technologies Program in 1994. Again, the RDCS program was not funded; however, the higher-risk Computational Aeroacoustics Analysis System (CAAS) program (Appendix H) submitted to NASA by the same team under the same solicitation was awarded funding.

The RDCS program was resubmitted to DARPA under the Rapid Design Evaluation and Optimization (RaDEO) program in 1995 after receiving an indication of interest following briefings to DARPA on the prospective program. DARPA funded the program starting in 1996. Initial program results promise to revolutionize the ability to analyze product designs by providing the ability to perform hundreds more analyses in a fraction of the time previously needed to conduct one analysis. This will have significant impacts on reducing future product costs while improving quality, performance, and reliability. It is proving to be a key program in the DARPA RaDEO program portfolio.

While a number of individuals were instrumental in putting the RDCS program forward, many without whom the program could not have been established, no one has been more instrumental than Gene Jackson. He had the vision of what might be accomplished by his team of rocket scientists, and persevered through a three-year struggle to get the program started. During this time he continued to fund what development he could, insisted on keeping the team together, and survived a heart attack. His initiative and leadership characterize the type of individual needed to be an end-user champion in a collaborative development program.

The following is a list of some of the individuals who have played the role of being an end-user champion in collaborative development programs. (Those whose names are asterisked were instrumental in starting the program.)

AT&T: Wyck Seelig* and Ted Polakowski in the PWB program.

Digital Equipment Corporation: Dwayne Poteet* in the PWB program.

Eastman Kodak: John Rueping in Light Flexible Mechanical Assembly and Optoelectronics Assembly; Ron Auble and Jean Orlicki in RRM, OSIC (Open Supplier Integration Center), and TEWE.

Ford Motor Company: Pete Sferro* in the RRM program; Howard Crabb*, George Joseph*, Ali Jammoul, and Dan Anderson in the RDCS program; Ken Kuna*, Sean O'Reilly*, and Bob Humphrey* in TEWE; and Rich Pearson in OSIC.

General Motors: Bob Early, Tom Kaczmarik, and Gary Patelski in RRM.

Hamilton Standard: Steve Pavlech in PWB.

Lockheed Martin Corporation: Keith Hunten* in Software Interoperability Standards development.

Pratt & Whitney: Frank Pijar in RRM.

Rocketdyne: Steve Babcock in RRM and OSIC; Bob Carman* in CIPE, AIMS, and TEWE; Gene Jackson* in CIPE and RDCS; Glenn Havskjold in RDCS.

Texas Instruments: Kurt Watchler*, Foster Gray, and Phil Gray* in the PWB program; John Richardson*, Mike Kennedy, and Allan Hrncir in the RRM program; Vern Lott in AIMS; Allan Hncir and Phil Gray were involved in many programs at NCMS that relied on Texas Instruments' support.

Center for Optics Manufacturing at the University of Rochester: Jeff Ruckman in Distance Learning and Flexible Opto-Electronics Assembly and Kodak Supplier programs.

CHAPTER 4

The Vision

Dr. Gene Jackson had a vision of how to move analysis up front in the product design process. Dr. Jackson's vision complemented that of Dr. Howard Crabb, recently retired from Ford Motor Company. Dr. Crabb's vision is well described in his 1998 book *The Virtual Engineer, 21st Century Product Development*, published by the Society of Manufacturing Engineers and the American Society of Mechanical Engineers. The end-user champions have to have a firm, almost religious, commitment to follow through on their vision. This is a requirement for collaboration.

These visions provide an idea of how a technology can be developed and applied to improve the company's business. The visions have to be solid enough to be able to rally interest. Each one has to be a vision people believe they can achieve, yet be challenging. It has to capture the imagination. It's the vision of a better product, a better process, a better world that provides the motivation to do the work needed to try to realize the vision. The realization of the vision becomes the driving force behind the program, the overall common objective for the good of the whole that justifies participation in the program. It's the sharing of common visions that forms the foundation for addressing decisions on technical development directions when collaborating with other companies.

Candidates for Collaboration

R&D visions are candidates for collaboration if:

- There is little customer differentiation between the products the partners produce (if they're in the same industry).
- Common development needs exist across a number of industries, such as the ability to more efficiently use information technology in business.
- The development is driven by a need to improve societal good (environment improvements, safety improvements).
- The end users have common suppliers that are essential to lean manufacturing.[1]
- No one company has all the best resources to develop and apply a needed technology.

Some classic ideas that have driven major collaborative development programs this century have been sending men to the moon and building the atomic bomb before the Germans during World War II. There are several grand visions that encompass a view of future manufacturing that have and continue to drive manufacturing R&D. These visions are at the core of several collaborative development programs. They include:

- Concurrent engineering
- Knowledge capture and use
- Free-form fabrication

As some of these visions may appear to be specific, overused, or unrecognized, a short description of each follows.

Concurrent engineering is the ability to get all the information involved in all aspects of a product over its lifetime simulated as part of the conceptual design process. This includes manufacturability, desired operational capabilities, different operational environments, product reliability and safety, product maintainability and support, product disposal, and

---

[1]Lean manufacturing is the efficient use of resources, teamwork, communication, elimination of waste, and continuous improvement described in *The Machine That Changed the World*, by James P. Womack, Daniel T. Jones, and Daniel Roos, Rawson Associates, 1990.

product cost. This vision is now sometimes referred to as Integrated Product and Process Deployment (or Development) (IPPD). The vision has inspired a number of programs and initiatives including the DARPA Rapid Design Exploration and Optimization (RaDEO) and Manufacturing Automation and Design Exploration (MADE) communities of programs (which include the Robust Design Computational System (RDCS) and Agile Infrastructure for Manufactured Systems (AIMS) programs), Continuous Acquisition and Life-Cycle Support (CALS) initiative, Rapid Response Manufacturing (RRM) program, Software Standards for the Exchange of Product Model Data (STEP) development for the International Standards Organization, and other programs. The challenge in implementing the concurrent engineering vision lies with:

1. The ability to get *interoperability* between the various information models that are used during different aspects of the product life cycle.
2. Ensuring that the models are *accurate* in reflecting reality.
3. Having a system that is *easy to use* for an average person.

While concurrent engineering envisions integrating all product engineering into the conceptual design of products, knowledge capture is needed to be able to get all of the information needed to conduct concurrent engineering. Knowledge capture involves defining what knowledge is. This has to be done in a manner that is readily understandable to people and other processes. It addresses the development and use of sensors to get data that can be refined to information. The understanding of all the information (how the product and associated processes interact with the environments they are in) constitutes the knowledge about the product. Knowledge capture encompasses all of the companies and individuals involved in the supply chain needed to build a product, market and sell a product, use the product, and dispose of the product. As the knowledge exists at many locations around the world, this vision involves the global harmonization of standards. This vision is the driver behind the Technologies for Enterprise-Wide Engineering (TEWE) initiative (Appendix C).

Free-form fabrication refers to the ability to build products in their final form directly from raw materials such that there is no waste—the concept of building products through additive processes as opposed to subtractive processes. In subtractive processes, raw materials are processed to create a new material (such as a steel ingot or whole cloth), which is then formed into the final product by removing and forming the new material. Subtractive processes generate a lot of waste from both product and process. This vision was the driver behind the Direct Metal Deposition (DMD) initiative (Appendix I), as well as numerous steriolithography and composite programs.

Starting a collaborative development program requires a common vision among the participants. But, where do these visions come from? How do you know if they're good visions? There's no shortage of visions of the future. The Internet is a valuable source of quickly getting visions of what the future might look like.

Many visions have evolved from thought focusing on how to address one of today's particular problems. One source of the general vision of concurrent engineering came from the Department of Defense in the mid-1980s as an answer to how to address the "threat" to U.S. industrial competitiveness believed to be coming from "Japan, Inc." The idea was for the U.S. industrial base to leverage the computational capabilities available into a tool to provide a leapfrog capability in manufacturing.

What's not known about a vision is whether there is a credible path from where we are today toward that future model. What's needed is a credible understanding of where we are today technologically, and where extensions of these technologies might take us. This requires an ability to learn and understand processes, which is further addressed in Chapter 13. It takes some degree of process understanding and ability to learn technology. With this capability a person can understand the particular part of today's technology environment, and extend the technology to meet the needs of a future vision. This can be captured in a concept paper, also referred to as a "white paper" or a "straw man."

The concept paper is a tool that can be used to generate consensus on how to pursue the realization of a vision. The paper should have a target audience. It should be able to capture and communicate a vision, with a course of action to achieve the vision, in no more than a couple of pages. The concept paper is a straw man that can evolve an idea. It provides a common starting point for a group to initiate a collaborative program. The question as to whether the vision is a good one will be determined by the actions generated by the concept paper.

A concept paper should generally consist of the following sections:

- Background—providing the reader with information on what issue is being addressed.

- Discussion—relaying to the reader what could be expected from extrapolating recent events.
- Recommendations—identifying actions that can be taken to influence the issue.

Exhibits 4.1 and 4.2 are two examples of concept papers. Exhibit 4.1 starts with a memo requesting a white paper and describing what points it should include, and is followed with the resulting white paper.

Exhibit 4.2 is a program concept paper put together after a December 19, 1997, meeting at the Ford Motor Company at which the participants agreed to pursue a NIST ATP program. The white paper was put together to harmonize the visions of the participants and to be used as a straw man for moving the program forward. It ensured that the group had a common reference for following discussions and evolution into a program plan.

EXHIBIT 4.1 White Paper Drafted for NIST ATP Focus Area

DATE: January 28, 1994
SUBJECT: ATP Program Area in Machine Tools

The following is a straw-man draft of a white paper for establishing an Advanced Technology Program area in machine tools that would provide $20 million to $30 million of ATP funds for a focused competition for projects to support the development and commercialization of the next generation of machine tools. This "program area white paper" was requested by Jack Boudreaux following a meeting he had with Fred Schierloh and Gene Allen on January 24. The paper is only a first step in developing a program area, and is being sent to you to develop further. The paper particularly needs additional empirical facts emphasizing the economic need for the program. Please provide drafts to John Decaire at NCMS, who will relay them to Jack Boudreaux at NIST.

The focus of the discussion was on the need to have a machine tool infrastructure to support new manufacturing processes that are starting to evolve, such as material additive processes, processes for manufacturing micromechanical and electrical systems, net-shape free-form processes, and other nontraditional manufacturing. The focus was on leapfrogging foreign competition by developing the next generation of manufacturing processes as opposed to attempting incremental catch-up improvements to metal milling, drilling, turning, and grinding. The development/commercialization of the wire electro-discharge machine (EDM) was a case in point where there

EXHIBIT 4.1 *(Continued)*

are no domestic wire EDM companies in a technology that has taken the jig grinding market from U.S. companies.

The white paper needs to address several key questions:

1. Why does the United States need a machine tool industry? What is the economic benefit of having a machine tool industry? What difference does it make if we do not have a machine tool industry? Note that we have lost most of this industry and U.S. manufacturers at present appear to be doing well purchasing overseas machine tools. Solid economic arguments are needed as opposed to patriotic flag-waving.
2. Given we need a machine tool industry, why should the government fund efforts to support the machine tool industry?
3. If the industry needs government funding, then why ATP funding (given that the amounts of funding are relatively small)?

The white paper advocating a machine tool program area needs to show that there is:

1. Strong potential for broad U.S. economic benefit.
2. A broad range of good technical ideas to be developed (i.e., there are a large number of potential high-payoff projects which could be pursued to develop the machine tool infrastructure needed to support new manufacturing processes).
3. A demonstrable strong industry commitment for pursuing development of machine tools for the next generation of manufacturing processes.
4. An opportunity for ATP funding to have a significant economic impact. The higher the potential leverage, the more likely to be selected a program area.

Machine Base for New Manufacturing Processes
A NIST ATP Program Idea White Paper 1/28/94 Draft

The growth of the U.S. trade deficit in commercial products occurred in parallel with the loss of the U.S. machine tool industry. The tie between producing competitive products and the ability to make the machine tools needed to produce competitive products is demonstrated by this trend in recent history. Japan and earlier the United States have demonstrated that the ability to make the machines capable of manufacturing products leads to a competitive advantage in making those products.

The United States has, for the most part, lost the traditional machine tool industry. Playing catch-up to the overseas conglomerates committed to making the best electronics assembly and metals milling, turning, drilling, and grinding tools is not likely to yield competitive results in the United States. One of the strongest competitive advantages available in the United

(continued)

EXHIBIT 4.1 *(Continued)*

States is the innovative characteristic of engineers raised in the U.S. culture. This characteristic has spawned a significant number of promising new manufacturing processes over the past decade. There is a broad range of good technical ideas to be developed into a large number of potentially high-payoff projects to develop the machine tool infrastructure needed to support new manufacturing processes. Some of these include:

- Free-form plastic and metal deposition processes.
- Composites of various combinations of metals, plastics, and other materials.
- Processes using light as opposed to electrons for information industry products.
- Electrochemical machining processes.
- Material removal processes using water jets.
- Environmentally sound fabrication processes.

These processes hold the promise of being more productive and hence replacing traditional manufacturing processes. However, the United States needs to focus on providing the machine tool infrastructure to support these new processes if our country is to capture the promised increases in productivity.

While this course would seem to be an obvious direction for the nation's industry to follow, we have a business environment that is not likely to embrace the investment needed to establish the manufacturing process machine infrastructure needed to capitalize on these innovations. An example is the development of the wire electro-discharge machine (EDM). There are no machine tool companies in the United States that make wire EDMs. The products made with wire EDMs used to be made with jig grinding machines. The United States was the dominant maker of jig grinders. Wire EDMs proved to be more efficient and cost-effective than jig grinders. As wire EDMs took over the jig grinder market the United States lost the machine tool infrastructure for making those products, principally the molds and dies used in forming products. Interestingly enough, some major U.S. companies now depend on importing molds and dies because they can be produced offshore more competitively. (This is the case in a major U.S. company in the toy industry.)

It has been argued that the United States does not need an indigenous machine tool industry, that U.S. manufacturers can stay competitive by purchasing machine tools made overseas. This is a faulty argument, as a strong competitive advantage exists for manufacturing companies that help develop and first use new manufacturing processes. The time to market advantage

EXHIBIT 4.1 *(Continued)*

gained by manufacturers developing process equipment to meet their needs is a major differentiator between those companies and their competitors.

Major U.S. manufacturing companies are now buying machine tools and other equipment developed by major Japanese manufacturing companies. These Japanese companies invested significant resources in the development of this equipment in the 1980s and have been benefiting from their investments for the past 5 to 10 years. When Japanese companies sell that equipment to companies elsewhere in the world, they are ready to install the next generation of improved equipment in their facilities. This is not a scenario which is likely to enable U.S. companies to produce products more competitively than their Japanese counterparts.

Ensuring that the United States can capture the competitive benefit of the new fabrication processes that are being developed in this country requires collaboration among:

- Companies dedicated to commercializing the new process machine tools,
- Manufacturing companies to establish the user requirements and become the eventual market for the new process machine tools, and
- Universities and national laboratories that are developing new manufacturing processes and established technical feasibility of those processes.

There is strong industry interest in major manufacturing companies having more competitive processes. There is also strong industry commitment in a number of small companies which are developing and attempting to commercialize new manufacturing processes such as free-form fabrication. There are unfortunately few incentives or mechanisms that will integrate these two industry groups into collaborative teams to ensure the commercialization of an infrastructure to support new manufacturing processes. Large manufacturers generally perceive a substantial business risk for becoming actively involved with small companies in these types of developments. Small companies rarely have sufficient resources to efficiently focus development and ensure market penetration.

The U.S. government can assist by stimulating changes to overcome these business barriers and reduce the development risk. The NIST Advanced Technology Program is well positioned to provide the needed incentives to industry to collaborate in the development of the machine tool infrastructure required to support the next generation of manufacturing processes.

(continued)

EXHIBIT 4.2 ATP Proposal White Paper—Enterprise-Wide Engineering

Overview

Boeing, Ford, Kodak, Raytheon and United Technologies–Pratt & Whitney propose to work with their supply base and technology development companies to develop a generic, interactive knowledge base accessible through the Internet. This interactive knowledge base will enable a company to work with its suppliers and partners, to capture, create, and reuse knowledge. The program will pilot the interactive knowledge base to improve product realization (design-manufacture), maintenance and support, modification and upgrade, and disposal. Goals for implementing this knowledge base are:

- 50 percent reduction in total engineering effort
- 75 percent reduction in engineering/unit in a specific product program
- 50 percent reduction in cycle time
- 50 percent improvement in quality

A metric in realizing this goal is the ability to provide the right information to the right person at the right time, integrating people, processes, and organizations.

Funding from NIST is being solicited to provide cash reimbursement for this effort. The initial program scope is for a five-year, $59 million effort with NIST providing $20.375 million in reimbursement. The program will be user-driven with each of the five users committing $1.5 million per year. The users will receive a NIST reimbursement of $375,000, or 25 percent, per year. Each user is to identify two product suppliers to work with, each of which will be requested to commit $200,000 per year with a $100,000 NIST (50 percent) reimbursement. Seven technology suppliers will be requested to participate with commitments of $400,000 per year, of which NIST would reimburse $200,000 (50 percent). The proposal for this effort is due to NIST on March 18, 1998.

Business Rationale

U.S. companies must ensure their competitiveness in today's global environment. While competitiveness is needed to be able to maintain a high quality of life in the United States, companies need to become flexible enough to rapidly design and make products around the world to meet varying regional market demands. At the same time, corporations will not be able to maintain a full, vertically integrated product development and production capability while also reducing the cost of their complex products. This leads to the need to employ the Internet to access the suite of

EXHIBIT 4.2 (*Continued*)

required core competencies from across the globe. Use of the Internet can extend a company's engineering competitiveness across the supply chain to effectively utilize all of the resources available to better conduct engineering in the design-manufacture processes used to get products to the market.

Technology Development Focus

The challenge of the program is to develop a generic, interactive knowledge base that can be accessed and used by all parties involved in the life cycle of a product. For such a knowledge base to be useful, it needs to be easily accessible and capable of providing knowledge to the user in easily understood terms relevant to the user's working environment.

Users need to be able to exchange information with other users through the knowledge base and update the knowledge base as knowledge is created. The knowledge base needs to be nonproprietary and commercially robust.

The knowledge process involves:

1. Data collection, including metadata (data describing the environment in which the data is captured).
2. Conversion of the data to knowledge, through people who are experts in specific domains.
3. Knowledge representation, through rules and underlying first principals of physics or fundamental market assumptions.
4. Knowledge exchange, through the World Wide Web, with established security and multiple user interfaces which provide varying levels of complexity and perspective.
5. Total product definition, information pertinent to all phases of the product life cycle.

The application of a generic, interactive knowledge base environment requires addressing business and cultural considerations. This proposal, however, is focusing on the technology development needed with the business and cultural issues being addressed in the major company environments.

The proposal will develop the following technologies relative to the knowledge process:

1. *Data Collection*—product data management (PDM), component descriptions and structure.

(continued)

EXHIBIT 4.2 *(Continued)*

2. *Conversion of the Data to Knowledge*—PDM–knowledge base (KB) inter-operability, component descriptions and structure, rule acquisition.
3. *Knowledge Representation*—simple modeler development, rule modeling, syntax, architecture, rule acquisition, KB–computer-aided engineering (CAE) interoperability.
4. *Knowledge Exchange*—Internet technology (including security), KB system interoperability, shared engineering sessions.
5. *Total Product Definition*—hierarchical, easy-to-use interfaces.

A baseline for developing and piloting the interactive knowledge base will be established through integrating a number of complementary standards and technology development efforts in which the partners are participating. These efforts include:

- The Joint PDM Enablers effort, presently being managed through NCMS and initiated in the RRM program to harmonize the proposals submitted to the Object Management Group to establish a common object interface to PDM systems.
- AIMSNET technology developed for information exchange on the Web through a DARPA-funded AIMS program involving Boeing, Raytheon, and CommerceNet.*
- National Industrial Information Infrastructure Protocols (NIIIP) Consortium technology accessed through ITI* and STEP Tools, Inc.*
- The Robust Design Computational System program being funded through DARPA involving Boeing, Ford, and MSC to enable robust product designs.
- Ford Direct Engineering efforts integrating KB into the design-manufacture process.
- KB applications at Boeing and Ford being pursued with Concentra ICAD.*
- STEP pilot programs being pursued by Boeing, Ford, Pratt & Whitney, MSC, SDRC, ITI*, and STEP Tools, Inc.*

Initial development in the program will establish a generic knowledge base architecture integrating these efforts. This architecture will comply with existing standards and be as open as practicable to evolving object-oriented software and Web standards.

The generic knowledge base architecture will be superimposed over product design, manufacture, or support processes at the five major users through pilot projects. These pilot projects will involve supplier companies providing products to a major user. Further development of the generic,

EXHIBIT 4.2 (*Continued*)

interactive knowledge base will take place based on the results of the pilots. The following are the pilot scenarios at each of the major users:

Boeing will use the RS-68 booster engine development program for the Delta IV launch vehicle to pilot teaming operations using the interactive knowledge base. Boeing–Huntington Beach is the prime, Boeing–Rocketdyne is the engine supplier, and the 30 or so suppliers to Rocketdyne will make up the remainder of the supply chain. Design of the production versions of the engines is now under way, with tooling design and production planning about to begin. Boeing military in St. Louis and Boeing commercial in Seattle will also be participating in the program.

Ford will leverage Direct Engineering^{SM} pilot projects involving suppliers, which will be used to validate and evolve the interactive knowledge base. Direct Engineering^{SM} pilots are Ford initiatives to create and capture and then use knowledge about a structure. The concept has been successfully demonstrated for designing an air conditioning hose assembly. Ford is pursuing several Direct Engineering^{SM} pilots to see if this experience can be scaled to other applications.

Kodak will leverage investments it is making to work with its supply chain to be able to design and make high quality (less than one defect per million) parts. The Open Supplier Integration Center (OSIC) has been established at the Rochester Institute of Technology to facilitate working with the supply base. Interactive knowledge base development will be piloted through the OSIC.

Pratt & Whitney's role is to be determined.*

Raytheon's role is to be determined.*

Management

The effort will be user-driven through a program Steering Group made up of representatives from each of the major participating companies. The companies providing parts will be represented through the company they are providing parts for. The technology suppliers will participate in the Steering Group. The program will be governed through a project agreement with a program manager provided through NCMS. This management process has proven to be effective, as it was used to govern the ATP Printed Wiring Board and Rapid Response Manufacturing programs.

---

*Potential participants, not yet selected.

CHAPTER 5

The Network

After an end-user champion has committed to a vision, the next challenge in establishing a collaborative development program is to identify and select the other companies and resources needed to productively pursue the vision. This is accomplished through the networks that are available to the end-user champion.

These networks consist of public organizations such as professional societies and the individual's personal network. The public organizations are sources of individuals who can potentially provide, either directly or through other people they know, the resources needed to successfully execute a collaborative development program. While introductions can be made and contacts identified through the public organizations, the relationships needed for business can only be established through developing personal relationships with and among the parties needed. The following provides an overview of public organizations and opportunities available as the source for establishing needed relationships, and identifies the types of parties you need to have relationships with. Chapter 12 provides further detail on what is needed to establish working relationships within a personal network.

The process can be likened to courting relationships with the opposite sex. The public organizations are like school dances. They provide forums where people can meet and get acquainted. Developing a meaningful personal relationship generally takes more than a first meeting at a dance, or only seeing each other at dances.

Public Organizations for Networking

There are a number of networking organizations available that can be used to establish collaborative R&D programs in manufacturing. Two organizations that exist for the explicit purpose of facilitating collaborative R&D programs in manufacturing are the National Center for Manufacturing Sciences (NCMS) and the Consortium for Advanced Manufacturing—International (CAM-I). The meetings these organizations hold are particularly valuable forums for exchanging and evolving ideas and visions that can lead to collaborative development programs. These organizations are described further in Chapter 7.

Networking can also be accomplished through professional associations such as the Society of Mechanical Engineers (SME), the Institute of Electrical and Electronics Engineers, Inc. (IEEE), the Institute for Interconnecting and Packaging Electronic Circuits (IPC), National Machining and Tooling Association (NMTA), Advanced Manufacturing Technology (AMT), American Society of Mechanical Engineers (ASME), and many others. In Washington, D.C., the Technical Entrepreneurs and Intrapreneurs Network (TEIN) provides a forum for area businessmen to exchange technical ideas and establish contacts outside the normal set of people they work with. Local service organizations, such as Rotary Clubs, can also provide an environment for networking.

Government-sponsored workshops, particularly those conducted by the National Institute of Standards and Technology (NIST), are valuable forums for networking the resources needed for collaboration. The NIST workshops are structured to promote collaboration in particular industries and technologies and to encourage participation in NIST's Advanced Technology Program (ATP).

Participants and Roles in Collaboration

PARTICIPANTS IN COLLABORATION

Getting the right participants involved in collaborative R&D is critical to pursuing any vision. The importance of end-user involvement in providing direction to any effort aimed at getting R&D applied was addressed in Chapter 3. Collaborative development efforts can involve a number of different combinations consisting of different organizations such as:

- End-users
- Technology development companies
- Manufacturing companies supplying parts to original equipment manufacturers (OEMs)
- Universities
- Government agencies
- Facilitators

For collaboration to work, each participant needs to benefit from the effort. All parties need to be selfish in this respect. The collaborative program has to be in line with the development that each organization would otherwise be pursuing as part of its core business. What is considered to be a benefit changes from one organization to another. Application of technology is needed to benefit an end user, while publishing a new theoretical foundation is a benefit to a university. The following are descriptions of how different organizations benefit from collaborative development (benefits for end-user organizations are repeated from Chapter 3 for comparison).

End-User Production Center

The principal benefits an end-user production center can realize from participating in collaborative development are increased productivity, more robust production processes, and improved product quality. An additional benefit is a potentially enhanced supplier base. Productivity increases result from the application of technology developed to address end users' needs. Many times, improved processes and quality result from the sharing of insights among collaborators as to how a process might work better. Information sharing can also result in finding suppliers that may be more highly skilled in a particular area.

End-User Research and Development Center

In-house R&D centers are under intense pressure to reduce technology development cycle times and cut costs. These organizations are also being required to devote more of their resources to short-term R&D and product programs. Benefits corporate R&D centers can realize from participating in collaborative development include leveraging the personnel expertise of other participants to get better results faster and reducing the amount of time it takes to get their development efforts adopted by one of their company's production centers. The applications of emerging technologies developed at corporate R&D centers are generally in the form of new process technologies. New process technologies need to be integrated into the companies' established processes to be able to realize benefit. Collaboration can assist companies in this integration. The development of new products can also result from collaboration.

Technology Development Companies

The principal benefit a technology development company can realize from participating in collaborative R&D is in gaining market acceptance of the technologies it's developing. Working with large companies enables market requirements to be better integrated with the technology being developed. This is particularly true for those companies whose business is to supply the technology they develop to a market. Other technology development companies form their business around getting contracts to do research, and may not have the sales and marketing staffs needed to take technology to the market. For these companies, collaboration focuses their efforts toward research that has commercial potential, which they can sell or license to sales and marketing companies.

Manufacturing Supplier Companies

Manufacturing supplier companies form the supply base that provides component parts to large automotive, aerospace, and consumer products companies. The objective of collaborative development programs involving manufacturing parts supplier companies is to improve the productivity of the combined total enterprise consisting of the end user and its suppliers. Principal benefits a manufacturing supplier company can realize from participating in collaborative development are improved business with its sponsoring customer and exposure to new customers. Those suppliers involved in this development will have a business advantage in adopting emerging technologies that can provide them with a competitive advantage.

Universities

Universities create not only the future talent for industry, but also the advances in frontier science and technology that underpin the development of breakthrough technologies. The principal benefit a university can realize from participating in collaborative development is recognition, as well as an opportunity to stay current with needs and applications of technology. Recognition attracts students and faculty with interest in a highlighted subject area and will attract potential complementary funding from government and industry, which needs a steady stream of the best and brightest people with the proper skill mixes. It is also important for research universities to enhance their research capabilities and resources, ensuring that their curricula are applicable to future market needs. Working closely with industry in collaborative projects will help to accomplish these critical needs.

Government Agencies

Government agencies can provide funding and technical expertise to collaborative R&D programs. The U.S. federal laboratories have unmatched supercomputer capabilities, specialized energy research, and large-scale engineering experience that are needed in industry applications. Federal lab collaboration with universities and industry benefits all three. The ability to solidify technological networks can be rewarding; however, continued improvement with intellectual property issues and red tape in establishing new cooperative research and development agreements (CRADAs) must continue.[1] A principal benefit a government agency can realize from participating in collaborative development is in recognition. Positive recognition generates political capital with the recognition that taxpayers' money is being well invested. This helps ensure that the agency receives future funding.

Facilitators

The principal benefit a facilitating organization can realize from participating in collaborative development is recognition. Recognition that an organization can establish and manage successful collaborative development programs helps ensure that the organization will continue to have a role as a facilitator. This recognition will attract additional companies interested in future collaborative R&D efforts, as well as assist in getting those efforts funded from industry and/or government.

ROLES IN COLLABORATION

The following describes the role of each of the organizations that might be involved in collaborative development (other than the role of end-user organizations, which is covered in Chapter 3). An overview of the business drivers that support their organization's existence is provided. Finally, some examples of benefits to these organizations with respect to their business drivers from their involvement in collaborative development efforts are given. These examples identify why each of these organizations should participate in collaborative development programs.

---

[1]*Going Global, The New Shape of American Innovation*, The Council on Competitiveness, September 1998.

Technology Companies

Technology companies include companies that are in business to develop technology and companies that are in business to sell technology. Often technology companies both develop and sell technology. Those companies that only develop technology frequently have relationships with other technology companies that sell their technology. This technology is often embedded in the products of the company selling a larger product, with royalties going to the technology developer for each product sold. Sometimes the technology sales company sells the developed technology outright, taking a sales commission for each technology product sold. If a technology development company does not sell its own products, or have a relationship with a company that can sell its technology, its business is not driven by the market. Companies such as this have government funding as their business base. These companies can conduct valuable research; however, a significant additional investment is often needed to ensure that the research can be robustly applied.

Technology companies represent both the R&D and the niche and general markets in the Technology Development Process described in Chapter 1. Technology companies that sell their technology need to be involved to provide a commercialization path for the results of a collaborative development program.

Technology suppliers should have personnel already working on development in a specific application area that may be proposed for a collaborative development project. The work of these personnel represent an in-kind contribution a technology supplier company can provide in a collaborative development project. These companies generally have a specific focus for their development activities. The collaborative development programs they get involved in need to map closely with their internal development plans. This is a requirement for them to realize benefits from a collaborative development program. Technology companies generally have a limited number of key personnel who work on their next-generation products. Diverting those personnel from working on next-generation products can undermine a company's existence. However, focusing their next-product generation and reducing the risk of market acceptance through collaborative development can significantly benefit the company. Its efforts will be leveraged through:

- Working with experts in the field from the user companies.
- Getting rapid feedback from testing at user sites on user problems.
- Obtaining potential funding from users to either hire additional support, hire consultants, and/or cover costs.
- Potentially interfacing with experts in the field from other technology companies.
- Obtaining funding to match in-kind contribution from the government (if a proposal is submitted and funded).

This can result in completing R&D sooner than doing it internally, and accomplishing it in such a manner that there is a certain market for the products being developed through working with the users.

Some examples in which collaborative development has benefited a technology supplier by enabling it to leverage its limited development personnel resources are:

- MSC was able to develop and demonstrate new interfaces and capabilities in its computer-aided engineering pre- and postprocessing software through an RRM project sponsored by General Motors,
- MSC was able to leverage its involvement in development of the Standard for the Exchange of Product Model Data (STEP) with Lockheed Martin and Boeing into additional business with those companies.

Collaborative development with technology end users helps technology companies cross the chasm in the Technology Development Process described in Chapter 1.

Parts Supplier Companies

Parts supplier companies are those that provide parts or subassemblies to original equipment manufacturers (OEMs) for assembly into their final products. They are members of the extended OEM enterprise. These companies can be large suppliers such as TRW, subsidiaries of large companies such as United Technologies Automotive, or small or medium-sized enterprises.

OEM parts supplier companies represent the general market in the

Technology Development Process. These companies are the users of new manufacturing processes, equipment, and information technologies. Parts suppliers, and the way they interface with the OEMs, represent the present manufacturing, information, and communications processes being used in the extended enterprise. Any new technology developed will need to be able to be integrated into these processes, or readily and cost-effectively replace these processes, while maintaining the ability to meet market demand for the products parts suppliers produce.

The personnel working in companies which provide parts to OEMs have process expertise and business acumen that form the backbone of the industrial base. Their primary business drivers focus around staying in business. They do not have the depth of resources to allow them the luxury of making mistakes. In many cases, they do not have personnel trained to efficiently use technology, and they do not have management trained to be able to make the process changes needed to take advantage of technology. This environment makes it very difficult for parts suppliers to participate in collaborative development programs. Their need to be able to show financial justification in a short period makes collaboration difficult.

The principal benefits provided to parts companies through collaborative development are the relationships with their customers. This is the primary driver of the involvement of parts supplier companies in the Technologies for Enterprise-Wide Engineering (Appendix C) and Open Supplier Integration Center (Appendix J) initiatives. There have been many cases in which a number of parts supplier companies work together through a regional economic development program to promote the application of new technologies to the local business base. This is the case with the National Institute for Flexible Manufacturing (NIFM) in northwestern Pennsylvania. The NIFM, on limited resources, was able to establish the requirements and training needed to integrate electrical discharge machining (EDM) technology into the regional infrastructure of small tool and die shops. A significant amount of this was done during the early stages of the NIFM through weekly breakfast meetings involving the presidents and technical experts of a number of local companies in Meadville, Pennsylvania. Those meetings proved to be an efficient use of time for all the individuals involved.

Universities

Universities range from those with research institutions such as the Massachusetts Institute of Technology (MIT), California Institute of Technology, and Carnegie-Mellon University to those focusing on applications to assist local manufacturing such as Rochester Institute of Technology, University of Missouri at Rolla, and Marshall University.

Long-term research has long been a forte of universities. Combined with investments from industry and government, this science infrastructure has benefited us all and had a positive impact on our economic and security needs. However, increased global competition, rapid technological change, and budget pressure have forced government to cut back and industry to allocate a higher percent of resources to product development and applied research. Companies that have long been supporters of long-term general research are channeling their investments more toward research areas which might leverage their own internal programs. Because of these shifting strategies, universities must now balance their levels of industry-targeted research and more basic long-term research. All of this means a larger research scope for universities with less discretionary resources. Clearly, more funding could help to solve this dilemma, but significantly more financial support from industry seems unlikely. A strategy designed to make maximum use of resources, including using in-kind resources from universities in projects with industry and industry resources assisting in university research, may prove to be a more productive collaboration.

The research conducted at larger universities represents the basic research and some of the development shown in the Technology Development Process in Figure 1.1 in Chapter 1. Smaller universities and colleges that are involved in working with manufacturing are a source of applied development that local companies can leverage. Most university involvement in collaborative R&D programs has been as a third party contracted to provide a particular technology expertise.

The primary drivers for university involvement in collaborative R&D are recognition, funding, and the foundation for spin-off companies. Recognition, as stated in Chapter 2, assists in attracting students, quality faculty, and private and public funds. The MIT Leaders for Manufacturing program has been of assistance in developing a strong relationship with Ford and involving students in helping develop and advance Direct Engineering[SM]. A number of universities receive funding for participating in collaborative development programs. Some examples include:

- The University of Texas at Arlington receiving funds as part of an RRM project to evaluate manufacturing applications of autonomous agent software.
- The University of Illinois receiving funding to assist in developing STEP standards to exchange the features of a product model.
- The Center for Optics Manufacturing at the University of Rochester receiving funds from Kodak, Texas Instruments, and other companies to advance optics manufacturing technology.

The evolution of companies can result from a university's participation. An example is the establishment of STEP Tools, Inc., spinning off from Rensselaer Polytechnic Institute as a result of the Defense Advanced Research Projects Agency (DARPA) Initiative in Concurrent Engineering.

Government Agencies

The role of the federal government, as defined in the Constitution, is to provide for the common defense and promote the general welfare of the United States. The two government agencies that principally provide cofunding for collaborative R&D are DARPA (for the common defense) and the Advanced Technology Program (ATP) of the National Institute of Standards and Technology (NIST) (to promote the general welfare). There are a multitude of other agencies that can provide funds and/or resources for collaborative development, including various labs and divisions in the armed services, the National Aeronautics and Space Administration (NASA), and the Department of Energy. Just about every agency has funds available to conduct research, and conduct competitions for contracts, but few at present have the contractual expertise needed to support collaborative development.

The availability of matching government funds often proves to be the catalyst for establishing collaborative development programs. This spur can be more valuable than the program funds. In the Rapid Response Manufacturing program, the participating companies contributed an estimated $15 million more than they were obligated to under the cooperative agreement with NIST. This estimate is likely low. The ATP contribution to the program was $19.8 million, which covered approximately 40 percent of the commitments made by the participating companies. While one could ask why the government provided any funds, it needs to be recognized that without the deadlines established by the government, the program would never have come into being. It's a credit to NIST and the program that the companies opted to provide effort well above their contractual requirement.

While government agencies can provide cofunding for collaborative R&D programs (further discussed in Chapter 6), the national and military labs also have some of the best personnel available to conduct research. These personnel can often be contracted through cooperative R&D agreements (CRADAs). The Printed Wiring Board program contracted Sandia National Laboratory personnel and the Rapid Response Manufacturing program contracted Oak Ridge personnel through CRADAs.

Facilitators

Facilitators consist of consortia, such as the National Center for Manufacturing Sciences (NCMS), Consortium for Advanced Manufacturing—International (CAM-I), SEMATECH, and others, which are generally nonprofits, as well as state and local government agencies.

Their principal role is to facilitate economic development of a particular industry segment or geographical area. While the establishment of collaborative development programs is not necessarily a primary objective for all facilitating organizations (with the exception of NCMS and CAM-I, which are further discussed in Chapter 7), they can provide assistance in networking and, depending on their experience base, assist in establishing the contracting and administration of any collaborative development. These aspects and their importance are addressed in Chapters 14 and 18.

Network Summary

Public organization and personal networks are used to identify potential partners for a collaborative development program. Personal networks are cultivated with individuals from all organizations that can play a role in a potential collaborative effort. The strength of the personal network, based on credibility and trust, provides the foundation for getting the corporate commitments needed for a program.

In getting commitments for collaborative development programs, it is important to understand and recognize the interests of the respective organizations. A simplified view of these interests is shown in Table 5.1.

TABLE 5.1   Table of Interests

Group	Interest/Metric
Major manufacturer	
Production center	Daily product throughput
Technology center	Development and application of technology to product/process
	Publishing
Technology supplier	Selling technology product (software, machine tool/ process capability)
Technology developer	Getting contracts to develop technology
Academia	Publishing
	Pushing the limits of understanding/knowledge
Government	Promoting the general welfare of the people
Facilitator	Providing value-added benefit to members

CHAPTER 6

Funding

Sustained innovation will require new types of R&D funding arrangements. The ability to leverage resources through collaboration and partnerships, to encourage vertical linkages among small and large firms (such as between material and end-user companies and their suppliers), and to find multidisciplinary programs that integrate research and process engineering will all be critical components for innovation.[1] In addition to having an end-user champion networking a vision to get the necessary organizations to pursue a vision, collaborative R&D programs need funding. Funding is needed for:

- The salaries and overhead of the personnel doing the R&D.
- Equipment and facilities used to conduct the R&D.
- "Collaborative overhead" needed to coordinate among partners.
- Cost of providing a contractual commitment among partners.

The personnel a company will be committing to an R&D effort are already on the company's payroll. These personnel are generally on the

---

[1]*Going Global, The New Shape of American Innovation*, The Council on Competitiveness, September 1998, p. 88.

payroll to perform a specific function for the company. In larger companies their job is likely to be conducting the same type of research that is being proposed through the collaboration with other partners. In smaller companies, these individuals are likely to have many other job responsibilities competing for their time as researchers. In all cases, companies need to be able to get value from their personnel involved in R&D, which should come in the form of future products or better processes that result in a positive cash flow for the company. Companies risk going out of business if this value is not sufficient.

In most cases, a company already has the equipment and facilities needed to conduct R&D in a collaborative team. It would not be participating on the team if it had not already invested in those types of facilities.

"Collaborative overhead" is the additional effort involved in leveraging development with other companies above the effort that would be involved for one company to conduct the R&D. This effort translates to the additional cost for collaboration. The additional effort consists of:

- The time needed to exchange information with other members of the development team.
- Travel to meetings of the development team.
- Effort needed to coordinate program planning and management of all the resources of the participating companies.
- Any extra accounting and administrative tasks that may need to be accomplished.

These are the overhead costs of collaboration. This effort and cost is, or should be, minimal relative to the benefits gained in quality and scope of the R&D performed. Chapter 18 goes into detail on administering collaborative R&D programs. In any event, the quality and scope of R&D will be enhanced significantly beyond the capabilities of what one company or organization can conduct. Participants still need to recognize that there is some cost involved with collaboration.

A valuable aspect of funding is that funding transactions are accompanied by legal documents that commit the parties to the collaboration. The presence of a binding document provides incentive for the participating companies to meet their commitments in a manner that reflects on the integrity of the company in the business world.

There are a few options available for funding collaborative R&D. These options consist of:

- *Self-Funding*—where all funds come from the participating companies.
- *Contract Funding*—where all funds come from a third-party organization, often a government agency, which is not involved in conducting the R&D.
- *Cofunding, or Joint Funding*—where the funds come from both the organizations conducting the R&D and a third-party organization.

Self-Funding

The question can be asked as to why funding is needed if the R&D personnel are already on a company's payroll. In some cases, additional funding is not needed. CAM-I, for example, provides a collaborative development environment in which funding (beyond member dues to CAM-I) is not sought. CAM-I pursues establishing collaborative R&D programs that focus on efforts that the participating companies have already made internal commitments to. CAM-I then provides the environment to leverage through collaboration. Participation in the Open Supplier Integration Center (OSIC, described in Appendix J) initiative has not required funding. These are initiatives that leverage efforts that are currently being pursued by the participating companies. The opportunity to leverage efforts by working with other companies is the principal opportunity being provided.

While self-funding of collaborative R&D programs is the ideal, there are some potential drawbacks that need to be recognized and addressed.

SMALL COMPANY RESOURCES

Small companies (under $500 million in annual revenue) often represent the commercialization path larger OEMs want to have in the program.

Some, if not most, of these businesses can't participate unless they get some degree of funding. Companies that do not produce a physical product, but instead contract out the expertise of their personnel, need to have full coverage for those people (coverage meaning the ability to credit the individuals' work time to a contract). If your people are your product, it makes it difficult to participate without full funding. In these cases, one or more of the participating end users can provide the funding (in the same manner they would do so to get needed expertise for the noncollaborative R&D they conduct).

PRIORITIZATION AND MOTIVATION

Self-funded programs, since there is no cash being exchanged, do not have particularly binding commitments from the participants. While a company's intentions may be good, there are other interests competing for the personnel resources being used in collaboration. Interests that result in funding for the company or organization usually take priority for resources. As a result of these competing priorities, collaborative development that is not associated with incoming funds or a critical timeline for a process or product that needs to be put in place often proceeds at a slow pace. Funding provides a degree of prioritization and corporate motivation that is sometimes lacking in programs that do not have outside funding. This has been the experience with OSIC and a concern voiced with some CAM-I efforts. These are issues that can be solved through involvement and commitment of senior management.

Contract Funding

The other extreme is to have the development effort fully funded by a third party through a contract or a grant. Companies and government agencies (particularly the National Science Foundation) fund universities in this manner. Past experience has shown that the participants are more motivated if they have their own resources committed to the success of the effort.

Cofunding or Joint Funding

Many collaborative R&D programs are funded by both the participating companies and a third party. Third-party funding is usually 50 percent or less of the cost of the program. The NIST Advanced Technology Program (ATP) and DARPA are the agencies most affiliated with providing matching funds for collaborative R&D. Chapter 11 provides additional detail on these programs, including contingencies that come with government funds, such as accounting procedures that need to be addressed. Funds could come from a commercial source, such as a bank or venture capital fund. However, the markets for private funding of collaborative development programs have yet to materialize. Several government agencies have programs that provide matching funds.

It is valuable to have personnel from government agencies as part of the network of contacts used to mature a vision. It is important to know the requirements the government has for its program dollars. Some agencies are mission-driven, meaning their R&D expenditures have to relate to performing a particular mission such as going to the moon or providing a particular defense capability.

In addition, government funding opportunities often provide the catalyst to get a collaborative R&D program started. The deadlines provided by the government to submit proposals for federal matching funds can be a valuable forcing function in the development of collaborative development programs, in addition to the matching funds which are awarded to successful project proposals.

CHAPTER 7

Organization

In creating a collaborative program, the program needs to be organized so that roles are recognized and understood, good communications are established, the legal framework for the collaboration is put in place, cash flows are managed between the participants, and means exist to constructively address problems that will arise. The organization structure that supports a collaborative R&D program can have a significant impact on the performance of the program.

Collaborative overhead needs to be minimized in any collaborative program. It needs to be easy for people in a company to be able to collaborate with the people in other companies involved in the joint venture. There can not be any significant overhead burden involved in collaboration, such as large amounts of legal work in putting together the joint venture agreement, additional accounting or timekeeping requirements, or other administrative work. Productively collaborating itself takes more time than a self-contained effort. Requiring additional overhead work from the personnel involved in collaboration can undermine the effort.

Our experience with successful collaborative R&D ventures has involved the following two models for addressing the organization needed for collaboration:

1. One of the participating companies takes primary responsibility for the organization.
2. A third party is used to coordinate the program.

Each approach has its advantages and disadvantages.

The first approach has been successfully used in the Robust Design Computational System (RDCS) program described in Appendix E. Rocketdyne (initially as a subsidiary of Rockwell and later as a subsidiary of Boeing) has coordinated all of the organizational infrastructure needed to establish and manage the program. Structuring the program was done in collaboration with the other partners, particularly their commercialization partner, the MacNeal-Schwendler Corporation. In this situation, Rocketdyne is the prime contractor, and manages the program through a Rocketdyne program manager. The rest of the companies participate at a nearly equal level, committed to the program through a program agreement. The program agreement among the companies followed the program agreement established in the Rapid Response Manufacturing program (see Chapter 14). This approach works well when there is one primary technology developer. Collaborative overhead is minimized, and the complexity of the organization is reduced. The program does become dependent on the ability of the prime developer to deliver technology to partners.

The second approach is preferable when there are a number of principal developing organizations involved. This approach has been successfully used in the Printed Wiring Board and Rapid Response Manufacturing programs, and is intended to be used for the Technologies for Enterprise-Wide Engineering initiative. In each of these, the National Center for Manufacturing Sciences (NCMS) was or is being used as the third party to provide the organizational structure for the collaborative development program.

In this approach the impartial third party provides program management, establishes the legal framework, interfaces with the government as appropriate, and coordinates cash dispersing. Services provided by NCMS include:

1. Administering the collaborative program's quarterly management team meetings:
   • Planning and organizing meetings at agreed sites.
   • Preparing and issuing meeting invitations and agendas.

- Preparing and circulating minutes of the meetings with action items and a schedule of follow-up activities.
2. Administering program communications:
   - Scheduling and facilitating telephone conference calls, circulation of minutes, action items, and schedules of follow-up activities.
   - Maintaining central program files.
   - Managing the production and distribution of progress reports and the final report.
3. Providing contract services:
   - Awarding subcontracts, CRADAs, and other required agreements as directed by the collaborative management team.
   - Closing the program on completion of the work
   - Resolving contractual issues and problems.
   - Processing approval requests to/through government agencies.
4. Responding to sponsor requests.
5. Filing antitrust reports to the Department of Justice under the National Cooperative Research and Production Act of 1984 and amended in 1993.
6. Providing accounting services:
   - Maintaining financial records.
   - Invoicing quarterly cost-sharing reports.
   - Preparing quarterly cost-sharing reports.
   - Preparing quarterly financial reports.
   - Updating program budgets annually.
   - Preparing final reports.
7. Providing technical management services:
   - Preparing statements of work for subcontracts.
   - Evaluating subcontractor proposals.
   - Preparing level of effort assessments.
   - Preparing sole source justifications.
   - Preparing and maintaining the program plan.
   - Evaluating deliverables.
   - Managing intellectual property as required.
   - Facilitating technical reviews and meetings.
   - Maintaining related activity awareness.
   - Managing technical activities to program plan and budget.

- Conducting technology searches when appropriate.
- Preparing program reports.

The collaborative overhead is often higher using the third-party approach than when having one of the participants administrate the program. This higher cost can be considered to be the cost of gaining the benefit of a "neutral broker." Other than the cost, some third-party organizations believe they need to control all the resources in the program. While this can work in some programs in which companies agree to provide personnel "on loan" to an organization, no company is going to let a third party direct what its personnel work on and how its other resources are to be used. (A company's membership in PDES, Inc., to participate in the development of the Standard for the Exchange of Product Model Data (STEP) requires a commitment of person-years of technical personnel. Many PDES, Inc., member companies provide highly qualified personnel to work at PDES's facilities.) Most collaborative development programs the authors have experience with involve a Steering Group which consists of senior managers from the participating companies who in turn direct how their internal resources will work in collaboration in the program. This process is detailed in Part V.

There can also be a so-called technological prejudice within some third-party organizations regarding the technological competency of different companies. Prejudices such as these can make it more or less difficult for a company to work with a third-party organization. There is also the issue of how well a third party can coordinate collaboration. The ability of a third party to facilitate collaboration is demonstrated by its collaborative program accomplishments and evidence of a collaborative culture, as opposed to advertising that it can coordinate collaboration.

The National Center for Manufacturing Sciences has shown itself to be a viable organization for coordinating collaborative R&D programs. NCMS is the largest manufacturing consortium in North America. When NCMS was originally established, it was not as an organization for managing collaborative development. It had been established through congressional legislation as an experiment to help the U.S. machine tool industry regain a competitive position through providing industry direction on how to invest $5 million per year in manufacturing research. NCMS had established a process to select and manage R&D programs among its member companies. The establishment of large collaborative development programs at NCMS took place outside this R&D selection process, and evolved a collaborative culture capable of effectively managing collaborative development programs. The experience of this evolution of business culture has provided the basis for this book.

PART III

Starting a Collaborative Program

The ingredients identified in Part II have to come together at the right times to start a collaborative program. A technology infrastructure has to exist as the foundation for a vision. The vision must address the business needs of a group of OEMs, or lead to the establishment of new OEMs. Funding may be necessary to reduce the technology and market risk. Controlling the dynamics involved in timing such that all of the ingredients come together to make a program is outside the control of any one individual, and usually outside the control of any one company or organization. The individuals championing a vision need to be aware of the dynamics involved in the evolution of the technology infrastructure and business, government, and social environments. They need to be able to tap into these dynamics as the opportunity permits, like a surfer catching a wave.

The source for starting a collaborative development program is the well of ideas in society that can be supported by a business case (the visions discussed in Chapter 4). Some portion of these visions form the basis for internal company business cases. Typically, this happens internally to a business through a process of evaluating and roadmapping emerging technologies. This technology selection evolves into budgetary discussions that lead to eventual winners in the decision on what technologies will be developed by the company. A collaborative development program is not an odds-on favorite to be a selected outcome from this process. This is due to the shortage of true believers in collaboration, and the natural tendency to take a good, or funded, idea and rush to develop it alone in an attempt to capitalize on being the first to market. A precipitating event is generally needed to extract commitments from prospective companies to work together in a collaborative program. Precipitating events can take the form of:

- A restructuring of the business environment.
- Budget pressures.
- The establishment of new regulations or markets (such as European consolidation).
- A deadline for proposals to get government funds.
- The good fortune to have an individual in the process who is a collaboration champion capable of steering the process.

The opportunity to obtain other outside resources, such as government funds to support a prospective program, can help make collaborators out of many technology managers.

Recent experience in establishing the Technologies for Enterprise-Wide Engineering (TEWE) initiative is used in the chapters of this section (Part III). The establishment of this initiative represents the cumulation of 10 years of experience in establishing collaborative development programs and a network of believers with common needs who understand the risks and rewards of such endeavors. The Direct Metal Deposition program is provided as an example of a program that had all the necessary ingredients, but did not materialize because the timing for getting funding was off.

The following four chapters describe a process for reading and riding these dynamics (in the same manner a surfer reads the water to catch a wave) to start a collaborative R&D program. These chapters identify how to:

- Network a vision by formulating and evolving ideas that have internal business commitments from companies to create a concept that can attract commitments from other companies interested in collaboration.
- Facilitate the initial meeting needed to start a collaborative program.

- Coordinate and assist in getting internal company/organization commitments.
- Get government assistance, if necessary, by working with government agencies to establish a collaborative program. (While most of the government focus in this book is in working with U.S. federal government agencies, there is also some reference to working with other governments around the world.)

CHAPTER 8

Network a Vision

The process of getting visions for collaborative development programs formulated and evolved into programs is a brokering process. The brokering, conducted by program champions, consists of getting a vision accepted by the people who can develop and implement the vision, and getting their commitment to pursue the vision. The broker is the one or more individuals who are the champions for the program. Good program champions will be able to get the commitments needed for the resources and funding to pursue the vision. Program champions can come from an end-user company, a third-party organization, or a technology supplier.

The key component needed in establishing a collaborative R&D program is having end-user companies involved in the program development. If the program champion is not an end user, the first priority of the program champion in establishing a program should be to get end user companies involved. If the program champion is an end user, that person may want to get a third-party champion to help network the vision. A good number of end users to have initially is three. Three is a large enough group to generate synergy among themselves, but is small enough to be manageable.

The program champion needs to network the vision among the

other organizations needed to establish and conduct a program with regard to:

- R&D resources
- Funds

While facilities and equipment are also needed, the personnel provide the core capabilities and are the true asset in any R&D program.
R&D resources can come from technology suppliers, universities, federal labs, or other end users. The end users are the primary source for
identifying the other companies and organizations that can provide the
additional R&D resources needed. This is subject to the corporate culture of the end-user company and its management's recognition of the
value of technology generated from outside the company. The organizational network is a secondary source for identifying companies and
R&D organizations with the capabilities needed to conduct the proposed R&D.

The effort needed to pursue a vision needs to be realistically scoped
to identify the types of personnel and material resources needed in the
effort. Personnel who have experience in developing and, just as important, deploying technology that is comparable to that being pursued in
development are the best source for estimating the effort and resources
that will be needed in a prospective program. These personnel should belong to a company or organization that will be participating in the
prospective program.

Networking takes place at the boundaries of organizations. The
boundaries could be between internal groups within a company, between
companies, or between a company and a government agency or university. The program champions networking a vision need to recognize this
and understand the boundaries of the organizations that need to be
brought into the program.

Program champions need to network funding sources, or provide a
compelling business case, to pay for the resources needed in the program. Most business executives, particularly those in operations, do
not look for collaboration opportunities. Collaboration is beyond the
resources they can easily control or influence, and hence is not generally considered. Funding coming with collaboration can get execu-

tives to consider collaboration as an option. Common funding sources for many collaborative R&D programs come from a government (such as a U.S. government agency, the European Commission, or the Japanese Ministry for Technology and Industry). Networking with these agencies is important to understand their interests, motivations, and timing.

The networking resources available to a program champion are:

- Public organizations.
- The program champion's individual personal network.

Personal networks are the most effective means for getting the resources needed to establish a collaborative R&D program. Establishing an effective personal network takes time and commitment. A key to establishing and expanding a good personal network is being able to establish successful programs. The recognition gained in establishing successful programs provides a reputation that attracts the needed ingredients for future efforts. The first successful collaborative development program established by Gene Allen was the Printed Wiring Board program. The experience and recognition derived from that program provided him with the credibility needed to start the Rapid Response Manufacturing (RRM) program. Success in establishing RRM led to:

- The Robust Design Computational System (RDCS) program.
- The Computational Aeroacoustics Analysis System (CAAS) program.
- Involvement in collaborative development of product model data software (PDES, Inc., STEP standards).
- The Technologies for Enterprise-Wide Engineering (TEWE) initiative.

The thrust behind all of the companies involved with these programs was the opportunity to come together to solve a common technical need more efficiently than any one company could by itself.

Networking OSIC and TEWE

The initial vision driving the TEWE program was networked through an already established personal network that greatly facilitated the effort. This personal network was that of the RRM program companies. The RRM program had ended on September 30, 1997, but the Executive Steering Committee had decided to continue having the weekly teleconferences as long as there was a strong business case to justify the time invested.

A white paper was drafted in the last six months of the program to capture the vision of where the development of future information technology would be directed at the RRM companies. This white paper is shown in Exhibit 8.1. This paper was circulated within the participating companies as well as NCMS and other organizations. In the last months of RRM, Ken Kuna from Ford had asked if Gene Allen could possibly put together another program. The year before, Scott Duval from Pratt & Whitney had made the same request.

Rick Jarman had worked with Gene Allen when Mr. Allen was at NCMS and with him in RRM as well. Mr. Jarman knew that Mr. Allen's skill and personal network could help him with a project he wanted to launch at Kodak. In October 1996, Mr. Jarman met with Mr. Allen to discuss how they could pull together a project to build on Kodak's intent to form a capability that would demonstrate how real product development teams, using existing tools, technology, standards, and processes, could rapidly engage Kodak and other OEM suppliers to cost-effectively produce 6 sigma quality parts (6 sigma quality is 3.4 defects per million parts). A demonstration facility was envisioned to be used to train interested suppliers in utilizing this capability in a way that fit their business needs. The facility would also offer a platform at which new or emerging capabilities could be evaluated. This demonstration center was to become the Open Supplier Integration Center (OSIC) at the Rochester Institute of Technology. The OSIC provides a key ingredient that was to become part of the TEWE initiative.

EXHIBIT 8.1 RRM II White Paper

RRM II
White Paper
6/17/97

Purpose

This white paper has been drafted by the Rapid Response Manufacturing (RRM) Steering Committee to gain support in establishing a follow-on program to the RRM program. The RRM Steering Committee proposes to continue the environment in which the participating companies can continue beneficial collaborative activities. These activities include:

1. Identification of collaborative opportunities based on a common vision.
2. Evaluation and execution of precompetitive development pilot projects.
3. Submission of proposals for funding from outside the participating companies.

Problem

The problem is how a company ensures that it continues to be competitive in today's global environment. U.S. companies need to be able to maintain the high quality of life in the U.S. while becoming flexible enough to rapidly design and make products around the world to meet varying regional market demands.

RRM Product

The RRM program has been valuable in enabling the participating companies to pilot developing technologies on applications in the company's design-manufacturing processes which they would not have independently pursued. RRM piloted over 100 emerging computer-based information, communications, and rapid prototyping technologies focused on the design-manufacture process for products characterized as mechanical assemblies (cars, planes, engines, etc.). Many of these technologies have been consequently adapted by the participating companies with significant return.

One the most valuable and effective capacities that has emerged from the RRM program is the highly effective working relationship established among the participating members of the Steering Group. These relationships have resulted in the exchange of valuable information on lessons learned in piloting new technologies.

EXHIBIT 8.1 *(Continued)*

New Vision

To preserve the value in maintaining the intercompany relationships established through RRM, a new vision has been adopted by the RRM Steering Group to guide in the development of pilot projects. This new vision is the concept of Global Engineering Efficiency: the ability to efficiently execute 24-hour contiguous engineering using integrated product development teams that can interact from any point around the globe. The RRM Steering Group believes that the pursuit of this vision will lead to solutions to the above-stated problem.

New Mission

To realize this vision, the RRM Steering Group has established this overarching mission, to which RRM follow-on pilot projects would contribute: Extend global engineering competitiveness across the supply chain to effectively utilize all the resources available to better conduct engineering in the design-manufacture processes used to get products to the market.

Pilot projects would balance people, processes, and technology focusing on design reuse and innovation. The Appendix provides further detail on these focus areas.

Objectives

Goals for implementing Global Engineering Efficiency are:

- 50 percent reduction in total engineering effort.
- 75 percent reduction in engineering/unit in a specific product program.
- 50 percent reduction in cycle time.
- 50 percent improvement in quality.

A metric in realizing this goal is the ability to provide the right information to the right person at the right time, integrating people, processes, and organizations.

Issue

With NIST funding for RRM ending in September 1997, should the RRM consortium companies continue to work together in piloting emerging technologies in their design-manufacturing processes?

Strategy

Given corporate support from the RRM consortium companies, the following strategy will be pursued:

(continued)

EXHIBIT 8.1 *(Continued)*

1. Establish the organizational infrastructure to extend the consortium of companies participating in RRM.
   • Under NCMS/TRC umbrella
2. Continue meeting for at least six months after NIST ATP funding for RRM ends.
   • Quarterly meetings
   • Weekly teleconferences
3. Pursue funding opportunities.
   • $40 to $50 million over several years
4. Identify collaborative pilots projects which balance:
   • People
   • Processes
   • Technology
5. In the event pilot projects have not been established after six months, the RRM consortium companies will disband.

Appendix
RRM II
Potential Common Focus Area

Past Value

The RRM program has facilitated the successful execution of a large number of precompetitive technology pilot projects over the five years of the program. Summary reviews of these projects may be reviewed in the RRM program quarterly reports. Perhaps one the most valuable and effective capacities that has emerged from within the RRM program has been the highly effective working relationship established among the participating members of the Steering group. These relationships have resulted in the exchange of valuable information on lessons learned in piloting new technologies. It is considered that the immediate discontinuation of the cohesive activities of the RRM Steering Group and represented companies would result in the loss of the capacity for this body to continue to influence and facilitate improvements to participating companies and the U.S. industrial base. Technology pilots are a proven and effective means to (1) accelerate the adaptation, (2) focus the development of new technologies, and (3) reduce risk within the participating companies. Successful pilots of new technology are precursors to the changes in company processes, structure, and culture needed to effectively use new technologies to stay in business. The ability of RRM to share the experience from technology pilots among the multiple companies and industries represented provides

EXHIBIT 8.1 (*Continued*)

(1) a proven and valuable method for industry to validate technology, and (2) a basis for evolving the participating companies.

The RRM companies, as a collective entity, provide a credible representation of the U.S. industrial base. The credibility of the group provides valuable leverage in efforts to get funding and resources committed to common efforts, either from the participating companies or from government agencies.

New Vision

While RRM is coming to a successful conclusion, the RRM companies recognize that there may be unique value in maintaining the intercompany relationships established through RRM. A new vision for the consortia of RRM member companies is needed.

The vision related to the proposed continuation of the RRM consortium is encompassed in the concept of Global Engineering Efficiency: the ability to efficiently execute 24-hour contiguous engineering using integrated product development teams that can interact from any point around the globe.

New RRM Mission

The overarching mission which RRM follow-on pilot projects would contribute toward is: Extending global engineering competitiveness across the supply chain to effectively utilize all the resources available to better conduct engineering in the design-manufacture processes used to get products to the market. Pilot projects would balance people, processes, and technology focusing on design reuse and innovation.

Effective implementation of this next generation of design automation will require that people, processes, and technologies be brought into balance and alignment.

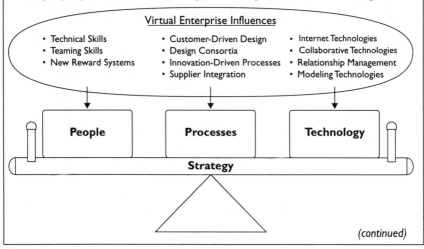

(continued)

EXHIBIT 8.1 (*Continued*)

People

- Engineers, manufacturers, quality control personnel, salespeople, marketing personnel, suppliers and even customers—all of the individuals involved with creating and communicating design intent—will need access to future systems for all design-associated information.
- New technologies (Internet, interenterprise product data management (PDM), relationship management tools, etc.) that will form the next generation of system architecture will require a new set of technology skills and training.
- Technology competency will need to move from the traditional bell curve where the vast majority of enterprise personnel simply use technology in a task-driven, individual productivity fashion (such as creating component models, processing change orders, etc.) to a new, more comprehensive program.

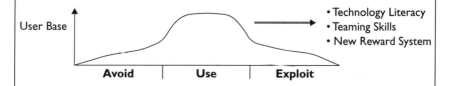

- The new comprehensive program (new set of incentives, rewards, and technology literacy) must be designed to raise the user's competency to benefit from the new technology (e.g., creating components models that can be reused or that fit properly in an overall assembly).
- To properly align the people element of the next generation product development strategy, an individual's and partner's team skills and technology competency must be valued and rewarded as highly as engineering know-how and creativity.
- Metrics in this paradigm will include: speed to create complete engineering models with first-time fit; fewest engineering change orders (ECOs) required; process know-how; and external collaboration.

Processes

- The process focus will continue to expand outward to foster greater collaboration among suppliers, business partners, and customers.
- This focus will produce designs of more specially tailored products that have a higher probability of market acceptance and generate closer working relationships with business partners and suppliers that can deliver high value-added products and services to meet new market demands.

EXHIBIT 8.1 (*Continued*)

- The product-centric, project-team style of engineering will evolve toward a market-centric organization whereby team members are collectively given tasks and rewarded for achieving competitive leadership along market lines instead of product lines.
- The new market-based organization will have greater freedom and flexibility to outsource or insource and select partners to respond more quickly and efficiently to market needs.
- Engineering action will be driven predominantly and more directly by the need to respond to specific external markets or customer needs (a customer opportunity order) vs. traditional, internally focused demands (an ECO, for example).
- The emphasis will shift from an ECO-driven, product-centric environment where engineering labor is focused on fixing mistakes to a mistake-free, right-the-first-time, customer opportunity environment where most engineering activity will be to develop new products or product variations aimed at capturing specific market opportunities.
- To achieve a customer opportunity driven process, engineering activity at all levels will need to be sensitized to the market and assume an innovation-driven posture.
- Market-centric teams will need to have organizational agility and the ability to leverage innovative ideas and technologies (internally and externally developed).
- These teams will be measured and rewarded by swift competitive market success.

Technologies

New technology advances and trends will dominate the design automation landscape during the next five years, including the emergence of the Internet, new modeling foundations, and tools for leveraging intellectual capital.

Product Innovation via Requirements-Driven Engineering Infrastructure

- Electronic processing of voice of customer requirements.
- Early definition of product characteristics leveraged throughout the product life cycle.
- Tools for decision support (e.g., Quality Functional Deployment, Design of Equipment diagrams, relationship managers, etc.).
- Integration with PDM and multidisciplinary analysis to track decisions and approval process, and access data.

(continued)

EXHIBIT 8.1 (*Continued*)

- Process knowledge leveraged for timely change propagation.
- Simulation, test and field experience electronically captured and leveraged in corporate memory/knowledge base for future product development.
- Mechanical product development process management—mechanisms for supporting the mechanical product development process with workflow simulation, project management, workflow management and control, and integrated PDM.
- Knowledge management—mechanisms for identifying, collecting, representing, storing, accessing, and managing engineering knowledge in any and all of its various forms including knack, know-how, subject-specific, company-specific, industry standard, and so on.
- Cost management—engineering support systems to: (1) assess nonrecurring engineering cost prior to the execution of mechanical design, (2) assess manufacturing cost at the completion of design and prior to manufacturing execution, (3) apply design advisors to assist in evaluating and recommending designs which minimize fabrication and assembly costs Design for Manufacture/Design for Assembly.
- Distributed analysis—improve the ability to conduct physical analysis of product designs early in the design process. Demonstrate a "distributed product development-manufacturing" capability by integrating suppliers into the analysis process. Provide any engineer involved in the distributed design process (internal to the user company or at a supplier site or subsidiary) with the ability to do any analysis on a part model and optimize that model.
- Tolerance stack-up Analysis and Simulation—develop and demonstrate an integrated and easy-to-use assembly level tolerance stack-up and simulation analysis.
- Manufacturing process planning—research and development for the application and implementation of multilevel planning using knowledge/agent-based technologies.
- Part fixturing—automation of modular fixturing techniques including possible use of knowledge-based applications for the use of hybrid and dedicated fixtures.

Component Management and Supplier Integration via Network-Based Virtual Enterprise Computing

- Broad information highway for linking enterprises for exchanging design information and accessing component libraries.
- Internet technologies such as Java graphical user interfaces (GUIs), Web

EXHIBIT 8.1 (*Continued*)

browsers, Virtual Reality Modeling Language (VRML) and HyperText Modeling Language (HTML) servers will play much larger roles, especially in conjunction with PDM.

- Additional expansion technologies in the shorter term will include VRML-type Computer Aided Design viewers, Internet read-only PDM clients, and Internet-enabled access to the supply chain.
- Supplier (supply chain) integration—proof of concept development of a truly integrated, geographically distributed, and tool-independent supply chain that can produce affordable 6 sigma quality products in order quantities of one.

New Modeling Technologies

The transition to the next-generation environment will yield significant changes to the mechanical modeling foundation and approach.

1. *Interoperability Services (Architecture)*—Enabling underlying software architecture to support integration of the software products required to execute and facilitate the product development process for Direct Engineering^{SM}.
2. *Data Exchange (STEP) Enhancement*—A broad range of implementation evaluation of STEP capabilities including product data management aspects.
3. *Federated PDM with Synchronized Product Structure*—Accessibility of PDM functions across business functions including design and manufacturing that will allow access to data that is spread across multiple PDM products and installations. Synchronize product structure across multiple views (as designed, per factory as built, as maintained, functional, etc.) with cross-structure mapping to relate the structures of specifications, functional breakdown, design detail, and so on, enabling the facilitation and integration of information from early project inception through production.
4. *Product Model Features Management*—Develop capabilities to support "feature mapping" from construction to design to manufacturing. Develop specific capabilities to support management of GM powertrain features.
5. The ability to effectively model and leverage design intent across the virtual enterprise.
   - The modeler has the ability to capture and edit geometric and non-geometric design intent that ultimately results in driving or influencing the physical design of the product.

(continued)

EXHIBIT 8.1 *(Continued)*

- The information to be captured will include tolerances, boundary conditions, performance criteria, packaging constraints, quality and compliance specs, and costing guidelines.
- Product will be built upon state-of-the-art hybrid geometric modeling utilizing variational geometry.

6. Increased usage and exploitation of top-down, assembly-driven modeling technologies.
   - Increased collaboration will require all team members work from an accurate, up-to-date, digital prototype of the design whereby sub-assemblies and components are checked for fit, interferences, and tolerances in real-time.
   - Large assembly navigation tools using neutral file representations (e.g., VRML) will operate in conjunction with CAD and PDM systems to provide access to and manipulation of models.

7. Beginning of the end of the engineering drawing as the primary mechanism for communication design intent.
   - Minimally dimensioned 2D drawings containing only relevant manufacturing information or call-outs will be generated to augment the 3D model; manufacturing will need 3D skills.

Technologies for Leveraging Intellectual Capital

Intellectual capital in the context of product development is defined as the collective design know-how of the corporation. This know-how translates to human assets (e.g., the experience of design team members) and digital assets (e.g., CAD/CAM/CAE/PDM databases).

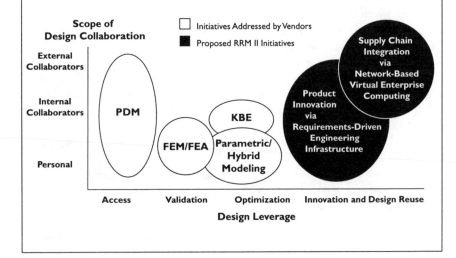

Mr. Jarman knew that Kodak's needs in this area were not unique and that by partnering with other companies that had similar needs the group could gain the functional expertise needed to realize this vision. The companies choosing to join Kodak in the OSIC initiative were Texas Instruments Defense Systems (now Raytheon), Rocketdyne Division of Boeing North America, Ford Motor Company, MacNeal-Schwendler Corporation, and forward-thinking smaller companies such as Harbec Plastics and Liberty Precision Industries.

In addition to the end-user interest in TEWE, NIST conducted workshops during the same time period in Collaborative and Distributed Design and in Knowledge-Based Systems Interoperability. These workshops were very synergistic with the white paper, and demonstrated that there was government recognition of these R&D topics as potential funding candidates. Many individuals from the RRM member companies participated in the workshops. The workshops also identified additional companies that could participate in TEWE.

Timing

Timing is a major factor involved in being able to establish a collaborative development program. In addition to having a vision supported by end-user champions and R&D resources available, infrastructure technology and the availability of funding need to converge with corporate commitments to start a collaborative R&D program. The time frame needed to put together a collaborative R&D program is typically a year or more. Table 8.1 shows the time frame needed to establish a sample of some collaborative development programs.

The criticality of timing was evidenced with the effort involved in networking the Direct Metal Deposition (DMD) initiative. The inability of this initiative to get started demonstrates the difficulty in getting a program to precipitate out of a vision.

The DMD initiative had started from a vision sponsored by Rocketdyne. Gene Allen was introduced to this vision at a 1993 meeting at

TABLE 8.1 Time Frame Needed to Establish Collaborative Development Programs

Program	Program Envisioned	Initial Meeting	Proposal Due Date	Award Announced	Contract Date
Printed Wiring Board (PWB)	June 1990	August 1990	September 1990	April 1991	September 1991
Rapid Response Manufacturing (RRM)	December 1990	July 1991	September 1991	April 1992	October 1992
Compressing Integrated Product Engineering (CIPE)/ Robust Design Computational System (RDCS)	January 1993	January 1993	March 1993/ September 1995	February 1996	June 1996

Rocketdyne (see Appendix K on the author's personal network with Rocketdyne). Rocketdyne had developed a laser as part of the Strategic Defense Initiative and was looking at how that technology could be commercialized for application in the general market. The vision was to build a machine that would support the laser and an applicator for powdered metal. Products could be built on a movable table that was programmed to move in the right directions and speeds such that the laser would continuously fuse the powdered metal and build the product. Steve Babcock and Gene Allen used NCMS as an organizational network and their personal networks to promote interest in this vision.

When Gene Allen, who was one of the program champions, left NCMS in November 1993, the DMD initiative seemingly had all of the ingredients needed to establish a program: end-user champions from United Technologies, Ford, Rocketdyne, and Hasbro teamed with a range of technology suppliers, national labs, and university personnel. The team met regularly for about six months in an effort to form a program. The only piece lacking was a precipitating event that could generate funding for this program, such as a proposal deadline for matching funds, a compelling business need, or some other comparable catalyst, to get the program started. All the ingredients seemed to be in place, like having gasoline and air being compressed inside an engine cylinder to the right mixture, but then not having the spark plug fire to get the engine going.

The concept paper in Exhibit 4.1 was drafted to assist in getting government funding, but the DMD group was not able to stay together long enough to wait for the catalyst that would have formalized the group. The individuals participating in the initiative all had jobs to do at their perspective companies and organizations. The group was not able to be held together without the prospect of funding. The technology risk was too great for the technology suppliers, even with end users involved representing a potential market.

The same situation existed with the TEWE initiative. Without the timing of the NIST ATP General Program competition, and the related NIST workshops, the last meeting of the RRM Steering Group on December 19, 1997, would not have led to the TEWE initiative, even with the white paper vision and end-user champions. The September 30, 1998, decision by the NIST ATP not to fund the TEWE initiative has not prevented the end users from independently pursuing efforts to better integrate their extended enterprises through developing the capability to better exchange knowledge. Efforts were still being explored in early 1999 to identify means to enable the end users to effectively leverage their development efforts and work with technology suppliers to ensure generic knowledge definitions and applications that are interoperable.

CHAPTER 9

Initial Meeting

Once a group of companies has expressed interest in a potential program, the next step is to have a meeting to structure a program. The first meeting is critical to forming a program. The participating organizations have to have enough confidence in the success of the effort that they are willing to make commitments. The initial meeting should establish this confidence. The direction resulting from this meeting will determine if there will be a program. The meeting should result in identifying concrete actions to be taken to establish a program.

A significant amount of the nation's most valuable asset—the time of its personnel—goes into meetings. The productivity of meetings can be greatly improved by effectively preparing for, facilitating, and following up with meeting minutes and results. The productivity of the initial meeting is key to reaching the objective of forming a collaborative R&D program.

Meeting Preparation

The initial meeting should identify:

- Technical objectives for the program.
- The commitment needed from the participating companies.
- Deadlines for establishing the program.
- Any program agreement that needs to be put in place.

The objective of the meeting needs to be stated and emphasized in communications before the meeting, at the beginning of the meeting, and at the closing of the meeting. This objective is to develop a program. Program requirements should be identified and agreed on at the meeting by all of the companies. These requirements may include program objectives and benefits, a time line, identification of existing design or manufacturing processes into which the developed technology will be integrated, levels of commitments needed to participate, and actions.

An agenda for the meeting should be established which will lead to a decision on whether to pursue a program, and, if that decision is yes, who needs to take what actions to establish the program. This agenda should be coordinated through all of the program champions prior to the meeting, and then provided to all of the participants prior to the meeting. Preplanning will lead to more efficient and shorter meetings.

The initial meeting that resulted in the Technologies for Enterprise-Wide Engineering initiative was ideal in the sense that all the participants already knew each other and had been previously working together under the Rapid Response Manufacturing (RRM) collaborative development program. During one of the weekly teleconferences held by this group, the decision was made to have a meeting to determine whether to develop a program along the lines described in the RRM II white paper shown in Exhibit 8.1. The forcing function was the upcoming general solicitation for proposals for the NIST Advanced Technology Program, which provides matching funds to selected efforts. RRM had been an ATP program, so the participants were familiar with the administration and operating practices of NIST.

The meeting was held at Ford's Advanced Manufacturing Technology Development Center on December 19, 1997. Bill Waddell, the RRM program manager, had circulated the agenda shown in Exhibit 9.1 to all of the participants on December 15, 1997. The meeting was held among the end-user companies that had participated in RRM, in-

EXHIBIT 9.1 Agenda for Initial Meeting Leading to the Technologies for Enterprise-Wide Engineering Program

---

Proposed 12/15/97

RRM Steering Group Meeting Agenda
RRM Central Site

Ford Advanced Manufacturing Technology Development Center
24500 Glendale Avenue
Detroit, MI 48239

Friday, December 19, 1997

9:15	Program manager comments
9:30	Department of Commerce Inspector General audit status review
10:00	Quantification of results of RRM I
10:30	Break
11:00	NIST background information

- ATP overview—new rules
- Workshop on collaborative and distributed design
- Workshop on knowledge-based systems interoperability
- Opportunity with Congress

12:00	Lunch
12:45	NIST ATP proposal discussion

- Review and discussion of proposed framework (30 minutes)
- Identification of key technology development areas needed (30 minutes)
- Scoping the size and duration of the proposed program (30 minutes)
- Determining cost-sharing scenario (30 minutes)
- Identification of recommended partners/suppliers (30 minutes)

2:45	Break
3:00	Identify action items

- Assign specific proposal drafting tasks
- Assign responsibility for gaining partner/supplier commitment

3:30	Adjourn

cluding Boeing-Rocketdyne, which had participated on some RRM projects on a nonfunded basis. The main reason for this meeting was to determine if any of the end users wanted to work together in a potential program.

Meeting Facilitation

A meeting needs to be facilitated to ensure that consensus decisions are generated and the group is quickly able to come to unanimous agreement on the needed technology focus areas and proposed actions. It's best to have the champions supporting the program control the meeting. The program champion should participate as a facilitator when requested, or if the meeting is not progressing toward meeting its objectives. Exhibit 9.2 shows the overhead slides used to facilitate and coordinate the initial meeting that led to the Technologies for Enterprise-Wide Engineering program.

These overheads highlight the purpose of the meeting (slide 1) and then provide background showing prospects and prospective NIST interest in a program from recent activities and discussion with NIST (slides 2 through 4), an overview of a prospective program (slide 5), identification of the technology development areas needed (slides 6 through 8), and an overview of the knowledge process (slide 9). It is interesting to note that a week earlier NIST had published new rules for the ATP which emphasized partnering and encouraged teaming large companies with small.

Not all meetings proceed as efficiently as the first TEWE meeting. The follow-on meeting that was required is more typical of the first meetings held to establish a program. This meeting was with all of the prospective participants in the program—the technology and parts providers as well as the end users who were able to identify commitments. The agenda for this meeting is shown in Exhibit 9.3. The need to have this meeting was identified at the initial meeting as documented in the initial TEWE meeting minutes shown in Exhibit 9.4. The end users identified

EXHIBIT 9.2 Overheads to Coordinate Initial TEWE Meeting

Slide 1
ATP 98
PURPOSE:
• **PROVIDE COST-SHARE TO INDUSTRY TO DO R&D ON TECHNOLOGIES THAT OFFER SIGNIFICANT, BROAD-BASED BENEFITS TO THE NATION'S ECONOMY, BUT ARE NOT LIKELY TO BE DEVELOPED IN A TIMELY FASHION WITHOUT ATP DUE TO TECHNICAL RISK.**
RULE CHANGE
• **STRONGER EMPHASIS ON CONSORTIA WITH A BROAD RANGE OF PARTICIPANTS.**
PROPOSAL DUE MARCH 18, 1998.

Slide 2
ATP DOES NOT FUND FOLLOW-ON PROGRAMS.
• **ENTERPRISE-WIDE ENGINEERING PROPOSAL NEEDS TO BE TECHNICALLY DIFFERENTIATED FROM RRM.**
• **COMPETITION IS KEENER THAN IT WAS FIVE YEARS AGO.**
• **THERE ARE MANY MORE COMPETITIVE PROPOSALS.**

Slide 3
NIST WORKSHOP
COLLABORATIVE AND DISTRIBUTED DESIGN

RECOMMENDS RESEARCH IN FIVE TOPIC AREAS
• **REPRESENTATIONS**
• **MOVING INFORMATION AMONG DESIGNERS**
• **ACCESSING INFORMATION THROUGHOUT THE LIFE CYCLE**
• **LEVERAGING INFORMATION BETWEEN PRODUCTS**
• **METRICS**

Slide 4
NIST WORKSHOP
KNOWLEDGE-BASED SYSTEMS INTEROPERABILITY

TWO MAIN THEMES
• **KB AND CAE INTEROPERABILITY**
• **CURRENT STANDARDS LACKING**

(continued)

EXHIBIT 9.2 (*Continued*)

FIVE CONCEPTS
- **KNOWLEDGE CHARACTERIZATION**
- **USABILITY**
- **VOCABULARY**
- **COLLABORATION**
- **COST**

Slide 5
ENTERPRISE-WIDE ENGINEERING INITIATIVE TO:
1. **DEVELOP THE CAPABILITY TO CREATE AND CAPTURE KNOWLEDGE.**
2. **DEVELOP THE ABILITY TO USE THAT KNOWLEDGE THROUGH CREATING A <u>KNOWLEDGE MANAGEMENT ORGANIZATION.</u>**

STRATEGY:
1. **DEMONSTRATE THE APPLICATION OF ENTERPRISE-WIDE ENGINEERING IN THE DESIGN AND FABRICATION OF ONE OR MORE COMPLEX PRODUCTS.**
2. **INTEGRATE ENTERPRISE-WIDE ENGINEERING INTO THE SUPPLIER BASE OF THE PARTICIPATING COMPANIES.**

Slide 6
KEY TECHNOLOGY DEVELOPMENT AREAS
- **WEB-ENABLED INFORMATION ENVIRONMENT.**
- **HOW TO STORE AND USE VERY LARGE PRODUCT DATABASES OVER THE WEB.**
- **HOW TO MIX STANDARD PRODUCT DATA WITH NON-STANDARD PRODUCT DATA.**
- **HOW TO EFFICIENTLY MAP LEGACY DATA INTO THE INFORMATION ENVIRONMENT.**
- **DEVELOPMENT OF DESIGN CAPABILITY MODULES AND INTEGRATING MECHANISMS (DEVELOPMENT OF MIDDLEWARE FOR COLLABORATIVE DESIGN).**

Slide 7
KEY TECHNOLOGY DEVELOPMENT AREAS
- **PILOT THE ESTABLISHMENT OF A LIBRARY OF "SMART" DESIGN MODULES.**
- **ESTABLISH INTEROPERABILITY BETWEEN KB AND CAE SYSTEMS.**

EXHIBIT 9.2 *(Continued)*

- **ESTABLISH A COMMON KNOWLEDGE REPRESENTATION SCHEME.**
- **ESTABLISH HIERARCHICAL MEDIATION AND NEGOTIA-TION LEVELS FOR INTERACTING WITH KNOWLEDGE BASES.**
- **ESTABLISH MEANS FOR KNOWLEDGE BASE VALIDA-TION.**

Slide 8
KEY TECHNOLOGY DEVELOPMENT AREAS
- **ESTABLISH A GENERIC MEANS FOR KNOWLEDGE-BASE COMPREHENSION.**
- **PILOT KNOWLEDGE-CAPTURE TECHNOLOGIES.**
- **PILOT KIF WITH EMERGING STANDARDS (STEP, CORB/OLE, JAVA).**
- **CAPTURE DESIGN RATIONALE.**
- **DEVELOP PROBLEM-SOLVING METHOD LIBRARIES.**

Slide 9
THE KNOWLEDGE PROCESS
      COLLECT DATA INCLUDING METADATA
           CONVERT DATA TO KNOWLEDGE
                REPRESENT KNOWLEDGE
                    DELIVER KNOWLEDGE
                        PRODUCT DEFINITION

the prospective technology suppliers and parts supplier companies they wanted to participate with in the program.

Many of the participants did not know one another during this meeting. At a first-time meeting, it is advisable to have all of the parties give brief presentations so that everyone knows who is at the meeting and what the potential roles are for their companies. The key technology areas that required development to realize the TEWE objectives also had to be identified.

The process used to quickly identify technology objectives that everyone could agree on was a modification of a Taguchi "House of Quality" approach. This approach had been used at the first Printed Wiring Board (PWB) program proposal meeting in 1990. At that meeting,

EXHIBIT 9.3 TEWE Proposal Team Meeting

Enterprise-Wide Engineering
February 2, 1998, Proposal Meeting
Ford Advanced Manufacturing Technology Development Center

Meeting Agenda
February 2, 1998
Technology Suppliers Meeting
Meeting Purpose—Select Technology Suppliers to Participate

8:00	Introductions	
8:15	Overview of ATP	MSC
8:30	Proposal drafting schedule	MSC/NCMS
9:00	Overview of program/white paper review	NCMS/MSC
	User company interest in program	
9:15	Ford—Direct Engineering^{SM}	Ford
9:30	Boeing—RS-68 Engine	Boeing
9:45	Kodak—Supplier Integration	Kodak
10:00	Break	
10:15	Overview of technology supplier selection process	NCMS
10:25	Proposed development coordinator	CMU
	Potential partners for emerging information exchange infrastructure	
10:30	CommerceNet AIMS	NexPrise
11:00	Infotest	NCMS
11:30	NIIIP	IBM
12:15	Lunch	
	Roles of MSC/SDRC	
1:00	MSC roles	MSC
1:15	SDRC roles	SDRC
	Potential partners for knowledge-base engineering	
1:30	Beam technologies	
2:00	Cognition	Cognition
2:30	Concentra	Concentra
3:00	Break	
3:30	Discussion: other technology development needs	
4:00	Review of selection process and expected action timeline to proposal	
4:30	End meeting	

EXHIBIT 9.4   Initial TEWE Meeting Minutes

Enterprise-Wide Engineering
Ford AMD Center
December 19, 1997

Attendees: Ron Auble—Kodak, Frank Pijar—Pratt & Whitney, Dave Prawal—Spatial, Peter Nies—Raytheon, Pete Sferro—Ford, Bob Carman—Boeing-Rocketdyne, Dick Wandmacher—GM, Bill Waddell—NCMS, Gene Allen—MSC

ATP Program Decision: The group determined that they would attempt to draft a proposal for the 1998 general ATP competition. Proposals are due March 18, 1998.

Program Description: The thrust of the program will be to develop an interactive knowledge base that can be used by a company with the company's suppliers and partners, to capture, create, and reuse knowledge. The program will pilot the interactive knowledge base to improve product realization (design-manufacture), maintenance and support, modification and upgrade, and disposal.

Scope: The initial program scope was for a five-year, $67.5 million effort with NIST providing $22.75 million in reimbursement. The program will be user-driven with each of the six end users committing $1.5 million per year. The users will receive a NIST reimbursement of $375,000, or 25 percent, per year. Each user is to identify two product suppliers to work with, each of which will be requested to commit $200,000 per year with a $100,000 NIST (50 percent) reimbursement. Seven technology suppliers will be requested to participate with commitments of $400,000 per year, of which NIST would reimburse $200,000 (50 percent). These commitments are outlined in the attached spreadsheet.

ACTIONS
User Companies
By 1/12/98   Identify internal work commitments that can be leveraged by working through this initiative.
By 1/16/98   Identify two product supplier companies to bring into the proposal effort.
             Provide recommendation on the technology supplier companies to be involved.
By 1/30/98   Have verbal commitments from all companies (users, product suppliers, and technology suppliers) to participate.

Gene Allen
By 1/16/98   Draft proposal white paper based on 1/12/98 company inputs.
By 2/2/98   Proposal storyboards prepared.
On 2/2–3/98 Proposal meeting at Ford AMD Center with all participants—one day each with product suppliers and technology suppliers. Writing assignments to be made.
By 2/27/98   First draft of proposal done.
By 3/18/98   Proposal submitted to NIST with written commitments.

AT&T, Digital Equipment Corporation, Texas Instruments, Hamilton Standard, and Sandia Laboratories all had very diverse perspectives on what key technologies needed to be developed to improve PWBs. Kurt Watchler, the program champion from Texas Instruments, used this Taguchi-like process to quickly get the companies to come to a consensus on the technology development needs for PWBs. He drew a matrix that identified PWB problems along one side and grouped causes along the other axis. The causes of PWB problems were broken down by constructing another matrix in which problem characteristics were grouped. The outcome was having all participants agree that the four key technology development areas for improving PWBs were materials, imaging, chemical processes, and soldering.

The Taguchi-like process used at the February 2 TEWE meeting was focused around the knowledge process shown in slide 9 in Exhibit 9.2. Key technology development areas were identified and prioritized by getting input from all of the experts in the room, which input, as was the case with the initial PWB program proposal meeting six and a half years earlier, was from some of the best expertise in the world on the topics being addressed.

This facilitated process identified 12 development tasks:

1. Knowledge Capture Techniques
2. Data to Knowledge Mapping
3. Smart Objects and Interfaces
4. Integrated Knowledge Framework
5. Knowledge Organizational Structure
6. Web-Enabled Tools for Real-Time Knowledge
7. Knowledge to Code Synthesis
8. Extended Enterprise Model
9. Collaboration Tools
10. Exchange through Firewalls
11. Notification Capability
12. Mediation Services

Another very valuable, and unscheduled, event that occurred at this meeting was when Ken Kuna, the director responsible for scaling Direct Engineering in Ford, was able to briefly address the assembled team and relay the importance to the future of Ford of what we were undertaking.

Mr. Kuna's spontaneous remarks provided an inspiration to all those present that we were embarking on a program that could really provide a positive change to tomorrow's society. Presentations from senior management are valuable in motivating a collaborative team. Spontaneous presentations are particularly effective.

Meeting Results/Actions

Meeting minutes highlighting decisions made and actions agreed on should be distributed to all the participants the day after the meeting.

EXHIBIT 9.5   2/2/98 TEWE Meeting Actions/Results

Actions/Results from 2/2/98 Meeting
Name—Technologies for Enterprise-Wide Engineering

2/4/98	Schedule coordination call with NIIIP*—Bill Waddell
2/4-6/98	Conduct NIIIP Coordination Call—Bill Waddell, Sean O'Reilly, Al Klosterman, Richard Bolton
2/6/98	Add technology suppliers
	EAI—Bob Carman
	Intercim*—Bob Carman
	Concentus*—Bill Waddell
	Engenious—Bill Waddell
	Netscape—Mo Rezayat
	InfoTest—John Sheridan
	*Based on agreement with NIIIP
2/11/98	Boeing, Ford, Kodak two to three-page drafts of internally funded pilot programs—Bob Carman, Sean O'Reilly, Ron Auble
2/12/98	Storyboards—Gene Allen
2/13/98	Identify LMES, Raytheon and InfoTest roles—Bill Waddell/John Sheridan
2/17/98	Technology suppliers meet at Ford—establish technology development foci for program, identify draft assignments
2/17/98	Draft program agreement for distribution
2/17/98	Sample commitment letter distributed
2/18/98	Parts supplier commitment package

Someone should be assigned to take the minutes and ensure prompt distribution. These minutes can be used by participants to coordinate any internal company actions that may need to be taken. They also serve to confirm the events that took place at the meeting. Next-day timeliness is important, particularly if there are actions assignments.

Exhibits 9.4 and 9.5 show the documented actions from the December 19, 1997, and February 2, 1998, meetings that resulted in the decision that the TEWE proposal be written and submitted to the NIST ATP program on March 18, 1998.

CHAPTER 10

Internal Company/ Organization Commitment

Every company has a set of business challenges that need to be addressed to justify committing to collaborative R&D as a corporate strategy. The internal organization of a company can produce barriers that make external collaboration difficult. For a collaborative R&D program to succeed, these barriers need to be addressed within each participating company.

Program champions need to get the support of their company while they pursue external interest in a collaborative program. This commitment can not be taken for granted. Collaboration has not been readily embraced in the U.S. business culture. Competitive instincts and fear of antitrust prosecution have compelled U.S. industry not to share information. However, global competition, the speed and agility needed to compete, and the explosion in information and computing technology has forced companies, as well as governments, to reconsider collaboration.

This change in U.S. corporate direction was evidenced at the Automotive Management Briefing Seminar conducted by the University of Michigan in August 1998. There the corporate leaders from the automotive industry presented a consistent theme that technical collaboration will become a way of life for both OEMs and suppliers across every level of the supply chain. Companies are finding that they need to be able to quickly establish, conduct, and conclude partnering relationships where they make sense for business. This need is particularly applicable to R&D efforts. Companies would like to be able to easily move in and out of collaborative efforts.

While this trend should make it easier to get company commitments to a collaborative R&D program, it's important to ensure that this commitment is understood and supported across the company. Collaboration can be difficult if its rationale and objectives are not understood by all those in the company who will be involved in the effort. The ease with which a company can make a commitment to a collaborative R&D program is dependent on:

• The size of the company
• The company's business culture
• The company's organizational structure

Company Size

For a small company that has around $20 million per year in revenue or less, the president and/or CEO of the company can generally decide if participating in a collaborative R&D venture is in the company's best interest. For a company of this size, collaboration needs to be part of the strategic business plan. The decision maker may get advice from a few trusted employees or peers, and will use this input to make a decision based on business sense. However, even in a small company, the commitment of the person in charge doesn't mean that the company will be able to effectively participate in the program. The individuals assigned to take part in the program must also be committed to it. This is often difficult in a small company as key individuals are often consumed by the company's day-to-day business. In some cases, the time and effort needed to collaborate (the collaborative overhead) are personally contributed by the company president and/or CEO.

For larger companies, the decision process gets more complex. In a large company, there needs to be a program champion committed to a technical vision willing to take risks to see the vision implemented. The program champion needs to have someone in corporate management to support him or her. In some cases, the official in corporate management may also need to champion the company's participation in collaborative R&D. This decision needs to be in line with the company's corporate strategy.

Corporate Business Culture

The acceptance of collaboration by a company's senior management is a prerequisite for participating in a collaborative R&D effort. Corporations are beginning to recognize that they compete more on their cultures than on their products. This recognition is dropping traditional barriers companies have had to sharing technology development. Relative to collaborative R&D, corporate business cultures can be divided into two camps: those that support collaborative R&D and those that will have to in the near future. Companies can be motivated to support collaboration if they recognize that it's the best way to conduct R&D. Another motivation can arise when a company does not internally know where the next technology developments will emerge and they choose to leverage their R&D and reduce risk through collaboration. Companies that choose not to collaborate do so because they believe they have a competitive advantage with their internal technology and believe that they can maintain their technological advantage through internal development.

Even with the support of a company's senior management, a compelling business rationale is needed for a company to commit to collaborative R&D. The prospective benefits of a collaborative R&D program must be significant enough, and the technology and market risk low enough, to justify the commitment of a company's key personnel to the effort. A company's most valuable resource is its personnel. Key personnel need to be working on programs that will improve a company's products or processes to ensure that the company stays in business. If these personnel are removed from company-centric work, it will hurt the company. The objective of a collaborative program is to help these people better do their company-centric job, by leveraging the collective knowledge and resources of others who have similar objectives and efficiently transferring that gain back to specific company applications.

The commitment of the company's key personnel should not be taken for granted. Many manufacturing engineers find collaboration hard to accept and are, in fact, threatened by the thought of it. When companies are faced with new metrics for continuous improvement in cycle time and the need to leverage all resources for the greatest return on assets, they ask their process improvement engineers to share their valuable expertise with others. This can be easily perceived to be a potential risk to their jobs. The companies that make this work are those where senior management demonstrates an ongoing appreciation as to the value of personnel who make the company's manufacturing processes work.

Some management personnel view collaborative R&D as a costly diversion of key resources, as opposed to being viewed as an opportunity to develop a technology or process with other major users and partners. Much of this may be the result of past experience with collaborative programs that were managed to find and address the common goals among all the participants. In these types of programs, more effort is expended toward identifying common objectives than actually doing research. Often the final objectives are so generic that they end up not meeting the objectives of any of the companies involved. For collaborative development to be valuable to a participating company, the company needs to be selfish in its participation to ensure that its objectives are met. Collaborative R&D projects that detract from this direction pose an unacceptable cost to a company.

If collaboration is perceived as taking a risk, it is not likely the company will collaborate. Risk taking is not rewarded in modern corporate management, as failure will risk an individual's career. Should collaboration be viewed as sharing a company's next-generation development with its competition, then it can easily be viewed as a risk. If collaboration is viewed as a means to take the risk out of conducting next-generation technology R&D, then it is viewed favorably. If a corporate culture fully embraces collaborative R&D, the company will consider collaboration opportunities in planning their R&D efforts, and will ensure that there is internal collaboration on R&D efforts to assist in successfully transferring new technology into production.

R&D PLANNING

The companies that have sustained success in joint R&D projects are the ones that make collaboration part of their competitive business strategy. In order for this to happen, senior management should have the commitment to include collaboration potential in the process of analyzing and planning R&D. The catalyst to do this, and form or join collaborative R&D projects, can be the enlightened vision of management, the awareness of benefits from a previous collaborative program, or other external knowledge influences. If this is the case, the company will commit to a strategic process that evaluates an R&D plan against a prospective model in which the company participates in multicompany consortia, university and government grant projects, or joint development with suppliers. But many times, collaborative involvement is born as an ad hoc situation where a company finds itself in an earnings and budget shortfall, or behind the curve of technology, and then turns to collaboration for first aid. As stated, this encounter could lead to a permanent commitment to an ongoing process; however, in many instances after the emergency passes, because collaboration is hard and requires new disciplines, the company reverts to the old behavior. When collaboration is viewed as a process in a company's strategy, there is a much greater chance that it will be embraced on its merits and transcend the various departmental organizations or other obstacles.

A company must start R&D planning with an accurate understanding of its strengths and weaknesses. If proprietary advantages are protected, collaboration may be the best way to achieve its goals. Once collaboration is part of the R&D business process, it can have a significant impact on the robustness of those plans. Technology planning which considers collaboration options identifies the broad financial and technological capabilities of multiple companies working together. Collaborative technology development planning is more likely to provide a realistic perspective on its outcome in terms of risk, cycle time, and necessary interoperability standards development than a more narrowly focused plan which seeks to identify technology gaps.

R&D TO PRODUCTION

The key to getting benefit from R&D is to transfer beneficial results of new R&D into production applications. Incorporating new technology into a production line requires changing the way a company does business. A change may be small or large, and while the process to change the way business is done in a company varies from company to company, a common trait among companies is their conservative nature relative to changing their processes. After all, a company is in business because the processes it uses are able to produce products or services that others pay enough for to cover their cost and generate some degree of profit. As long as those processes work, there is little motivation to change the processes.

Most companies are aware that it might be possible for another company to provide a better product or service than they do at a reduced price through the use of some new technology. Companies usually follow their industry and watch for emerging technologies that could improve their processes. However, the decision to adapt and install a new technology or a new process is recognized as taking a high risk, usually based on past experience. Risk aversion such as this reflects a lack of flexibility and commitment to continuous improvement, and is a function of the corporate culture that has been put in place by the company's management.

However, due to the rapidly evolving information and computation infrastructure, companies have to have the flexibility to be able to integrate and adapt new technologies and evolve with this infrastructure or risk going out of business. Companies need to demonstrate to themselves that they can significantly reduce the risk of integrating new technology into their products and processes. Collaboration can be used by companies to reduce the risk of R&D applications through the use of pilot projects. Having a number of companies involved in integrating a technology into a pilot process reduces the risk to all parties, and provides lessons on what needs to be done to modify or adapt a technology and how this can be accomplished. Pilot projects were used to significant effect in the Rapid Response Manufacturing program.

Company Organization

The business rationale for participating in collaborative R&D needs to be communicated to and understood by all the personnel in a company who might be involved in or with the collaboration. This includes corporate administration and legal organizations, sales and marketing, product development/production, as well as a company's R&D organization. The company president and CEO and the board of directors need to support and at times champion collaboration.

The personnel in a company's different divisions often have different incentives and drivers motivating their performance. The ability to collaborate and support collaboration should be included in personal performance measures and appropriately compensated. Collaborative R&D leverages a company's efforts to develop new products and processes. As such, personnel in new product development are the individuals who are most impacted by any new collaborative effort. These individuals need to be actively involved in and support any participation in collaborative R&D programs.

Sales and marketing personnel can use collaborative relationships with other companies to establish long-term strategic relationships which can provide a secure revenue base. Legal personnel need to understand the need to be able to support collaboration, as opposed to identifying why the company can't collaborate. It is often difficult for legal departments to come to grips with sharing information. Sharing information is viewed by lawyers as risky. They need to recognize that collaboration reduces the overall corporate risk involved with staying in business in a changing world.

Dr. Al Klosterman, SDRC vice president and chief scientist, summarized the position progressive companies are taking with intellectual property when he relayed, "If you're putting all of your energy into protecting your past, you're not putting effort into the future."[1] Administration and accounting personnel need to be aware of and involved in decisions having to do with collaborative development. Some programs have the potential of needing changes in administration and accounting that would require the company to change procedures. This is particularly the case when U.S. government funds are involved. Administrative and accounting requirements need to be understood and negotiated if significant change is required. If this portion of the collaborative overhead is too high, it may not be worth it for the company to receive any funds. If there is financial reimbursement involved in the program, how these funds will be credited and how they may be used by the company should be determined.

Collaboration among the internal organizations in a company is needed to ensure that the company's external relations with its partners is consistent. An internal process should be used when starting a collaborative R&D program to ensure that all the personnel in the company that might be involved with the effort are aware of and support the effort. Exhibit 10.1 is an example of an Internal Sign-Off process used at the MacNeal-Schwendler Corporation.

Confidence in Collaboration

The ability to get company support for a collaborative R&D program is dependent on the confidence senior management in the company has in the abilities of the team to meet the company's objectives. This confi-

---

[1]Dr. Al Klosterman, TEWE initiative meeting, October 1, 1998.

EXHIBIT 10.1 Internal Form for Coordinating Collaborative Program Development

---

Proposed Collaborative Program (page 1)   No.:
                                            Date:

Program Title:
Customer:
Business Unit:
Products:
Partners:
Proposal Managers:
Key Individuals:
Contract Type:
Contract Value:
Business Case:

Preproposal Review and Sign-Off:
Business Unit: Date:
Collaborative Programs: Date:
Production: Date:
Government Contact Administrator: Date:
Proposal No.:   Date:

Proposed Collaborative Program (page 2)   No.:
                                            Date:

Background:
Competitive Analysis:
Program Risks:
Next Action(s):

White paper attached if available.

---

dence comes from the credibility and past experience of the program champion as well as the organization coordinating the effort. If the organization and champion have demonstrated a capability to generate results from establishing and managing collaborative R&D, companies are more likely to make the needed commitment. The program champions need to be able to instill a high degree of confidence that collaboration will work toward meeting company objectives.

Internal Communications

Some companies have a job position for coordinating their collaborative development. More likely, the role for internal and external coordination of R&D will fall to a program or technology champion in a more traditional part of the company organization. This individual should meet with the company's business unit managers at least once per year, and establish at least monthly communications with key business units. Communications should focus on establishing strategic relationships with major accounts through leveraging existing collaborative R&D programs or establishing new collaborative R&D programs. The process for establishing collaborative development programs should be communicated to the company's business units.

Even in a company that is supportive of collaboration, a degree of timing is still needed to commit to a program. An action from the first TEWE meeting was for the end users present (Kodak, Pratt & Whitney, Raytheon, Ford, Boeing, and GM) to identify internal work commitments that could be leveraged by working through the proposed program initiative. This action was assigned December 19 and had to be completed by January 12—not the most convenient time to get a multimillion-dollar commitment from a company. Pratt & Whitney, Raytheon, and GM were not able to get the needed commitment. Timing with Pratt & Whitney's internal budget process and the recent merger between Raytheon and Texas Instruments Defense Electronics Systems Group prevented either of those companies from being able to make the needed commitment prior to the proposal submission deadline in mid-March of 1998. While GM was able to coordinate a commitment two weeks before the proposal due date and be integrated into the proposed program, the program would not have proceeded if Boeing, Ford, and Kodak had not been able to commit to the program by January 12. It would not have been possible to put a viable collaborative development program together without these commitments in place.

The basis for getting internal support at the MacNeal-Schwendler Corporation (MSC) for any collaborative program was established

EXHIBIT 10.2 Executive Summary of MSC Network Distributed Analysis Software Collaborative Development Plan

Network Distributed Analysis Software
Collaborative Development Plan
Executive Summary

Background

MSC Collaborative Development has been involved in two strategic initiatives with major, process-centric customers over the past six months. These process-centric customers are Boeing, Ford, General Motors, Kodak, Lockheed-Martin, Raytheon, and United Technologies Corporation. The focus of these strategic initiatives is to enable these customers to take advantage of emerging Web technologies to develop and fabricate components with subsidiaries or contractors located anywhere in the world. The initiatives are to: 1) establish a follow-on to the successful Rapid Response Manufacturing program, and (2) assist in the establishment of an Open Supplier Integration program.

Purpose

This collaborative development plan:

1. Identifies the role of collaborative development in getting new technologies integrated into MSC products.
2. Coordinates MSC's efforts in working with the above customers with the plans of MSC business units.
3. Focuses collaborative development on projects creating the ability to "efficiently conduct analysis in a distributed environment."*
4. Facilitates MSC's strategic evolution to a new business model—a model in which MSC provides customers a combination of CAE products and CAE services to increase their productivity. This plan reviews the new business model, and identifies how MSC Collaborative Development can assist the MSC business units by:

   • Establishing technology pilot projects with customers to provide input to MSC product development.
   • Providing funding to integrate new technology into MSC products and services.
   • Establishing and expanding MSC strategic partnerships.

The focus on the development of network distributed analysis software involves improving the interoperability between CAE and CAD and PDM, improving the ease of use of CAE, developing MSC software products that are client-server-efficient, and improving in software quality. MSC can leverage our unique competencies (analysis codes/algorithms, EXPRESS, open architecture, and engineering) through establishing collaborative development programs with customers. Any funds received as a cost reimbursement would flow to the business units. The plan identifies the availability of MSC personnel as the key resource issue and provides recommended solutions.

---

*A distributed environment is a set of computers—personal computers (PCs), workstations, mainframes, or supercomputers—located in different geographical locations connected via an intranet or the Internet. Efficient analysis is the ability to provide the right answer quickly and cost-effectively.

through drafting an internal MSC development plan. The Executive Summary of this plan is shown in Exhibit 10.2. This paper was distributed internally within MSC in the summer of 1997 before the TEWE program materialized. The plan provided the foundation for rapid MSC approval for participation in TEWE. When TEWE actually materialized, formal MSC sign-off was obtained using the Internal Form for Coordinating Collaborative Program Development, shown in Exhibit 10.1, with the ATP Proposal White Paper—Enterprise-Wide Engineering dated January 16, 1998, shown in Exhibit 4.2.

CHAPTER 11

Government Assistance

The availability of matching funds from the government is often the motivation driving a company to participate in a collaborative development program. The Technology Development Process can be optimized when the ingredients of collaboration identified in Part II are in place. These ingredients are not found only in industry. Many times the best R&D is accomplished with industry working with government and academia. While industry should be the principal driver in this process, governments play an important part in establishing an infrastructure and providing incentives for collaboration.

Governments are responsible for establishing the financial and legal boundaries for conducting business; they define the business environment and have a significant impact on the status of the infrastructure available. Recent changes in the business environment have been driven by more societal and environmental regulation but more relaxed antitrust positions. The politics regarding the role of government in society is not the subject of this book. We can say that without government support acting as a stimulus to bring scientists and engineers together, it is unlikely that we would have seen as many of the highly successful collaborative projects that have given global business such momentum in recent years. In this chapter we will identify:

- Government programs that can assist in establishing collaborative R&D programs.
- Concerns to be aware of in accepting government funds.
- Ways to network with the government to identify and foster collaborative R&D opportunities, including an overview of the U.S. government funding process.

Government Collaboration Programs

Technology advances in information and computers are requiring companies to be more efficient with their resources, as well as making speed to market a competitive advantage. It has already been identified that these changes are driving the need for a company to be able to collaborate if a company is to be able to compete. Collaboration to enhance national economic competitiveness began and gained momentum in Japan, and then spread to Europe, before being adopted by U.S. industry.

United States Government Programs

In the early 1980s it was realized that U.S. industry was being handicapped by the business environment defined by federal government antitrust laws in effect from the early part of the century. In response, the U.S. federal government passed the National Cooperative Research Act in 1984 that permits companies to work together on generic, precompetitive research. While the law changed in 1984, business practices did not and change has not been quick in coming to U.S. industry. Companies, in which employees had been repeatedly trained not to work with others outside their company, found it difficult to change habits and cultures to enable employees to work with others, including their competition.

The U.S. government is responsible for roughly half of all of the R&D spending in the United States every year. The U.S. government is also the largest single employer of scientists and engineers. While the U.S. government has spent billions of dollars annually over the past half century, programs to promote corporate collaboration in R&D have only been established in the past decade. This book addresses only those federal programs that promote the establishment of collaborative R&D programs.

NATIONAL INSTITUTE OF STANDARDS AND TECHNOLOGY (NIST) ADVANCED TECHNOLOGY PROGRAM (ATP)

The NIST ATP (http://atp.nist.gov), established in 1990, is assisting firms in changing their business environments to adopt collaboration. The ATP is a key component in the United States' technology strategy for economic growth, generating broad-based benefits through industry-led innovation. The mission of the ATP is to stimulate U.S. economic growth by developing high-risk and enabling technologies through industry-driven, cost-shared partnerships. The ATP encourages a change in how industry approaches R&D, providing a mechanism for industry to extend its technological reach.

The ATP has been a catalyst that has provided incentive for U.S. companies to work together. The incentive is in the form of cost-sharing technology development. However, the private sector is required to provide the majority share of the costs. Experience with the Printed Wiring Board (PWB) and Rapid Response Manufacturing (RRM) programs has shown that the participating companies put more funds into the efforts than required by the government to get matching funds. This is because the collaborative R&D environment enabled them to effectively leverage resources with other companies. The ATP has provided a means to change the business environment in the United States. The authors' experience with the PWB and RRM programs has shown that the ATP is one of the best uses of U.S. taxpayer dollars being applied to conduct the U.S. government's constitutional responsibility to promote the general welfare of U.S. society.

The ATP has several critical features that set it apart from other government R&D programs:

- The goal of the ATP is economic growth and opening new opportunities for U.S. business and industry in the world's markets. This is accomplished by fostering enabling technologies that will lead to new, innovative products, services, and industrial processes. For this reason, ATP projects focus on the technology needs of U.S. industry, not those of government. The ATP is industry-driven, which keeps the program grounded in real-world needs. Research priorities for the ATP are set by industry: for-profit companies conceive, propose, cofund, and execute ATP projects and programs based on their understanding of the marketplace and research opportunities.
- The ATP does not fund product development. It supports enabling technologies that are essential to the development of new products, processes, and services across diverse application areas. Private industry bears the costs of product development, production, marketing, sales, and distribution.
- ATP awards are made strictly on the basis of rigorous peer-reviewed competitions designed to select the proposals that are best qualified in terms of the technological ideas, the potential economic benefits to the nation (not just the applicant), and the strength of the plan for eventual commercialization of the results. Expert reviewers (without conflicts of interest) drawn from the business community, government, and academia carefully examine and rate each proposal according to published selection criteria that focus on both business and technical potential.
- The ATP has strict cost-sharing rules. Joint ventures must pay at least half of the project costs. Single companies working on ATP projects must pay all indirect costs associated with the project. (This provision encourages small companies, particularly start-ups, that often have much lower overhead rates than large firms.)

The dominant feature of the ATP program is the selection criteria used to award programs. These criteria were simplified in November 1998. The criteria used from 1990 to 1998 are shown in Exhibit 11.1, as they provide a good outline for establishing a business plan for a technology company.

EXHIBIT 11.1 NIST ATP Selection Criteria, 1990–1998

The five Advanced Technology Program (ATP) selection criteria used in selecting proposals for funding and their respective weights are listed below.
The subfactors under each criterion are weighted equally. No proposal
will be funded unless the program determines that it has high scientific
and technical merit, no matter how meritorious the proposal might be
with respect to the other selection criteria. Similarly, no proposal will be
funded that does not require federal support or that is product development rather than high-risk R&D.

1. Scientific and Technical Merit (30 percent).
   a. Quality, innovativeness, and cost-effectiveness of the proposed technical program; that is, uniqueness with respect to current industry practice. Proposers shall compare and contrast their approaches with those
taken by other domestic and foreign companies working in the same field.
   b. Appropriateness of technical risk and feasibility of the project, that is,
is there a sufficient knowledge base to justify the level of technical risk involved, and is the risk commensurate with the potential payoff? Projects
should press the state of the art while still having credibility with regard to
technical approach.
   c. Coherency of the technical plan and clarity of vision of technical objectives, and the degree to which the technical plan meets the project and,
in the case of focused program competitions, program goals.
   d. Integrated, forward-looking, team approach to the project. This factor
includes the extent to which the R&D team will take into account aspects
such as research and raw material suppliers and considerations of manufacturability and requirements of customers, regulatory concerns, safety issues,
and environmental impacts. It also includes the extent to which all of the
necessary technical disciplines will be brought into the R&D and how R&D,
manufacturing, and marketing will work together in an integrated fashion.
   e. Potential broad impact on U.S. technology and knowledge base.

2. Potential Net Broad-Based Economic Benefits (20 percent).
   Potential to improve U.S. economic growth, taking into account the
timeliness of the proposal; that is, the potential project results will not occur too late or too early to be competitively useful, and the degree to
which ATP support is essential for the achievement of the broad-based
benefits from the proposed R&D and appropriateness of proposed R&D
for ATP support. This criterion takes into consideration the likelihood of
the results being achieved in the same general time frame by the proposer
or by other U.S. researchers without ATP support, and whether other federal agencies or other sponsors are already funding very similar kinds of
work. Projects will not be selected if the Program judges that federal support is not needed. In assessing the potential for broad-based economic
benefits, emphasis is placed on a strong potential for spillover benefits extending well beyond those accruing to the awardee(s). Benefits are com-

(continued)

EXHIBIT 11.1 (*Continued*)

pared against the costs of the proposal to determine cost-effectiveness of the proposal.

3. Adequacy of Plans for Eventual Commercialization (20 percent).

a. Evidence that if the project is successful, the proposers will pursue further development of the technology toward commercial application, either through their own organization(s) or through others.

b. Degree to which proposal identifies potential applications of the technology and provides evidence that the proposer has credible plans to assure prompt and widespread use of the technology if the R&D is successful and to ensure adequate protection of the intellectual property by the participant(s) and, as appropriate, by other U.S. businesses.

4. Level of Commitment and Organizational Structure (20 percent).

a. Level of commitment of proposer as demonstrated by contribution of personnel, equipment, facilities, and cost-sharing. Extent to which the proposer assigns the company's best people to the project. Priority given to this work in relation to other company activities.

b. For joint ventures, the extent to which the joint venture has been structured (vertical integration, horizontal integration, or both) so as to include sufficient participants possessing all of the skills required to complete successfully the proposed work.

c. For joint ventures, the extent to which participation by small businesses is encouraged and is a key component of the proposal.

d. Appropriateness of subcontractor/supplier/collaborator participation and relationships (where applicable). For large-company single proposers, the extent to which subcontractor teaming arrangements are featured and are a key component of the proposal.

e. Clarity and appropriateness of management plan. Extent to which the proposers have clarified who is responsible for each task, and the chain of command. Extent to which those responsible for the work have adequate authority and access to higher level management.

5. Experience and Qualifications (10 percent).

a. Adequacy of proposer's facilities, equipment, and other technical, financial, and administrative resources to accomplish the proposed program objectives. This factor includes consideration of resources possessed by subcontractors to the proposer or other collaborators.

b. Quality and appropriateness of the technical staff to carry out the proposed work program and to identify and overcome barriers to meeting project objectives.

c. Past performance of the company or joint venture members in carrying out similar kinds of efforts successfully, including technology application. Consideration of this factor in the case of a start-up company or new joint venture will take into account the past performance of the key people in carrying out similar kinds of efforts.

The ATP has used general and focused program competitions as investment mechanisms. General competitions are open to proposals in all areas of technology. Focused program competitions, established in 1994, are developed in response to specific suggestions received from industry and academia (focus competitions were discontinued in 1999).

ATP projects typically run from two to five years, the commercialization phase could add several more years, and the full economic impact may not be realized for some years after commercial introduction. It also is costly—companies must spend additional time, effort, and money on their own to pursue product development and marketing. Because of the risks involved—commercial as well as technical—some ATP projects fail. Others may proceed faster than anticipated, and intermediate results may lead to marketable products even before the ATP project ends. Regardless of whether initial commercialization takes place before an ATP project ends or long after, the company must invest its own money to design specific products incorporating the technology and to pay any other costs associated with commercialization.

The ATP Web site also provides valuable information on how to establish alliances with companies to perform collaborative R&D. The specific Internet address is http://www.atp.nist.gov/alliance.

ATP funds enable the establishment of potential markets for emerging technologies. The ATP funding can lead to the coordination of otherwise independent efforts across different industries. This coordination across industries can result in sufficient market demand for emerging technologies to justify the commercialization costs for technology suppliers. In addition to reducing the commercialization risk, ATP funds enable several technology suppliers to work together across several industries in coming up with generic technology solutions. This enables the establishment of consensus infrastructure technology development, as opposed to a number of independent technology developments pursuing the same objective.

The NIST ATP requires matching funds from industry which do not originate from government contracts. As such, companies that support the Department of Defense (DOD) or the National Aeronautics and Space Administration (NASA) are not eligible to participate in the NIST ATP with funds from government contracts. Differences in the overhead required to do business with the government and commercial industry have led to the segregation of the U.S. industrial base. Companies that are predominately government contractors such as Lockheed Martin, Raytheon, General Dynamics, and Newport News find it difficult to participate in ATP programs. When the Rapid Response Manufacturing program started, Sikorsky Aircraft was to be the pilot end user for United Technologies participation. This had to be shifted to Pratt & Whitney commercial end-use applications because Sikorsky R&D funds could not be used as a match for the NIST ATP as those funds came from DOD contracts.

At one time, DOD and NASA had established programs to enable government contractors to cost share in R&D efforts. These programs—the Technology Reinvestment Project run by the Defense Advanced Research Projects Agency (DARPA), which coordinated efforts among DARPA, NASA, the Department of Energy, the National Science Foundation, and the Department of Transportation; and the Aerospace Industries Technology Program run by NASA—were programs that allowed government contractors to match funds. While these programs could not be supported politically and are no longer in place, they generated new ways for the U.S. government to work with industry through cooperative agreement authority. Many DARPA programs now encourage or require cost sharing from industry.

DEFENSE ADVANCED RESEARCH PROJECTS AGENCY (DARPA)

DARPA (http://www.darpa.mil) is the DOD funding organization for high-risk, high-payoff technology R&D. Each of the armed services (Army, Navy, Air Force, and Marines) conducts R&D as well. The service R&D is differentiated from DARPA's in that the service R&D is more mission-driven and lower in risk. DARPA's primary responsibility is to help maintain U.S. technological superiority and guard against unforeseen technological advances by potential adversaries. Consequently, the DARPA mission is to develop imaginative, innovative, and often high-risk research ideas offering a significant technological impact that will go well beyond the normal evolutionary developmental approaches, and to pursue these ideas from the demonstration of technical feasibility through the development of prototype systems.

Many DARPA solicitations have required industry cost sharing and evidence of a commercialization path. None are as focused on economic benefits as the NIST ATP. They instead require a defense mission focus. The Robust Design Computational System (RDCS) is a collaborative development program cofunded by DARPA. The majority of the industry cost share in this effort is provided by Ford, which is not receiving any government funding.

NATIONAL AERONAUTICS AND SPACE ADMINISTRATION (NASA)

NASA (http://www.nasa.gov) is the government agency with a space mission focus. NASA's overall program, as outlined in the agency's strategic plan, is comprised of four strategic enterprises. Each enterprise covers a major area of the agency's research and development efforts. The four NASA enterprises are aeronautics, earth science, human exploration and development of space, and space science. NASA's interface with industry has been primarily to contract for products and services.

The Computational Aeroacoustics Analysis System (CAAS) program was funded through the NASA-run Aerospace Industries Technology Program. Like the DARPA cofunded RDCS program, the bulk of the private-sector cofunding for CAAS came from Ford.

OTHER U.S. GOVERNMENT AGENCIES

Other government agencies have programs that support collaboration or can be sources of technology development resources. The U.S. Department of Energy (http://www.doe.gov) provides contractual vehicles (cooperative research and development agreements, or CRADAs) through which companies can work with the national labs. Federal laboratories within the Department of Defense, National Institutes of Health, and United States Geological Survey (http://www.dtic.mil/techtransit) are also able to participate with industry through CRADAs. CRADAs are used to get the personnel resources available at the labs to work with industry. In some cases, CRADAs can be used to get funds for the industry participants as well.

In recent years, these agreements have been simplified and made more flexible in an overt effort on the part of the government to create and promote federal laboratory and industry collaboration and technology transfer. It is in the transfer area that much work remains. Issues regarding technology transfer stem from the fact that none of the ingredients for collaboration identified in Part II were present when the research was being conducted. This was primarily because much of this work was classified and specific to federal agency missions and so did not lend itself to commercial needs. However, these laboratories continue to be a valuable source of talent, skills, and knowledge, and provide a significant opportunity for collaboration. The Department of Energy laboratories help support American leadership in science and technology. The Department of Energy laboratories have over 30,000 scientists and engineers who are conducting breakthrough research in energy sciences and technology, high-energy physics, superconducting materials, accelerator technologies, materials sciences, and environmental sciences in support of the DOE's mission.

The mission of the U.S. Small Business Administration (SBA) Office of Technology (http://www.sbaonline.sba.gov/sbir) is to strengthen and expand the competitiveness of U.S. small high-technology research and development businesses in the federal marketplace. Each of the 10 U.S. federal agencies that conducts R&D is required to set aside a percentage of its R&D budget for the Small Business Innovation Research (SBIR) program, which amounts to over $1 billion per year. The SBIR program provides grants to companies to conduct research. Follow-on Phase II SBIR grants require a commercialization path for the development, with Phase III efforts primarily dependent on private funding. The Small Business Technology Transfer Pilot Program was also established to encourage private and public resource support for the commercialization of federal R&D efforts.

The National Science Foundation (http://www.nsf.gov) is an independent U.S. government agency responsible for promoting science and engineering through programs that invest over $3.3 billion per year in almost 20,000 research and education projects in science and engineering. The National Science Foundation funds research and education in science and engineering. It does this through grants, contracts, and cooperative agreements to more than 2000 colleges, universities, and other research and/or education institutions in all parts of the United States. The NSF accounts for about 20 percent of federal support to academic institutions for basic research.

These are also numerous state and regional economic development initiatives that provide incentives for collaboration.

European Union Programs

Participation in European Union (EU)–funded development projects is driven by end-user requirements for specific industry solutions. In Europe, there is a strong perspective that teaming and collaboration are the keys to being globally competitive. These countries have recognized that research and development needs a critical mass of financial support that is often beyond the capabilities of individual industries or countries. The aim of the EU is to facilitate development and the evaluation of new technologies, to help speed up and simplify industrial processes. This allows industrial users to evaluate the benefits of new technologies and techniques for their own businesses.

Participants in EU R&D projects can be divided into three groups: end users, research institutes, and technology providers (Figure 11.1). All three groups work as a team, within a framework or plan developed to maintain project impetus and to allow progress to be evaluated.

EU EUREKA Program

EUREKA (http://eureka.belspo.be) promotes pan-European, market-oriented research and development across almost 30 European countries. It's a Europe-wide network for industrial R&D to strengthen European competitiveness by promoting market-driven collaborative research and technical development (RTD). RTD involves industry and research in-

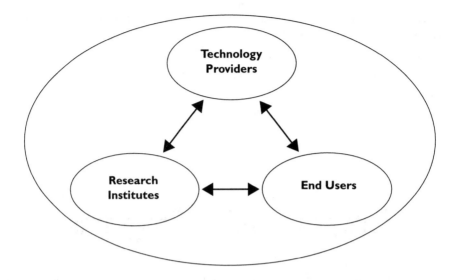

FIGURE 11.1 European Union Program Collaborative Program Composition

stitutes across Europe using advanced technologies, and results in cost-effective products, processes, and services.

Launched in 1985, EUREKA has already changed the face of pan-European cooperative research and development. It is a framework through which industry and research institutes from 25 European countries and the European Commission develop and exploit the technologies crucial to global competitiveness and a better quality of life. Today 25 countries and the European Commission are full EUREKA members, while many more countries, particularly in Central and Eastern Europe, have some form of associate status.

The EUREKA project portfolio as of September 1998 included 653 running projects worth an estimated investment of 5.227 billion ECUs (European currency units) involving almost 3000 different organizations across Europe, of which just over two-thirds are from industry and just under half are small to medium-sized enterprises. So far 675 projects have been finished worth an estimated investment of 11.611 billion ECUs.

Although the European Commission is one of the EUREKA members, the research projects run under its RTD programs are very different from EUREKA projects, as can be seen in the following comparison.

European Commission	EUREKA
Precompetitive R&D.	Development of marketable products and services.
Top-down program generation by the European Commission.	Bottom-up project generation by partners.
EC supervision.	Business agreements between partners.
Large central funding source.	Decentralized funding source—the EUREKA label improves chances of national funding support.
Research results are property of both EC and partners.	Research results are property of partners.

EUREKA's ground rule for project formation is that a market-oriented R&D project is best run by those aiming to market its results. They, and no one else, are the best judges of what will succeed. This means that the partners, rather than EUREKA or any government, propose and define their project. And once the project is launched, it is the participants who run it and exploit its results. Participants decide on:

- The project's aims.
- Who is involved.
- Who runs the project.
- What each partner contributes.
- How each partner uses the results.

EUREKA exists to create EUREKA projects—transborder, market-oriented, high-tech European RTD projects. A EUREKA project meets the EUREKA criteria if it:

- Is a high-tech, market-oriented R&D project.
- Involves partners from at least two EUREKA members.
- Aims to develop a cutting-edge civilian product, process, or service.
- Is funded by the partners themselves, who receive public financing from their national governments.

There is enormous scope for variety within these constraints, with projects ranging from the 100+-partner, 3.8-billion-ECU Joint European

Submicron Silicon Initiative (JESSI) project to two-partner feasibility projects involving less than 1 million ECUs in investment.

EU ESPRIT PROGRAM

Esprit (http://www.cordis.lu/esprit/home.html), the European Union's information technologies (IT) program, is focused on user requirements and the need to accelerate and broaden the take-up of IT. These projects are specifically focused on the integration of information processing in flexible manufacturing, office automation, software, and microelectronics. For these reasons, Esprit integrates cutting-edge R&D projects with preparatory, support, and take-up activities. This approach fosters the collaboration between technology users and technology suppliers that sparks off innovation. Suppliers benefit by getting feedback from users about their current and future needs; this helps them to better direct their research and exploit the results in the fast-moving world of IT. By interacting with user groups via the program, they also improve their chances of establishing their technologies in the marketplace. Through Esprit, users as a whole gain the opportunity to influence the technology and product development process. Those keen to adopt new information technologies get access to the latest developments and assistance in trying these out, while those looking for proven technologies and standardized products are brought into contact with suppliers, and with more experienced users, via dissemination and best-practice networks. The Esprit program, in short, can help everyone using or developing IT.

Several years ago, while evaluating the potential opportunities for Kodak to participate in the Esprit program, Rick Jarman met with a senior manager from a large U.S. computer company that was actively involved in this program. His perspectives on the Esprit program were that his company's participation was extremely valuable to the company for the following reasons:

- The R&D projects in which the program was involved were among the most cost-effective projects being done in or out of his company at the time.
- The best prospects for future customers in Europe were also participating in the program.

- The relationships developed through the program had already yielded technology which could be transferred to products representing customer solutions at a faster pace.
- The company could not afford not to be involved, as most of their competition was also involved in the program.

It was during this exchange that the benefits of collaboration became most apparent to Mr. Jarman.

Esprit forms part of the EU's Fourth Framework Program, which runs from 1994 to 1998, and is expected to be part of the Fifth Framework Program from 1998 to 2002. The Fifth Framework will be expending between 14 and 16 billion ECUs. Framework programs set the overall aims and priorities for the EU's R&D activities and define their content in broad terms. Specific programs—of which Esprit is one—define the more detailed basis for R&D in a particular technological area. Esprit works in close cooperation with other specific programs, particularly ACTS (telecommunications), IMT (industrial and materials technologies), and Telematics Applications. Esprit is managed by DG III, the Directorate General for Industry of the European Commission. The R&D that each specific program will support is described in a work program that contains descriptions of the tasks to be undertaken. Esprit is a so-called rolling work program, as it is adapted each year, after extensive consultation, to take account of industry's changing priorities.

There are two types of calls for project proposals in the ESPRIT program:

1. Domain-specific calls address particular parts of the Esprit program. Each call makes reference to the tasks in the work program for which proposals are invited, and specifies the submission deadlines. Most tasks are open for particular calls, though some can be submitted at any time.
2. Thematic calls address themes that cut across the different domains and tasks in the program.

Proposals are then evaluated by independent experts, and the best are selected for funding. Industrial partners have half their costs met via the Framework Program budget, while research institutions can have all their marginal costs covered (i.e., the additional costs incurred through participating in a project).

A condition of most R&D projects is that they bring together companies and research institutions from at least two EU/EEA or associated countries (such as Israel). There are many opportunities for organizations from other countries to take part, and Esprit particularly favors the involvement of researchers from the countries of Central Europe and the Baltics (CCE), the Mediterranean region, and the new Commonwealth of Independent States (CIS) of the former Soviet Union.

Esprit's PROSOMA service has been launched to help industry benefit from the many successes achieved in the program. For most organizations the completion of an Esprit project is only the first step toward commercializing their work. The remaining hurdles can be formidable: finance, legislation, marketing, and distribution all need to be addressed. Experience shows that social contacts, or networking, is a key factor in overcoming these barriers. Networking brings information technology providers into contact with systems developers, equipment manufacturers, venture capitalists, technology brokers, and end users—any or all of whom can provide what is needed to bring a result to market. Such networking helps bridge the gap between research and the marketplace, and so helps turn innovation into business.

PROSOMA helps companies looking for innovative IT solutions to identify relevant Esprit R&D results by making professionally produced, multimedia presentations of these results available on CD-ROM and via the World Wide Web. It also enables businesses to learn from the experiences of others in taking up and making use of information technologies. Each presentation may be linked to the Web site of the company concerned, providing searchers with useful background information and putting the results into context with the company's other products and services.

Japanese Programs

Some of the earliest postwar Japanese collaborative R&D programs started in the 1960s. The government established engineering research associations (ERAs), which were designed to help small and medium-sized companies gain technical expertise. This program subsidized collaborative projects at nonprofit organizations, with partial funding coming from the government. These programs, which were similar to recently established "manufacturing extension centers" in the United States, were such a success in Japan that the government used this model to extend collaboration activities to larger-scale programs in the 1970s and 1980s. An example was the Very Large-Scale Integration (VLSI) program, which provided financial support for advanced technology areas like integrated circuits for television, semiconductors, and other computer-based research. Again, these collaborative efforts were successful, and they played a key role in the later industrial growth in Japan. Today, the Japanese commitment to collaboration is evident through their key technology centers (KTCs). KTCs are aimed at conducting more basic research than previous programs, which were weighted more toward development efforts.

While Japanese industry has provided the world with the example of how collaboration can improve the competitive position of companies, the extension of this collaboration to companies outside the Japanese culture has been difficult. The Japanese ability to rapidly commercialize proven R&D has made them appear as threats to many companies. The 1998 Japanese financial crisis appears to have been brought on by an all-too-free flow of funding. The availability of commercialization funds was not balanced with the market in their system. The correction of this financial system appears to require a change in Japanese business culture. While cultural changes take time, Japanese society has proven to be one of the most adaptable over the past 150 years.

If the commercialization of technology in Japan is artificially high, the commercialization rate of U.S. government–funded technology appears to be low. It is important to recognize that collaboration in Japan has been easier than in other regions of the world as Japan has a homogeneous, monolithic society that shares the same culture and values. In a very consensus-oriented society, it's been easier for the Japanese to come up with a common goal which everyone agrees with and commits to realizing. Collaboration efforts in the United States are harder to establish due to the broad social and cultural diversity. Conversely, the opportunity for success can be greater for collaboration in the United States due to the range of views that are made available in a collaborative team.

Perhaps an optimal situation can be achieved as collaboration takes on a more international trend.

International Trends

Today, many countries around the world recognize the impact that advanced technology and its resulting innovation have and will have on their economies. Interconnectedness is one of the keys to competitiveness in the knowledge-based economy. Nations that foster an infrastructure of linkages among and between firms, universities, and government gain a competitive advantage through quicker information diffusion and product development. Collaboration and partnerships enable faster rates of learning.[1] Many of these countries are promoting government-subsidized collaborative research and development as a means to achieve their economic goals, which will inevitably raise standards of living.

The world business environment is becoming less nationalistic in companies' efforts to stay competitive. Ford vice president Bill Powers sees the evolution of the world business environment toward "coopetition." This evolution is taking place through the creation of transnational relationships that respond to global markets. Many of today's companies serve global markets. In doing so, companies usually employ local personnel and are developing new relationships with suppliers and customers which benefit the local economies where their markets are located. Most companies' global strategies do not differentiate the world by geography, and try to integrate and coordinate the companies' development and sales worldwide. This enables companies involved in collaborative R&D to leverage investment from both the U.S. and other governments in a manner that complements their own internal development.

---

[1] *Going Global, The New Shape of American Innovation*, The Council on Competitiveness, September 1998, p. 16.

It is important to ensure that there are no national restrictions on development funded through a government, particularly on potential future sales of technology. It is very hard for a commercial company to differentiate markets at the technology level. This is an issue that needs to be addressed up front in getting government funds for collaborative R&D. This is rarely a problem when a government is providing less than half the funding needed.

Government Funding Concerns

Ideally, government funding would not be required to establish a collaborative development program. In some cases government funds are not needed. Rocketdyne and Fiat were able to jointly develop both information and laser technology due to the mutual respect and noncompetitive aspects of the two corporations. The Consortium for Advanced Manufacturing—International (CAM-I) and the Technologies Research Corporation (TRC), an NCMS subsidiary, put together collaborative development programs without government funding. The resources in CAM-I and TRC programs are based on what the member companies provide. In addition, CAM-I provides an international business environment for its members. TRC leverages the administration and program management expertise of NCMS, including its proven success in establishing the legal base needed for project agreements.

Still, the bottom line is that the government funding and time lines provide incentives to industry to establish collaborative R&D programs that are not otherwise present, and without which most of the programs described in this book would not exist.

Personal experience with programs that do not have government funding as a program stimulus has shown that these programs often take longer to generate results. The stimulus for these programs has to be from end users with product and process deadlines. Most of industry has not progressed to the point that they are willing to risk placing key company product and process programs in collaborative environments.

There are, however, many downsides involved with industry working with government:

- *Timeliness.* The time it takes to work with the government to get a program funded is usually a year or more. The process used to solicit, write, and evaluate proposals takes at best several months. Then there are contract negotiations, which can take many more months. In addition, this process moves at the government's schedule and pace, which is often driven by election dates.
- *Uncertainty.* Person-years of effort can go into proposal writing with no guarantee that the effort will result in funding. The uncertainty lasts from the time a proposal is submitted to the time the contract is signed. There is additional uncertainty in established programs that a change in political direction can reduce or eliminate funding.
- *Networking Overhead.* A significant amount of effort is involved in establishing working relationships with federal government agencies and with congressional staffs. This can be particularly difficult for commercial industry, as few individuals in government have experience in industry. Details on what is involved are described next.
- *Administrative Overhead.* Government contractual requirements can lead to additional administrative and accounting work, as well as audits. These requirements have prevented many companies from doing business with the government. In some cases, if the administrative and accounting requirements were followed to their fullest detail, a company would go out of business, as the overhead costs would be higher than the profit companies are restricted to taking in government contracts. Cooperative agreements and grants generally require less overhead than contracts.
- *Market Risk.* Doing business with the government presents a company with a risk of losing commercial business. Establishing the overhead staff needed to administer government contracts can lead to commercially noncompetitive overhead rates. Private-sector pursuit of government business in the United States has led to the segregation of the U.S. industrial base into a defense, or government, industrial base and a commercial industrial base. This segregation needs to be recognized by program champions trying to broker the development of a vision for a new technology.

Government Networking

In networking with the government, it is valuable to understand the process through which the government provides funding. Funding is the lifeblood of a government agency. It's the metric those in federal government use to measure importance. An overview of how the U.S. government works follows.

FEDERAL GOVERNMENT FUNDING PROCESS

Federal agencies submit a budget to the President, who in turn submits it to Congress. The President submits a budget for the following fiscal year (which starts the following October 1) to Congress on February 1 of every year. Thus the federal agencies have to submit their budget inputs to the White House generally a year in advance of the next fiscal year.

The President's budget goes to the authorizations and appropriations committees in both the House of Representatives and the Senate. The authorizations are scheduled to go through Congress first, with legislation that authorizes the uses for the government funding. Both the House and Senate vote on the coming fiscal year budget authorizations. After being passed by both houses of Congress, the authorizations bill goes to a conference of the House and Senate authorizations committees to work out any differences in the House and Senate versions of the bill.

Generally, after the authorizations bill has passed, the appropriations go through the same process, with the House and Senate voting on respective versions of the appropriations bill and differences being resolved in a conference of the House and Senate appropriations committees.

The congressional authorizations and appropriations bills are submitted to the President, ideally before the end of the fiscal year, to be signed into law. The President has the option to veto a bill if it deviates significantly from the President's budget request. In the event that the President has not signed an appropriations bill into law before the end of September, a continuing resolution is passed to keep the government operating while the appropriations process is completed.

At any event, items can be added or dropped for funding. The most straightforward way to track how a particular funding line is proceeding is to outline it as follows:

Budget Line	Line X
President's Budget Request	$XX
House Authorization	XX+–
Senate Authorization	XX+–
Authorizations Conference	XX+–
House Appropriation	XX+–
Senate Appropriation	XX+–
Appropriations Conference	XX+–

This method of tracking identifies what committee in the House or Senate is adding or deleting a particular line in the budget. This is a basic tool used by lobbyists to get the programs they support through Congress.

Federal agencies get their budget, ideally at the beginning of the fiscal year. This is approximately the same time the agency needs to be submitting its budget for the next fiscal year to the President. A federal agency's job is to execute its budget. How well the agency executed its budget in the past year will influence what its budget will be in the following year. (Couple this budget process with the continually changing political climate and personnel turnover, and it's easy to see the complexity of the process. The process does do a remarkable job of preventing any one person from gaining an indiscriminate amount of power in our system.)

To execute their appropriated budgets, the agencies have funding vehicles in place to cover their operating expenses and contractual obligations from multiyear contracts approved in years past. There is usually an amount of new funding which they can use to pursue their mission. Most agencies (DOD, DOE, NASA) have a specific mission to accomplish and are permitted to use the funds in the manner most fitting to accomplish this mission. The DOD has a planning, programing, and budgeting system that was put in place by Secretary of Defense Robert McNamara in the early 1960s to develop a defense industrial base capable of winning the Cold War. (A by-product of this system was the segregation of the U.S. industrial base into commercial and defense bases.) The NIST ATP has been differentiated from the mission agencies in that its mission is to work with industry to further the economic well-being of the United States.

Any new funds are to be used toward obtaining the objectives required by the governing legislation. While there is usually some portion of congressionally directed funds that are a result of our political system, the vast majority of new funding available has to be competed for. Competition is intended to enable government agencies to get the best capabilities for the funding they have. While it can be argued that the overhead involved in the process does not likely achieve the goal of being the most efficient use of funds, it is the fairest system that has evolved to date.

Agencies make public announcements for programs to perform their missions, identifying the funds they have available in the *Commerce Business Daily* (CBD). CBD announcements of funds available for selected proposals are called requests for proposals (RFPs) or broad agency announcements (BAAs). RFPs and BAAs identify:

- The program, product, or service being requested by what agency.
- The amount of funding available.
- Selection criteria that will determine who gets awards.
- The contractual means that will be used (contract, cooperative agreement, or grant) to provide funds.
- A deadline for proposals.

Proposals are usually requested two to three months after the appearance of the RFP or BAA. The selection process then takes another several months. After awardees are selected, contract negotiations start, which takes another several months. The total process from RFP publication to award takes up most of the fiscal year.

NETWORKING OVERHEAD

If there is interest in getting government funds, it is important to understand and appreciate the government funding process. It's easy to see how the level of funding becomes the dominant metric in the administration of our government (as opposed to the effective utilization of those funds). A significant effort is required to budget and obtain funds in an agency and then contract the funds. The way in which the funds are spent and the mission program conducted or product or service provided depends to a significant degree on the contractor involved in performing the work. Much of this is left to trusting that the contractor will do the best job possible.

In industry, the market generally does not permit investments of funds that do not generate a return. The returns are generally measured quarterly. The government funding helps industry justify a longer-term perspective for needed industry investment in R&D. As such, if it is possible to get industry funds to drive a program which can be complemented by federal government funds, the program is more likely to produce needed results that both the government and industry want.

Commercial industry needs to be proactively involved with government to promote the business environment it needs to be competitive in the world marketplace. As much as this business environment requires government funding to promote and initiate collaborative R&D, business needs to be involved in working with both government agencies and the legislative branch to establish a win-win balance in which government and commercial business work together to bring about a business environment that is best for society.

However, there is an overhead cost involved for commercial businesses to work with government. While this overhead expense can be justified by providing an environment for long-term corporate stability, commercial companies need to stay in business. The overhead costs involved in networking with the government need to show some return for the companies to justify the overhead investment.

The U.S. defense industry knows how to work the government, as government funding is the lifeblood of that industry. Taken to the extreme, this can be to the detriment of an industry, as for example with the U.S. shipbuilding industry. U.S. commercial shipbuilding has been ranked 23rd in the world for most of the past decade, and as of 1998, no longer builds commercial ships. The U.S. Congress is the only market for the U.S. shipbuilding industry, and it now procures around six ships a year for the U.S. Navy at an average cost of approximately $1 billion per ship using the six main shipyards left in the country. The U.S. Navy is powerless to get the ships it needs in a more cost-effective manner, as U.S. shipbuilding has become a political jobs program rather than a competitive industry.

Large government contractors expect around a 90 percent success rate in the proposals they submit to the government. They do not submit a proposal unless they know the customer, its intentions, expectations, and budget resources. This involves working with the appropriate federal agencies and congressional representatives and their staffs. The time and effort needed to establish these relationships generate a significant overhead cost.

Commercial companies should ensure that the government is informed of their capabilities and interests. The best way to do this is through meeting with the representatives from the company's congressional district and meeting with the government agencies relevant to a company's interest. The U.S. government is reflective of the involvement of those who interface with it. Elected governments generally want to help ensure they have a competitive economy that provides the foundation for social stability.

If a company has ideas on how the government can assist in industry, it should provide input to help guide the direction of government. This can be accomplished through participating in workshops and working with the government in developing the plans and road maps used to influence future laws and appropriations. While this provides no guarantee to a company that it will get funding, it does establish relationships that will be used in evaluating the credibility and competence of potential future proposals.

Examples of the value of participating with the government are:

- Boeing, Ford, General Electric, Knowledge Technology International, Kodak, IBM, Engenious, the MacNeal-Schwendler Corporation, and other companies working with NIST to establish potential focus programs for ATP competitions on Collaborative and Distributed Design and Knowledge-Based Systems Interoperability.
- Any one of the many companies participating in the Integrated Manufacturing Technology Roadmapping Project being coordinated by the Department of Energy with DARPA and NIST support.
- Participating with the government when requested to participate in government-industry working groups such as for the Integrated Product/Process Development (IPPD) Task Group of the Aeronautics Materials and Manufacturing Technologies (AMMT) Working Group of the National Science and Technology Council (NSTC). The objective of this group is highlighted in Exhibit 11.2.
- Ensuring that your Congressman and Senator are aware of your company interests.

EXHIBIT 11.2　Example of Industry-Government Working Group Charter

---

Aeronautics Materials and Manufacturing Technologies (AMMT) Working Group Integrated Product/Process Development (IPPD) Task Group

Charter

Survey the use of IPPD in industry and delineate the needs for additional work (i.e., enterprise culture affecting manufacturing, computer-aided design tools, manufacturing process integration into design, relationships of the customer/assembler/supplier, vertical partnering, information systems to support decision making, workforce training, etc.) to accelerate agile manufacturing operations in the aerospace industry.

Scope

Use existing plans and programs as examples. Industry and government sources should be considered along with existing literature and the Lean Aircraft Initiative and Agile Manufacturing efforts.

Objective

Evaluate IPPD process to bring technology and manufacturing people together more effectively earlier in the process. Affordability, operational use, and sustainability must be considered in design, not just in production.

Approach

Convene a group of generalists, people with broad experience in product development as well as design, to look at experience/case studies to determine where opportunities exist to generalize or improve the process. This would include coordination with the Standardization, Intelligent Materials and Processes, Environmental, and Education and Training Task Groups.

While there is no formal interface between U.S. government and industry, and many of these initiatives come and go with the winds of the prevailing politics, there is value in industry maintaining a continuing dialogue with government. While private company participation in these efforts is at the expense of the company, the resulting industry-government relationships provide a foundation for furnishing recommendations for legislation, for RFPs or BAAs, or in contract negotiations which better promote commercial industry involvement with government. A rule most commercial companies have in establishing collaborative R&D programs is that any government funding should not require the company to change how the company does business. Government needs to better understand the commercial business drivers and culture if it is to succeed in establishing a competitive business environment.

While some commercial companies can afford to make the investment in providing direction to the government, they also expect some rate of return on the overhead costs involved in establishing these working relations. However, most government employees do not differentiate commercial and government industry. In addition, most of them do not have any experience in industry or understanding of what is needed to sell enough product or services to be able to make a payroll. As such, the risk for commercial companies in getting a return on the effort spent in establishing working relations with the government is relatively high. Commercial industry needs to be selective in establishing government relationships that provide a good probability of a return.

An additional reason for commercial industry to work with government mission agencies is that they can also serve as customers for the technology being developed, with the caveat that considering government agencies as customers needs to be viewed from the perspective of the total commercial market. Specific government requirements can sometimes make the cost of doing government business too high to make a profit.

If nothing more, attendance at government workshops and meetings can provide a forum for commercial companies with like interests to network and potentially establish joint relationships.

PART IV

Tools for Collaboration

There are a number of resources and capabilities that can assist in establishing collaborative manufacturing research and development programs. They are:

1. Individual relationships and trust
2. Process understanding
3. Contractual agreements

Individual Relationships and Trust

The development of relationships in which individuals trust that they are all working for their common good is critical for the establishment and conduct of collaborative development.

Process Understanding

The ability to understand processes of all types is important. Process understanding is needed to provide the framework for collaboration. The individual's role in a process needs to be understood as well as how processes relate together in a company or organization, and how the company in turn relates to the processes in the economy and society.

Contractual Agreements

Agreements need to be put in place to establish a collaborative development program. The process of establishing contractual agreement among participating companies can take longer and be more cumbersome than developing the technical program. It is important to understand the framework and rationale behind the needed contractual agreements early in the process of establishing a program. Without proper attention, a fully developed program can be terminated before it starts due to contractual difficulties.

CHAPTER 12

Individual Relationships and Trust

Successful collaboration requires successful interaction among individuals. The relationships established in a collaborative environment require a high degree of trust and understanding. The participants need to be secure in who they are, in what they know, and with their position in their company or organization. It generally takes people who are the best of the best to collaborate—people who are innovative, action-oriented, and capable of (and receptive to) learning new processes. In addition, these people are committed to make collaboration work.

For example, while Michael Jordan won the league scoring titles in his first few years in the NBA, he wasn't able to win championships. Larry Bird and Magic Johnson told Michael that he wouldn't win any championships until he learned to be a team player. Michael learned. As a result, the Chicago Bulls became the dominant basketball team of the 1990s with Scotty Pippen, Dennis Rodman, Michael Jordan, and the rest of the team working together to complement and supplement each other's play. Michael learned to work with and depend on the team. He realized that "the team including Michael Jordan" was better than Michael Jordan alone could ever be. Michael and coach Phil Jackson worked to make sure that everyone on the team recognized the importance of the team. When one person went cold shooting, the ball was passed to other teammates to score. They had developed confidence in the capabilities of their teammates, and knew their own capabilities and limitations. All the players were trusted to have the same objective—to win the game.

Trust and confidence in the team works the same way in a collaborative R&D program. Everyone involved in the team knows each one is dependent on the others to make the program work. Everyone needs to know what has to be done. They also need to have the capabilities each participating company will bring to accomplish the R&D objectives. Decisions on appropriate actions to be taken by each participating company are discussed. These discussions will formulate the R&D direction and the goals of the program. Care needs to be taken to ensure that discussions lead to actions on the part of one or more of the companies involved in the program. If discussions can not result in actions, it's likely that the group is wasting time discussing that topic. All of the personnel working in a collaborative R&D program should recognize and assist in realizing the common interests and goals of the program. What's more, all of the personnel need to recognize, respect, and assist in realizing the specific interests and goals of each company in the program. Individual company goals and interests in the program need to be self-serving.

Steve Babcock, a champion of many collaborative R&D programs at Boeing-Rocketdyne, shared a key feature of this relationship building when he relayed, "You can't be secretive about collaboration, or have a 'hidden agenda.' Everything has to be out in the open. You must have a passion for the subject at hand, and be willing to go to all ends to make it happen. You need to do this in spite of potential opposition in your company from those who do not understand the power of collaboration. You also may have to do a lot on your own time, since most everyone has more to do than time in a day. Also, keeping the collaboration subject very high in your priority and schedule is imperative. Too often, people think about commitments and actions only five minutes before a teleconference, or leaving for a meeting. Delays from people who have made commitments are dangerous and can be contagious."[1] The authors have found that professional actions taken by collaborative team members in meeting commitments with quality products can also be contagious.

Building trust between companies is a challenge, particularly be-

---

[1] E-mail from Steve Babcock to Gene Allen dated October 5, 1998.

tween large original equipment manufacturers (OEMs) and their component parts suppliers and technology suppliers. This is often due to past history, where OEMs dictated to suppliers what they wanted and what price they would pay. As part of the effort to build trust between OEMs and suppliers, the suppliers participating in the Open Supplier Integration Center (OSIC) initiative were asked to write down what they thought a customer could do to help them build trust. The OEMs in OSIC were asked to do the same for the suppliers. The following answers are the compiled results.

To build trust from the supplier's perspective, the OEM customer:

• Gets the supplier involved early, preferably at the concept stage.
• Has a real project and proper funding.
• Identifies the real decision makers and the criteria and time line for making decisions.
• Is able to separate cheapest price from the best overall solution.
• Pays in a timely fashion.
• Has stated priorities of quality and performance.
• Supports new and innovative approaches to manufacturing (especially new technologies).
• Understands the supplier's needs and is willing to discuss, with an open mind, what is reasonable or possible.
• Will not quote out the job once the supplier has helped put it together.
• Is willing to share in the burden of additional costs that comes with new technologies or processes, especially high-risk efforts.

To earn trust from the customer's perspective, the supplier:

• Has a history of performance in doing what the supplier says.
• Demonstrates openness and honesty in all interactions as determined by the character of the people involved in face-to-face meetings.
• Has plans and shares future investment strategies and resources with a goal of improving the combined team's competitiveness in the marketplace.
• Listens openly and not with a preconceived solution.
• Provides honest inputs. (Uses facts, doesn't fabricate.)

- Says what the supplier will do, and then does it.
- Shares cost drivers for processes.
- Shares demonstrated capabilities, quantitatively if possible.
- Is willing and able to link internal information systems to those of the customer.

All parties need to recognize that each company will always have different processes and practices governing their businesses; no two processes will be the same. This is important for all participants to understand, particularly in a collaborative R&D program developing "process" technologies. The R&D tasks pursued in a program developing process technologies can only be loosely coupled to each other due to the different company processes and practices. If a group of companies are pursuing technology development focused around product improvement, then the R&D tasks can be more tightly coupled. This distinction became apparent through the establishment of the Rapid Response Manufacturing (RRM) program, and was important to realize before the participants started to trust each other's motivations in the program. RRM had to have a loosely coupled R&D plan recognized by the participants as the foundation to building cooperative relationships between the participants.

Good working relationships are a precondition for being able to effectively leverage a collaborative environment, and the only way to be able to generate the results from collaboration that are significantly better than going it alone. The Printed Wiring Board (PWB) program, with its common product focus, was able to establish a more focused or tightly coupled R&D plan. Good working relationships were able to be established faster in the PWB program than in the RRM program. This was because the RRM participants did not initially recognize the distinction between process and product collaborative R&D plans needing to be loosely coupled versus tightly coupled. It is easier for most people to visualize efforts based on product, versus process.

The team relationships established in the RRM program were observed by Boeing officials at an RRM meeting hosted by Boeing in Everett, Washington. Boeing had expressed interest in joining RRM and had invited the RRM Steering Group to Seattle to discuss respective programs. Boeing had personnel from a number of different internal organizations at the meeting (commercial, defense, corporate, information systems). The Boeing officials were impressed that the RRM team, consisting of people from over 10 different companies from different industries, was more harmonized and cohesive in their thoughts and direction than the personnel from Boeing. They were surprised to hear someone from Pratt & Whitney finish a sentence started by someone from Ford. The RRM group at that time was a team, with individuals knowing each other to the point that they could anticipate reactions. The RRM team could have had a similar reaction in meeting with any large corporation, even within those who were RRM member companies. The RRM had formed into a team from working common issues at quarterly meetings and weekly teleconferences over the previous two years.

A collaborative program will not produce significant results until a team environment is established. Creating a team environment requires the development of individual relationships based on trust, integrity, and credibility. Individual working relationships and trust can be established prior to the establishment of a collaborative R&D program. In many cases a collaborative program is the result of the relationships developed in personal networks.

Trusting, working relationships can be established by assisting those within the network. Establishing oneself as a valuable asset to others is vital in creating a personal network. This book is the result of the working relationship established between the authors while establishing and conducting collaborative R&D activities between Eastman Kodak, the National Center for Manufacturing Sciences, and the MacNeal-Schwendler Corporation. Gene Allen has had the opportunity to provide value to champions for collaboration at a number of companies. His experience in establishing a network with personnel at Texas Instruments, Ford, and Rocketdyne is shown in Appendix K. Key points highlighted in these relationships include the corporate commitment demonstrated by the OEMs, and the value Mr. Allen was able to provide through coordinating efforts among the participants and facilitating the establishment of a team environment. Another feature characterized in these relationships is that Mr. Allen's contacts with these companies resulted in actions that were of benefit to the companies. The three actions that resulted from Rocketdyne's first meeting with Mr. Allen provided a foundation for a continuing relationship.

The Collaborative Animal

Larry Johnson describes himself as a collaborative animal. He exhibits characteristics that promote collaboration. He is very personable and very intelligent. Larry Johnson exemplifies the optimal characteristics required for a person to be successful in collaborative development. They are the best people in an organization, and they are committed to the collaborative R&D assigned. They have to be people who are capable of (1) independent thinking and (2) taking constructive action. They have to be:

- Confident in their own intelligence.
- Smart enough to know what they don't know.
- Capable of learning quickly.
- Willing to share information.
- Confident in their own position.
- Able to understand other's perspectives such that they can help make the best decisions on actions that need to be taken.
- Able to take actions and make things happen within their company or organization.

While at Texas Instruments, Mr. Johnson worked with others in drafting the basis for developing software that can operate with ultimately any other software across all computers, a computer software architecture for interoperability. This work became the foundation for the computer architectures that were later adapted by the Rapid Response Manufacturing (RRM) program and the National Industrial Information Infrastructure Protocols (NIIIP) Consortium. Mr. Johnson then worked through the RRM program to validate and evolve this architecture. He became the chairman of the RRM Interoperability Services Working Group, where he coordinated efforts to develop a standard interface to Product Data Management (PDM) software systems to enable them to interoperate. The conclusion of this effort, which piloted a Common Object Request Broker Architecture (CORBA) interface to the Metaphase PDM system, coincided with a call from the Object Management Group (OMG)[2] for inputs to develop the CORBA PDM standard. Mr. Johnson coordinated the results of this RRM work with seven other inputs from software companies that develop and sell PDM systems, efforts that continued after he went to work for the MacNeal-Schwendler Corporation. In coordinating the development of the Joint PDM submission to the OMG, the acceptance by OMG of the submission as the standard followed. Mr. Johnson is now a cochair of the OMG Manufacturing Domain Task Force, continuing efforts to evolve software interoperability, a mission that can be likened to getting everyone in the world to be able to understand each other in the same language.

The individuals in collaborative development, like Larry, are intrapreneurs (an entrepreneur employed by a large company). They need to then be able to implement the actions they decide on. They have to have the support of corporate management to do what they do. Often they do not have the resources to perform all the needed actions, and have to depend on their relationships within the organization to be able to get others to take action. These people are an organization's best doers. They know what needs to be done, and ensure that it gets done regardless of their position. These are the people in an organization you turn to in order to get things done.

The credibility of the companies and individuals involved in collaborative development is enhanced by their ability to follow through with their commitments. The manner in which commitments are met provides the basis for building the trust needed to build strategic relationships. Meeting commitments must not only benefit the participating company, but should be done in a manner that is beneficial to all participating parties. Failing to meet commitments, or meeting them in a way

---

[2]OMG is a consortium of over 800 software vendors, software developers, and end users. OMG moves forward in establishing the Common Object Request Broker Architecture (CORBA) as the "middleware that's everywhere" through its worldwide standard specifications: CORBA/IIOP, Object Services, Internet Facilities, and Domain Interface specifications. Established in 1989, OMG's mission is to promote the theory and practice of object technology for the development of distributed computing systems. The goal is to provide a common architectural framework for object-oriented applications based on widely available interface specifications.

that is not beneficial to the other participants in a collaborative development program can undermine the reputation of an individual or a good company.

The ability and enjoyment of working with other very capable people generates a camaraderie within a successfully operating collaborative development team. The group becomes a fraternity of individuals who know that they can trust one another.

Collaborative Team Characteristics

Warren Bennis and Patricia Ward Biederman in their book *Organizing Genius: The Secrets of Creative Collaboration* validate the collaborative premise that "none of us is as smart as all of us" by identifying common characteristics among six case studies on recently conducted collaborative efforts that have had significant impact on society. The case studies are:

1. The Manhattan Project's development of the atomic bomb.
2. The Xerox Palo Alto Research Center's development of the personal computer.
3. The Lockheed Skunk Works' development of high-performance aircraft.
4. The Disney development of animation.
5. The Democrats' 1992 presidential election campaign.
6. Black Mountain College's impact on the arts.

The common characteristics the book lists as lessons are:

1. Greatness starts with superb people.
2. Great groups and great leaders create each other.
3. Every great group has a strong leader.
4. The leaders of great groups love talent and know where to find it.

5. Great groups are full of talented people who can work together.
6. Great groups think they are on a mission from God.
7. Every great group is an island—but an island with a bridge to the mainland.
8. Great groups see themselves as winning underdogs.
9. Great groups always have an enemy.
10. People in great groups have blinders on.
11. Great groups are optimistic, not realistic.
12. In great groups the right person has the right job.
13. The leaders of great groups give them what they need and free them from the rest.
14. Great groups ship.
15. Great work is its own reward.

Much of what is characterized in this book was in evidence in creating and conducting the Printed Wiring Board, Rapid Response Manufacturing, Robust Design Computational System, and Technologies for Enterprise-Wide Engineering programs. A complementary list of characteristics needed to establish successful collaborative efforts is:

1. Having a common focus for the group. The focus should be based on a higher purpose. The focus should be centered around making something or accomplishing a particular objective to allow for tangible completion.
2. Having capable people committed to the effort.
3. Establishing mutual respect and trust among the group such that everyone is comfortable that each individual's actions are in the best interest in achieving the desired group objective. Collaborative efforts require as much development in culture and social dynamics as in technology.
4. Recognizing that leadership is required to maintain focus and ensure results.
5. Demonstrating the power of true believers led by a messiah.

CHAPTER 13

Process Understanding

An important part of being able to successfully establish, manage, and participate in collaborative development efforts involves the ability to understand processes. Process understanding is not taught well, or even generally understood, although we live in a world governed by processes. A process is a continuous operation or action that leads to a particular result. Processes are dynamic, constantly changing in reaction to their environments—making them more difficult to conceptualize than static objects. An easy process to understand is driving a car. The driver controls the process by using the gas pedal, the brake, and the steering wheel to get the car to transport him or her to a particular location. The processes that govern how the car actually works are more complex. Processes we encounter include:

- Natural processes governed by the laws of physics.
- Social processes governed by law and culture.
- Business processes governed by commercial market survival or government procurement practice.

In addition, all processes can relate to, and influence one another, as explained in Dr. Edward O. Wilson's book *Consilience: The Unity of Knowledge* (Knopf, 1998).

Being able to communicate and learn processes is an important tool for all people involved in collaboration. A good process baseline provides all the participants with an understanding of where they fit into the development efforts.

Process Perspectives

For individuals to be able to add value, it helps if they understand the business and technical processes and the key characteristics driving those processes. It is impossible for everyone involved in a collaborative program to know everything about every process. What's important is that the people be able to understand and, as appropriate, learn processes that are new to them that impact the program. Understanding these processes provides a foundation for collaboration.

There are different levels of process understanding. There are high-level views that should be able to be understood by all of the people in the effort, and detailed views that require particular expertise to understand. An example of a high-level view is the understanding that:

> a company that employs a person has to make money to stay in business. If the company doesn't make money, it can not continue to pay its personnel.

This is a high-level concept that most people understand.

Going from this high-level view to a more detailed overview involves:

> the employees of a company knowing the processes by which their company makes money (manufacturing, sales and marketing, distribution, finance, administration, etc.), and more importantly, knowing how their role in the company helps the company be profitable and stay in business.

This is a broad view of a company that does not go into a lot of detail. Even so, experience has shown that the processes used in a company to make money are not necessarily well understood by anyone in the company, in many cases even by management. Today, many companies are attempting to communicate metrics for process improvement that enable an employee to understand the relationships various functions in the company have to one another. By communicating these interrelational measurements, it is hoped that employees will better understand how their individual roles support the entire company mission. An example of such a metric is return on net assets (RONA). RONA equals net earnings divided by net assets. To calculate RONA, divide net earnings (sales minus operating costs and taxes) by total net assets (cash receivables and property minus liabilities such as accounts payable). When the functions of a business are expressed and built into a formula such as this, the effect different functions have on each other and on overall company performance can be more easily understood. The impact of the cost of quality and goods on sales becomes more evident, and the effects of inventory and machine utilization become more understandable to employees responsible for those functions. Collaboration usually gets high marks when measured this way. Collaborators know it, and appreciate its benefits more easily than those who have not experienced this kind of phenomenon.

Small tool and die companies are a fundamental portion of the supply base supporting manufacturing. Almost every mechanical product built uses a die to form some part of it. Die fabrication companies are under high pressure to reduce costs. However, the costs of the machine tools used to make dies run into the hundreds of thousands of dollars. The prices a company charges for making dies have to cover the cost of the equipment used to make them, as well as the cost of the personnel operating the equipment. The way to lower die costs is to be able to produce more dies with the equipment and operators a company has available. Machine utilization is a good metric that the company's personnel can monitor that ensures they have a competitive position in the market.

Even though the understanding of the company's business processes is beneficial to all the employees (good employees will want to improve what they do in order to help the company stay in business, as it provides them with both security and self-satisfaction), few in the company will have even the high-level view of all of the company's business processes. Those who do have a high-level view encompassing all of the company's processes are generally in management, making decisions based on their total understanding of the enterprise. These individuals generally do not have a detailed understanding of each of the company's business processes; however, they can usually understand detailed presentations of the processes and how the detail fits into the corporate Big Picture. It is important to recognize that there are various levels of process understanding which are known to varying degrees by different people in an organization. All of this understanding is needed to make things work.

While understanding the company's processes provides a broad view of the company, a person working on the manufacturing plant floor has a detailed understanding of the processes describing how the machine tool that person operates works. An experienced die cutter will know to change the parameter settings on the equipment to compensate for the air temperature in the plant to hold a particular tolerance. A plant engineer will know to check the material properties of a new batch of raw feed stock the company received to make an aircraft engine compressor blade. These are examples of highly detailed process knowledge that even though it can and should be predictable is often difficult to communicate to others. Much of the detailed knowledge and understanding of these processes comes from experience.

Process Presentation and Learning

Collaboration requires communicating with all members of the research and development team such that they can understand how joint development can impact their internal processes. Fast diffusion of information through public-private partnerships and alliances turbocharge the learning process.[1] The ability to present and learn processes is an important tool for collaboration.

---

[1]*Going Global, The New Shape of American Innovation*, The Council on Competitiveness, September 1998.

Process Presentation

As described, the process views of a company can be expressed to varying levels of detail at varying levels of both breadth and depth. All of the process views should be consistent with one another for the company to operate and stay in business. The specifics in the detailed process have to support the generalizations presented in the high-level view of the process.

The ability of a company to understand and control its processes has much to do with its success. Controlling processes requires the ability to understand and make decisions on how and what inputs to the process need to be changed. Usually process decisions involve more than one person, requiring communications about the process. The ability to communicate about processes is important across all levels in a company, organization, or even society. If the experience and education level of an audience is not known, the process needs to be accurately simplified. The key is being able to understand the process and reduce the complexity of the process such that it can be communicated.

Senior decision makers have many things on their minds. To be able to communicate with them and empower them to take action, briefings to senior personnel have to reduce complexity of the process to enable understanding and decision making. Should further details be needed, they have to follow from the high-level view provided. Guidelines to brief senior military personnel on the politico-military situation in a particular part of the world are limited to three minutes. In those three minutes, the background on the region needs to be presented, issues identified, and recommended actions provided. In billion-dollar presentations to decision makers, such as those on the congressional appropriations committees or in Fortune 500 companies, written presentations have to have all the same type of information (background, issues, recommendations) on one $8^{1}/_{2}''$ by $11''$ piece of paper, in big print, double-spaced, and with wide margins. The ability to reduce process complexity and communicate it is a tool that can facilitate collaboration.

Learning Processes

Different people learn in different ways. Some learn better by listening; others learn better by reading; almost everyone learns best by doing. Learning to drive a car is a good example; you can listen to a teacher explain how to drive, and you can read a manual on how to drive, but the best way to learn is to get behind the wheel and learn by experience. While experience is the best way to learn, it's good to have some degree of learning accomplished prior to getting behind the wheel of a car. The driver should know ahead of time that forcing the transmission into reverse while moving forward will damage the car.

Understanding and controlling processes provides the basis for business. Process understanding and control, as highlighted in the driving example above, requires both a theoretical understanding and practical understanding. Different institutions teach varying degrees of both. In the world's research-oriented universities, such as MIT, the problem is often considered solved if a solution can be conceptualized. Details are often left for others, as they were not an interesting part of the problem. In vocational institutions, understanding the specifics of operating a process is more important than understanding the mathematical details of the theory that explains the process.

One of the best educational environments for learning to understand and control processes is provided in the U.S. Navy's nuclear power training program. The operation of nuclear power plants requires not only theoretical knowledge, but also detail knowledge. A ship's nuclear-powered propulsion system consists of a complex of interrelated mechanical, electrical, chemical, and radiological systems which need to operate reliably and safely. Reliability is needed to keep the ship under way in the water in any weather or combat condition. A loss of power in heavy weather or under attack could result in the loss of the ship and its crew. Safety is needed to prevent a reactor casualty which could cause radiological contamination outside the ship. To address this balance between reliability and safety, the Navy nuclear power training program emphasizes continuous theoretical and practical training on all of the integrated systems making up the power plant. The Navy's nuclear-trained operators are trained to the extent that if the reactor automatically shuts down (scrams), operators will be able to identify the cause and fix the problem so that they can start up the reactor as soon as possible.

This training extends throughout a career in the nuclear Navy. Advancement requires demonstrated technical competence in making the decisions needed to safely and reliably operate a nuclear propulsion system. Those Navy officers who are assigned as engineering officers responsible for the engineering plant on a nuclear-powered ship have to complete a rigid qualification process that demonstrates their understanding of the various systems and system interactions that make up a nuclear propulsion plant. Only qualified engineering officers are selected to command nuclear-powered ships and then only after they pass another qualification process which demonstrates their ability to make the best decisions possible regarding the operation of a ship's nuclear power plant. The commanding officer of a Navy nuclear-powered ship has a full understanding of the processes that govern how that ship works, to the degree that the commanding officer can take knowledgeable action under any contingency to ensure the safety of the ship while performing its mission.

A very valuable trait of the Navy nuclear power program is learning how to quickly comprehend new processes. This is indoctrinated into nuclear-trained Navy personnel because each different class of ship has different systems that interrelate in different ways. Being able to learn new systems quickly is an aptitude that would be valuable to everyone, and is particularly valuable in a collaborative development environment.

This same combination of theoretical and practical training is used in other professions. One notable example is with the medical profession, which uses teaching hospitals to train interns under the masterful eyes of experienced surgeons. Teaching factories have been established in many areas around the country to provide theory and practice in operating and managing new manufacturing technologies. Teaching factories are often established in conjunction with local colleges and universities.

The Navy nuclear power continuous training model can be readily extended to a manufacturing enterprise. Much of this model was based on the apprenticeship programs that used to be taught at General Electric and Westinghouse. An outline of how such a training program might exist is provided in Exhibit 13.1.

The availability of corporate training programs is an aspect of a corporation's culture. Training is a foundation to ensure that a company has

EXHIBIT 13.1   Process-Centric Enterprise Training Program

Personnel Selection

A rigorous selection process limits the training program to personnel who have demonstrated aptitude to perform the needed operations in an enterprise. A student's scholastic background must demonstrate aptitude prior to being given written exams and interviews by senior personnel in the enterprise.

Employees hired to be specialists in one of the enterprises processes will receive training focused on that particular process, with cross training in each of the other processes used in the enterprise's businesses. Managers are required to have the same knowledge as the specialists in all of the fields.

Schooling

A classical instruction program is required to learn the theory behind the enterprise's processes. A passing grade is required for each topic taught. Failure on any topic results in dismissal from the program.

Demonstration/Application Training

Additional training in the enterprise working environment, or a prototype of that environment (as in a teaching factory) is required after completion of the classical instruction program. Training is conducted through filling out "qualification cards," which are booklets outlining required knowledge to work a given position in the working environment. The student must get signatures from the employees in the working environment for:

1. Verbally relaying to the employees:
   - How equipment and processes work.
   - Why equipment and processes are designed in a particular manner.
   - What means are used to operate the equipment/processes under different conditions including casualties.
2. Observing various evolutions involving the equipment and process.
3. Demonstrating to the employee that they can operate the equipment and processes under normal and abnormal conditions.

After completing the qualification cards for each position in the enterprise, qualification time is spent with a particular employee, in which the student performs all of the employee's functions in the enterprise process while being monitored by the employee. Qualification performance is graded and must be completed satisfactorily. Failure to satisfactorily demonstrate the ability to perform results in dismissal from the program.

(continued)

EXHIBIT 13.1 *(Continued)*

After successful completion of the qualification portion of learning the enterprise's processes, students are interviewed by senior enterprise personnel in a final oral board, which must be satisfactorily completed to graduate from the program and be hired for a position in the enterprise.

Continuous Enterprise Training

Personnel must repeat the qualification process after reporting to a new position or process in the enterprise. Once qualified to operate a process, all employees have at least one hour of classroom refresher training each day, and training evolutions conducted two to three times a week during regular work time. Managers study to become qualified to be senior managers, which cumulates in a series of written and oral exams conducted by the personnel who design and build the systems and processes which make up the enterprise.

Training Emphasis

Next to the actual operations of the enterprise, training is the highest priority. The best personnel are selected to be instructors. Managers are evaluated by how well they have trained their personnel, and are personally involved in the program, conducting lectures and overseeing qualification boards.

and continues to evolve the processes it needs to stay in business. Collaborative development benefits and complements internal company training programs.

Basic Processes Needed for Collaboration in Manufacturing

It is important in a collaborative environment for those managing the effort to know and support the businesses of each of the participants. There are some basic high-level business processes that everyone involved in a collaborative development project should know as a foundation for their collaboration, the most important of those being the processes being impacted by the collaborative research being performed.

As an example, the Rapid Response Manufacturing (RRM) program had as an objective the reduction of the design-manufacture time for mechanical products. To reduce the design-manufacture time, one needs to know the design-manufacture process. Figure 13.1 shows a generic product design-manufacture process.

The generic product design-manufacture process highlights the steps from getting an idea about what a product might be to making the product. The application of computers to this process has resulted in computer-aided design (CAD) being used to help draft designs, computer-aided engineering (CAE) being used to simulate the physical interactions a design might encounter, and computer-aided manufacturing (CAM) digitizing the instructions to the controls of manufacturing equipment. While CAD, CAE and CAM have improved the performance of steps in this process, they have, in many cases, lengthened the process, as product data can only be exchanged between CAD, CAE and CAM systems through translators.

The black arrows show process steps that are ideally avoided. These steps characterize the build-test-fail-fix cycle that represents

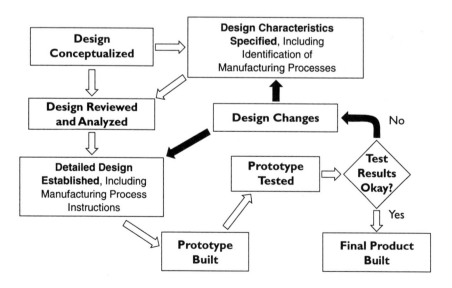

FIGURE 13.1   Generic Product Design-Manufacture Process

the large cost hill in Figure 1.2. The better defined the product design characteristics can be relative to the real physical product form and function, and the better actual manufacturing process capabilities are understood and specified, the more accurate the design review and analyses will be. The more robust the detailed design manufacturing process instructions are, and the better the prototype testing processes are, the higher the chances are that there will be fewer design changes needed, and that a quality product will be cost-effectively produced.

While Figure 13.1 describes the particular process that was being addressed for the RRM program, there are other generic processes that are helpful to understand as a foundation for conducting collaboration. These include the government funding process described in Chapter 11, and the technology commercialization process described in Chapter 1. The establishment of the Technologies for Enterprise-Wide Engineering (TEWE) initiative focused around the knowledge process simplified in slide 9 shown in Exhibit 9.2. Other processes in the manufacturing business environment for which a high-level perspective is a valuable tool for collaboration include a generalized product life cycle process shown in Figure 13.2, and the generic enterprise shown in Figure 13.3.

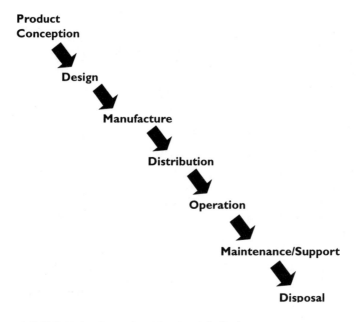

FIGURE 13.2 Generalized Product Life Cycle

The generalized product life cycle is a simple recognition of the process a product goes through from being someone's idea through being designed, made, used, supported, and disposed of. In considering systems, it is useful to remember that everything we know of has a life cycle, from subatomic particles with life cycles measured in millionths of a second or less, to the known universe with a life cycle of tens of billions of years as far we know.

The generic manufacturing enterprise is driven by a strategy that incorporates market demand for products with the capabilities the enterprise has in its people and physical assets (black arrows). This strategy directs the product realization processes (further detailed in Figures 13.1 and 13.2). Costing processes are used to price the company's people's efforts and asset use and to put a price on the product. Products are then sold in the market, with the funds from sales being used to pay the enterprise's personnel and cover the cost of its physical assets. Cash flow from the products made in the enterprise should also generate dividends for investors, which in turn attract additional investment. Training supports the enterprise's personnel. The company's physical assets are supported

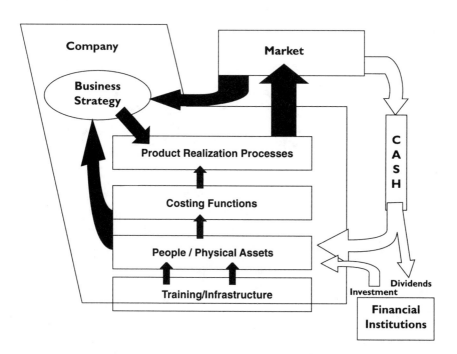

FIGURE 13.3 Generic Manufacturing Enterprise

by the infrastructure. Much of the training and infrastructure support originate outside the company.

Every company has its own internal company processes. Every chief executive officer, chief financial officer, and manager of information systems follows his or her own established processes and views the other systems from one's own perspectives. These processes should be able to be roughly mapped to the generic model. The more others can understand the personal process their compatriots use, the more effectively the enterprise can work together as a team.

The understanding of the roles of people in society, and how those roles evolve as society evolves, gets us back to a Big Picture perspective. Technologies being applied to manufacturing will lead to improved capabilities to generate wealth employing fewer people directly, but supporting more employment in total. The service industries associated with directly supporting new technologies support more jobs, as well as provide the wealth generation to support improved health care, education, and entertainment. The agricultural base provides us with food for survival. The manufacturing base provides us with wealth to support political stability and a higher quality of life.

General Technology Development Direction

We live in exciting times, with the emergence of new information, communications, and process technologies promising significant improvements in the quality of life around the world. To facilitate getting new technologies adopted, there are some general considerations that should be taken into account for all emerging technology development. These are:

- New technologies must be easy to use if they are to be accepted by the market. The complexity underlying how the product operates needs to be removed from the user, particularly for the mass consumer market.

- New technologies need to easily interoperate with the existing legacy infrastructure and related systems in the enterprise.
- New modeling and simulation technologies need to be accurate in their portrayal of physical reality.

Many multinational manufacturing companies are embracing new technologies to improve their competitive posture. Ford Motor Company provides an example of this with its Direct Engineering^SM initiative, an effort to dramatically improve product quality, decrease time to production, and reduce cost. This effort has been evolved by Ford through the Rapid Response Manufacturing program through several pilot demonstrations. Other large companies are pursuing internal initiatives similar to Direct Engineering^SM, which has promoted collaboration in the Technologies for Enterprise-Wide Engineering (TEWE) initiative.

Direct Engineering^SM is an initiative to create and capture knowledge and then establish the ability to use that knowledge through creating a knowledge management organization. The vision is to have "a single engineer who develops a completely defined product" using knowledge bases. The Direct Engineering^SM methodology gives the engineer all the applicable design rules, manufacturing rules, system constraints, and best practices during the initial phase of product design. This approach significantly reduces the product redesign that typically occurs because manufacturing, or system constraints, were not considered early in the design phase. All these rules and best practices are approved and kept up to date by a cross-functional knowledge management organization composed of subject matter experts from product design, manufacturing, plant layout, production, shipping, and service. The information is delivered to the engineer, when it is needed, by knowledge-based engineering software tools.

Building the structure to integrate Direct Engineering^SM into Ford's product development process requires identifying the changes that are needed in individual attitudes, in Ford's corporate culture, in continuous technology development, and, most importantly, in implementation. Ford personnel have identified the following six fundamental principals of Direct Engineering^SM:

- A single unified concurrent engineering process (design-manufacture)
- An integral knowledge management process
- Seamless knowledge delivery and application
- Rapid development of a total product definition
- An engineer-centric environment
- The home organization owning and leading the effort

Direct Engineering^{SM} captures the direction major companies are heading in applying emerging technologies. The only thing certain about this direction is that it will change. It is most likely that the changes will be minor, like the course changes a ship makes in changing destinations from LeHavre to Antwerp as it leaves New York. The final destination for the applications of emerging technologies is improving business processes for the benefit of all in society, as the final destination of the ship is Europe.

In any event, the use of good engineering practices will dominate the direction of the Technology Development Process. Good engineering practices simply require that a problem be clearly defined with a description of the environmental constraints known as boundary conditions. Once the problem is understood, the resources available to solve the problem need to be defined and understood. Then it's just a matter of applying the available resources in the best possible manner to address the problem. This is a high-level view of the engineering process. As with most high-level views, the devil is in the details. Collaboration in process understanding and development can exorcise the devil.

CHAPTER 14

Contractual Agreements

One of the capabilities needed in establishing collaborative development programs is the ability to establish a legal business framework for a program. This is accomplished through drafting:

1. Agreements among parties participating in the collaborative development program which spell out the details for sharing and protecting any intellectual property contributed or developed during a project.
2. Agreements addressing any funding.
3. Agreements with a government for technical services—cooperative research and development agreements (CRADAs) in the United States.
4. Subcontracts the group may put in place with a third party.

Establishing these agreements constitutes part of the overhead involved with collaboration. The work needed to establish these agreements can be significant. When the Printed Wiring Board and Rapid Response Manufacturing programs were put in place, it took as long (or longer as was the case with the CRADAs) to put the program agreements in place as it took to develop and agree on the technical work plan.

The objective of a company's legal staff should be to provide a legal mechanism to enable you to do what you want in collaboration. However, legal and contracts experts in large manufacturing companies have been well educated and trained in the discipline to protect the companies' intellectual property and to err on the side of too much protection.

To do this, they have built fortresses of fire walls and layers of protection around products and processes that come in contact with knowledge property deemed key to existence of the business. While companies must continue to protect and defend the real knowledge-based jewels that have competitive value, they must also be flexible and clever enough to find ways to peel away the layers that are not critical, so that value-adding operations can be performed. Today, companies choosing collaboration are faced with inflexible legal and contracts people who do not understand or believe in collaboration as a viable means of doing business. Aligning these departments as early as possible in the process is very helpful and time-saving.

The National Center for Manufacturing Sciences (NCMS) has performed an invaluable service in getting a large number of corporate legal staffs from companies in the U.S. manufacturing base to agree on terminology for these agreements and establishing a precedence for collaborative program agreements. Having a proven legal precedence for agreements that resulted in successful collaborative development programs removes the risk perceived in the past to be affiliated with collaboration. Organizations such as NCMS provide their members with a significant service in reducing the collaborative overhead related to putting the contractual agreements in place.

Partnership Agreement

The first consideration to be addressed is whether a partnership agreement is needed. In some cases a simple nondisclosure agreement signed by all of the participants at a meeting is sufficient. Many projects do not even need a nondisclosure agreement if the information being exchanged is nonproprietary.

A partnership agreement is needed when the group performing the collaborative development work is getting funding from the government or another third party. An agreement is also needed if the group plans to collectively subcontract work.

Partnership agreements[1] are used when it is necessary to define the parameters for collaboration, project management, funding, and intellectual property protection and dissemination of project technology. Means of how to dissolve an agreement in cases where no progress is being made or the wrong parties are on the team should also be addressed. A partnership agreement should also protect the partners from antitrust considerations. This agreement should reference any funding agreements and incorporate any provisions required by the funding source.

The following discusses a generic project agreement that has been developed by the National Center for Manufacturing Sciences (NCMS) through the legal staffs of their member companies (the Table of Contents is shown in Exhibit 14.1). We discuss what is included in each of the sections, with excerpts from a generic NCMS agreement where relevant.

The NCMS Project Agreement starts off by defining and identifying the participants and stating that each participant has one vote in the program. A background section is provided which uses a number of "WITNESSETH" and "WHEREAS" phrases resulting in the "NOW, THEREFORE, in consideration of the foregoing and the mutual covenants and promises set forth herein, the parties hereto agree as follows:" comment, with the rest of the agreement following. The registration of the group under the National Cooperative Research and Production Act of 1993 is sometimes identified in this section. Registra-

---

[1]Variously referred to as project agreements, program agreements (NCMS uses the term *project* for what the authors consider to be a program), joint venture agreements (the term for a partnership agreement used by the National Institute of Standards and Technology Advanced Technology Program), or joint research and development teaming agreements.

EXHIBIT 14.1 Draft NCMS Project Agreement Table of Contents

Draft

Table of Contents

Project Agreement
Number _____

SECTION I	Research Project
SECTION II	Participation and Administration
SECTION III	Cost and Funding
SECTION IV	Reports and Publications
SECTION V	Term and Termination
SECTION VI	Technology Rights
VI.A.	Definitions
VI.B.	Participants' Background Technology
VI.C.	Research Project Technology
VI.D.	Patent and Copyright Enforcement
VI.E.	Warranty of Sublicense(s) to Subsidiaries of Participants
SECTION VII	Participants' Responsibility and Release
SECTION VIII	Additional Party Participation
SECTION IX	Notices
SECTION X	Additional Provisions
SECTION XI	Governing Law
SECTION XII	Entire Agreement
SECTION XIII	Agreement Execution
APPENDIX A	Funding Summary
APPENDIX B	Project Funding Summary
APPENDIX C	Sample Format of an Invoice
APPENDIX D	Background Technology Summary

tion provides antitrust protection, and is an action that should be pursued by all U.S.-based collaborative R&D efforts.

Section I—Research Project, provides a description of the program and references either a proposal or a work scope, which would be attached as an appendix.

Section II—Participation and Administration, identifies the participants, the Steering Group which oversees the program, and the project manager. The voting process and the guidelines for other administrative processes the group will use are covered. The evolution and rationale for some of these procedures are discussed further in Chapters 15 and 18. The Section II excerpts in Exhibit 14.2 show the program manager as being from NCMS, which is recommended for complex collaborative programs as addressed in Chapter 15.

Section III—Cost and Funding, provides an estimated total cost of the research project and identifies where the funding is coming from. It also contains flowdown conditions that accompany any funding vehicle from the government.

Section IV—Reports and Publications, identifies any reporting requirements and addresses the process for news releases and other publications.

Section V—Term and Termination, identifies the duration of the project and the process participants can use to terminate their participation, or have their participation terminated by the rest of the group.

Section VI—Technology Rights, is the most important portion of the project agreement. It defines background technology as separate from the R&D performed under the project and research project technology as the R&D performed under the project. Exhibit 14.3 is a general description of Section VI from a generic NCMS project agreement, which has evolved through NCMS coordination with corporate lawyers from many companies.

Section VII—Participants' Responsibility and Release, states that each participant shall be solely responsible for its own activities and those of its employees, agents, and assignees under the research project and shall have no liability or responsibility for the actions or inaction of another participant or that participant's employees, agents, and assigns.

Section VIII—Additional Party Participation, identifies the process to add other participants to the project.

EXHIBIT 14.2 Excerpts from Section II of NCMS Generic Project Agreement

---

Section II—Participation and Administration

The Participants hereby agree to carry out the Research Project as herein set forth. Participants shall perform, directly and through the use of subcontracts, research and development work under the Research Project. NCMS shall manage and administer the Research Project on behalf of the Participants in accordance with all applicable legal and regulatory requirements. Each Participant shall appoint one representative to serve on the Project Steering Group, and shall advise the Project Manager in writing of the name of its representative. The Participants may appoint a new or alternative representative to serve on the Project Steering Group by providing due notice to the NCMS Project Manager, with copy to all Participants. The Project Steering Group shall be responsible for providing general direction to the Research Project. The Project Steering Group shall also hear disputes between and among Participants. Finally, the Project Steering Group will be responsible for directing the formal close-out of the Research Project and subsequently documenting in meeting minutes or otherwise in writing that all technical, administrative, financial, and other salient considerations relevant to this project have been timely and appropriately concluded. . . .

Except for those circumstances requiring unanimous consent as specified herein, the Project Steering Group shall be governed by majority vote of the voting Participants. The USERS and NON-PROFIT Participants shall each have one vote; each PRODUCTION SUPPLIER shall be represented in voting by its respective USER with no additional vote being allowed; the TECHNOLOGY PROVIDERS shall collectively have only one vote which shall represent the consensus of the TECHNOLOGY PROVIDERS at large (the NCMS vote shall be a tie breaker vote if required). The Project Steering Group shall meet as often as necessary to discuss and review the status of the Research Project, but no less frequently than quarterly.

NCMS's representative to the Project Steering Group shall serve as Project Manager for the Research Project. The Project Manager shall ensure that the research work progresses timely and efficiently and conforms to the general spirit and intent of this Agreement. The Project Manager shall also be responsible for all aspects regarding the administration of the Research Project. In this capacity, the Project Manager shall be primarily responsible, on behalf of all the Participants and on an ongoing basis throughout the term of the Agreement, to monitor and assure completion of Participant obligations regarding project matters including but not limited to technical performance, project reporting, adherence to project budget (including expenditures, contributions and documentation of actual matching/in-kind) and Background Technology review and invention disclosure reporting. . . .

In the event the Project Steering Group elects to award research contracts, NCMS, or other qualified Participants as directed by the Project Steering Group, shall award contracts to the contractors selected on the basis of competition or sound sole source justification criteria. The contracts shall include all required flowdown and Section VI provisions from this agreement and from (any funding agency contract). . . .

EXHIBIT 14.3 Excerpts from Section VI of NCMS Generic Project Agreement

Section VI—Technology Rights

VI.A. Section VI.A of the project agreement provides definitions of Project Agreement terms and conditions. "Technology" is defined to be the entire body of technical knowledge related to the research project, and includes "Background Technology" (i.e., Technology in existence prior to the effective date of the project and Technology developed during the term of the agreement but separate and apart from the project), and "Research Project Technology" (i.e., Technology developed under the project). "Intellectual Property" is defined to be protectable Technology such as patents and registered copyrights, whereas "Technical Information" is a defined much more broadly to consist of various forms of data. The term "Necessary Background Technology" is also defined to be Background Technology which is necessary for and essential to the implementation of Research Project Technology.

VI.B. Participants' Background Technology

Section VI. B describes how Background Technology may be contributed to the project. Essentially, each participant retains the discretion over the Background Technology it will contribute to the project and the conditions under which it will contribute such Background Technology. All such contributed Background Technology is identified on an appendix to the Project Agreement—Appendix D. This section also describes how receiving participants will administer the Background Technology contributed by other participants during the term of the project and thereafter. While project participants are not obligated to license Necessary Background Technology to other participants, project participants are required to make a good faith effort to identify the existence of any Necessary Background Technology they may possess.

VI.C. Research Project Technology

Section VI.C details provisions for ownership and licensing of Research Project Technology. Generally, the developing participant owns such Research Project Technology and licenses it to the other project participants on a nonexclusive, royalty-free basis. Licenses include the right to make, have made, use and sell articles and processes under any inventions or patents developed under the research project as well as the right to copy, distribute and make derivative works and to use any mask works. Companies are free to sublicense wholly-owned and majority-owned and controlled subsidiaries throughout the world. This section also sets forth the requirements for disclosure of inventions to the project participants and funding sources and mechanics governing the prosecution of patent applications and the payment of patent prosecution and maintenance fees.

VI.D. Section VI.D identifies how the participants intend to handle patent and copyright enforcement issues and deal with potential infringers.

Section IX—Notices, identifies the points of contact for the project who would be the recipients of any formal written communications.

Section X—Additional Provisions, identifies any additional considerations to be included in the agreement, such as power of attorney, or order of precedence relative to other related agreements.

Section XI—Governing Law, identifies the state whose laws govern the agreement.

Section XII—Entire Agreement, identifies any other documents that constitute the total agreement, and identifies that the agreement can not be modified or rights assigned except by written consent of all the parties.

Section XIII—Agreement Execution, contains the signatures of all the parties participating in the agreement.

Appendix A—Funding Summary, summarizes the projected funding to be provided.

Appendix B—Project Funding Summary, summarizes the total resources determined necessary to complete the program identifying the expected obligations of the participants.

Appendix C—Sample Format of an Invoice, provides and example of how funds would be invoiced in the program.

Appendix D—Background Technology Summary, identifies the background technology each participant expects to provide in the program and the conditions under which the background technology will be provided.

Funding Vehicle Agreements

Most of the firsthand experience the authors have with external funding for collaborative development programs is with matching funds coming from government agencies, or industry-sponsored programs with universities. Collaborative development programs also take place when the participating companies agree to collaborate on a particular project and to provide the needed funding to cover the common overhead costs.

These funds have historically been paid to contract a third-party service agency, which might be a consortium-type organization, or a law or accounting firm. The third party would administer and manage the program, as well as be the contractor for any subcontracting the program might need.

In the event that a collaborative R&D program is being self-funded, the participation of smaller technology supplier companies usually requires some form of payment for any significant work that they would perform. Recently, the member companies of the National Center for Manufacturing Sciences (NCMS), which have realized and appreciated significant benefits from past collaborative R&D projects with government funding, have turned to the Technologies Research Corporation (TRC), an NCMS subsidiary, in order to collaborate when a government presence is unavailable or not needed. As mentioned in Chapter 11, government assistance may lack timeliness, flexibility, and certainty, while adding risk and overhead. The TRC is experiencing significant growth, as it efficiently adds value to industry-led and -sponsored projects by providing many of the services needed to support collaboration. The TRC contracts professional services to a group of client companies to manage collaborative R&D projects. These services include:

1. Project formation, development, and management:
   • Identifying opportunities.
   • Managing projects.
   • Evaluating and justifying projects.
   • Monitoring projects.
   • Identifying funding sources for projects.
   • Reporting project status.
2. Legal, administration, contracting, purchasing, and subcontract management.
3. Financial, accounting, and supplementary fund raising.
4. Government relations.

Government financial assistance awards can take one of three forms: contracts, grants, or cooperative agreements.

Contracts generally require specific deliverables and have a payment schedule for meeting particular milestones. Contract research is generally performed by companies that have overhead structures in place to deal with the government, as contracts are governed by the rules in the Federal Acquisition Regulations (FAR). Commercial companies generally can not afford to have the overhead structures required by the FAR and be competitive in the commercial marketplace. If a commercial company, such as Boeing or United Technologies Corporation, does do business with the government, it does so from a business unit separated from the commercial business units. As government research contracting does not readily lend itself to commercial business, government research contracts are not the most viable vehicles for collaborative R&D. Government contracts are also a generally unlikely vehicle for getting a major end user involved in collaborative R&D. The government, except in a wartime economy, generally does not represent a significant enough market for the finished technology to enable cost-effective commercialization.

Government grants are often used for funding research. With grants, the government provides funds with no deliverables required to be provided back to the government. The National Science Foundation and National Institutes of Health use grants as their primary funding vehicles. Most grants go to academic institutions. The Small Business Independent Research (SBIR) program provides grants to small businesses to conduct research. The record of SBIR programs getting R&D commercialized, however, leaves a lot to be desired. The authors are not aware of any SBIR Phase III efforts, which are the commercialization stage in the SBIR program. Grants have a similar tendency as government contracts to get companies dependent on an artificial government market for their existence. The effort needed to get follow-on and variant SBIR funds is less than that needed to get the significant funding usually required to commercialize technology. As such, the incentives end up with government grants becoming the business base for a company.

The cultural differences between the government and commercial sectors of the U.S. economy are significant, with too few people recognizing that we have two insulated business cultures. A number of individuals in the government continue to believe that the government's role is to develop technology, and that industry should come to the government to get the technology it needs.

Cooperative agreements are the preferred government contractual vehicle for government cofunding of collaborative R&D. Cooperative agreements enable industry to direct the program, and provide the flexibility to change program scope and evolve with new technology development. The leverage of government funds through getting industry to provide a majority share of the effort is significant for the taxpayer. R&D funds used in this manner are more likely to get commercialized, as that is industry's objective for R&D.

All of the NIST ATP awards are provided as cooperative agreements. The applicable federal regulation that governs NIST cooperative agreements with for-profit organizations is Office of Management and Budget (OMB) Circular A-110, "Uniform Administrative Requirements for Grants and Agreements with Institutes of Higher Education, Hospitals and Other Non-Profit Organizations." The fact that a standard for nonprofits is being applied to for-profits, and that this is done because it is preferable to using the FAR, indicates the divergence between government and commercial business practices. (There is no OMB Circular for working with for-profit commercial companies.)

In the Department of Defense, "Other Agreements Authority" has been expanded for use across the department to enable contractors to significantly improve the ability for the private sector to deal with the Department of Defense. "Other Agreements" were piloted in the Defense Advanced Research Projects Agency (DARPA) in the early 1990s, and have been effective in getting industry to cost share development efforts.

While cooperative agreements are the optimal contractual vehicle for government cofunding of collaborative R&D for improving the Technology Development Process, the ensuing auditing requirements can still be a substantial burden on a commercial company. The auditing requirements can generate significant collaborative overhead, and have driven some companies away from accepting government funds for their participation in collaborative development programs. These concerns are further addressed in Chapter 18.

For companies that serve the commercial market, a third-party organization, such as the National Center for Manufacturing Science (NCMS) or Consortium for Advanced Manufacturing—International

(CAM-I), or a company that is a defense or government contractor, is best used to provide the interface with the government.

Cooperative Research and Development Agreements (CRADAs)

CRADAs are the means used for collaborative development programs to involve personnel from government laboratories in the program. CRADAs basically are government mechanisms to pay lab personnel to work with industry on a program. CRADAs stipulate that the labs can not be held accountable for conducting R&D needed by industry, and as such the R&D performed by the government labs involved in collaborative development programs is not on any company's critical technology path. Another unfortunate reality is that the time it has historically taken to establish a CRADA makes the traditional multimonth government contracting process look fast.

The benefit is that the quality of the R&D personnel in the labs often more than compensates for the often clumsy CRADA process. The value that the world-class talent in the government labs brings to a collaborative development program can significantly impact a program.

Again, having NCMS or CAM-I as an interface to establish CRADAs with government labs can be a cost-effective means to reduce the collaborative overhead involved in working with government labs.

Subcontracts

Another type of contractual agreement often needed in collaborative development programs is the ability for the collaborative team to contract third parties. Often a common service, such as Picturetel being used in RRM for video-teleconferences, is desired. It makes more sense to be able to have the consortium subcontract than have one of the members contract the service and attempt to coordinate compensation from the rest of the group. A third-party organization such as an NCMS or CAM-I can readily provide this service.

PART V

Making Collaboration Work

The most important aspect of being able to put a collaborative development program together is having a high degree of confidence that the program will achieve its goals. Confidence results from the credibility of the individuals and organization involved in putting the program together, and their past ability to make collaborative development programs work. Once a program is successful and has met or exceeded objectives, then it is easier to establish other collaborative development programs, as there is a basis for having confidence that the program will work.

While it's not easy to put together a collaborative development program, it can be harder to make the program work. The Rapid Response Manufacturing (RRM) program took nearly two years after the first meeting in July 1991 to coalesce into a productive organization which generated results for the participants. Some of the keys to making a collaborative development program work are:

- Good management.
- Effective means of selecting projects.
- Effective means for implementing projects.
- Effective administration.

Collaborative Program Management

The management of a collaborative development program can be difficult, as no one person or organization controls all of the resources being committed to the program. A collaborative program management model that has proven effective in practice is the model used for the Printed Wiring Board (PWB) and Rapid Response Manufacturing (RRM) programs. PDES, Inc. (Appendix F) has a roughly parallel program management process that was independently evolved. These models center around a Steering Group (called a board of directors in the PDES, Inc., model) made up of all the members of the consortium. The Steering Group empowers a program manager, who coordinates the activities of technical teams established by the Steering Group and made up of personnel from the participating companies.

Project Selection and Approval

There are different means for determining the specific technology research and development tasks and projects to be pursued in a collaborative development program. Some programs are loosely coupled with broad objectives that could be addressed through a number of different approaches. Other programs are tightly coupled with more specific objectives and defined approaches. An effective means for selecting projects has proven to be through focused workshops. Ultimately, in both cases, the projects or tasks selected should be driven by an OEM need.

Project Implementation

Conducting collaboration on the project level maximizes the benefits of collaboration. Getting people to collaborate can be accomplished through workshops, effective communication, learning, teaching, being proactive, and identifying opportunities.

Program Administration

The execution and management of any program requires some degree of reporting to keep the organization legally and financially accountable. Programs receiving government funds require specified reporting requirements and audits. Companies have to demonstrate to themselves that the internal commitments they are making are worthwhile. Administrative actions should be minimized to the extent that they meet the requirements of all the participants, including the government. Administrative work beyond the minimum takes valuable time and effort away from pursuing the technical objectives in a program.

Experiences from the recently completed Rapid Response Manufacturing (RRM) program are used as the source of most of the examples in this section (Part V). The management of the RRM program was particularly effective as the participants contributed approximately $15 million in additional resources to the program over their original commitments (for which no government reimbursement was available).

CHAPTER 15

Collaborative Program Management

While establishing the Printed Wiring Board program in 1990, there were no known processes in place on how to establish a collaborative development program. The program champion from AT&T, Ted Polakowski, had been involved with several past collaborative development efforts and consortia. He relayed that most collaborative efforts fail to meet their potential, due to the managing group not controlling the resources provided to the program. His concern over this point was echoed by Kurt Watchler, the Texas Instruments program champion, and supported by the program champions from Digital Equipment Corporation (DEC) and Hamilton Standard Interconnect.

Mr. Polakowski pointed out that if the managing group doesn't have control of the resources the group will not be able to manage the program. These people recognized that each company in a collaborative development program is like a player on a basketball team. Each team member is in control of one's own capabilities, and determines when to run, shoot, or pass. Companies in collaboration need to be able to act in the same manner, controlling and using the companies' capabilities in the most efficient manner to meet the development objectives.

The structure shown in Figure 15.1 was established to manage the PWB program through the initial meetings and teleconferences among the group that came to be the PWB Steering Group—the individuals who championed the program in each of their companies and had control over the resources their companies were committing to the program. The group established processes for managing the program that ensured, as much as possible, that the program would meet its objectives. This structure was adopted and evolved in the Rapid Response Manufacturing (RRM) program. RRM was managed through an executive Steering Group using weekly teleconferences to coordinate the overall effort.

The Steering Group is the managing entity of the program. Personnel on the Steering Group have to be in a position to control the resources being committed to the program by their company. While each participant in the collaborative development program should have a representative on the Steering Group, the direction of the Steering Group needs to be controlled by the end users of the technology being

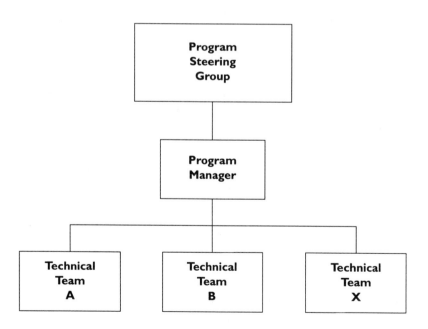

FIGURE 15.1 Collaborative Program Organizational Model

developed. The RRM consortium was managed through an executive Steering Group. This Steering Group consisted of six voting members. Each of the manufacturing companies (Ford, General Motors, Texas Instruments, and United Technologies) had one member as did the National Center for Manufacturing Sciences. The five technology supplier companies selected a single representative as the sixth member. The NCMS program manager was authorized the tiebreaker vote if required. Over the five-year program all votes were unanimous. The Steering Group used weekly teleconferences to manage the overall effort. The Steering Group empowered a program manager, who coordinated the activities of technical teams. The technical teams were established by the Steering Group to focus on particular R&D objectives. The technical teams are generally made up of personnel from the participating companies.

While the PWB program was blazing new ground in the process of getting U.S. companies to work together, it was limited in that the participating companies were all large companies. The RRM program proposal was written by the large companies participating in the program: Ford, General Motors, Texas Instruments, and United Technologies. The president of NCMS, Ed Miller, directed the inclusion of technology suppliers into the program before the proposal was submitted to NIST. This evolution strengthened the ability of the collaborative development team to ultimately commercialize technology by ensuring that technology commercialization paths were integrated into the program through the technology suppliers. These companies also have some of the best technical expertise available in their respective fields. To ensure that the size of the controlling group was effective, the executive Steering Group was established to manage the RRM program. The PWB Steering Group had five members, and the RRM executive Steering Group had six members. It should be noted that even though the PWB program did not have technology suppliers directly involved, it was largely successful in developing and deploying the technology needed to maintain a competitive capability to build PWBs in the United States.

The following sections describe the Steering Group, program manager, and technical teams, with the general operating procedures that have evolved from these National Center for Manufacturing Sciences (NCMS) programs.

Steering Group

According to SEMATECH's chairman and CEO, Bill Spencer: "The operation of effective consortia requires, above all, agreement on achievable common goals based on a sense of shared interests. It also requires skilled management and strong long-term commitment on the part of participants to make available adequate resources in terms of high-quality personnel and financial support. Senior management of participants must be regularly involved in the strategy of the consortium, with meetings and transparent communication with all levels of member companies."[1] As evidenced in this quote, it is critical to the success of a program to have the right people involved, people who are responsible for implementation of the technology being developed within their company. Steering Group personnel can be generally characterized as strong, proactive individuals interested in getting things done to improve their company.

The project Steering Group is responsible for:

- Providing general direction to the research project.
- Considering additional project participants.
- Hearing disputes between and among participants.
- Selecting a program manager.

If the Steering Group does not select the program manager, it should at the very least have some influence over who will fill that position. Many times a program manager is an employee of a third party such as NCMS. In this case the final decision on employing an individual as a program manager is that of the employing organization.

The voting procedures for the group need to be agreed on by the group. While voting procedures need to be identified, the group should strive to obtain unanimous decisions.

Generic operating procedures for a Steering Group are shown in Exhibit 15.1. These procedures can be modified as appropriate to meet the circumstances of specific programs.

---

[1]William J. Spencer, SEMATECH.

EXHIBIT 15.1 Generic Steering Group Operating Procedures

The Steering Group is responsible for the review and approval of the technical program, and resource budgets required to accomplish the program technical plan as established contractually with any government agency providing funds. The Steering Group will review and approve all program operating procedures, as well as any revisions to the approved technical plan, resource budget, and/or operating procedures.

1. *Steering Group Structure.* Each of the participating organizations shall designate a representative on the Steering Group. This representative cannot also lead a technical team. Each participating organization shall also designate an alternate to vote in the absence of their representative. The designated alternate may also serve as a leader of a technical team. Alternates, as well as all technical team leaders, will be invited to all Steering Group meetings.

2. *Conduct of Meetings.* The program manager shall chair Steering Group meetings. Steering Group Members can submit suggestions for inclusion on the agenda prior to each meeting. While it is important to provide free communication in meetings, it will be the responsibility of the chairman to assure that the issued agenda is adhered to. As necessary Robert's Rules of Order will prevail to provide for orderly contact and progress in meetings. Decisions will be documented in the minutes of each meeting.

3. *Frequency of Meetings.* Meetings of the Steering Group will be held as required, but no less frequently than quarterly. Meetings will be called by the program manager, or requested by members through the program manager. Effort shall should be made to vary location of meetings on a round-robin basis.

4. *Task Plan Management.* The Steering Group will authorize master task and resource plans for technical teams to be managed by the program manager. Progress against authorized plans will be reviewed periodically as arranged by the Program Manager to provide for insight in to how overall technical components are being covered, how the resources available to the program are being used, and how each technical component is progressing toward achieving planned milestones. The Steering Group may commit and authorize additional, or dissolve technical teams from time to time as deemed necessary.

5. *Compliance.* Each member of the Steering Group is responsible for assurance of their respective company efforts, and reporting any changes to people within their company.

6. *Operating Procedures.* The Steering Group shall be responsible for the review and approval of all operating procedures and any amendments to them.

Program Manager

The job of managing a collaborative development program is to ensure that the program works effectively toward meeting its development objectives. Collaborative development program managers, when compared to traditional company program managers, are confronted with needing to produce better results, with less direct control over resources, even though there may be larger resource commitments available. Still, it is the job of those managing a collaborative program to exceed the objectives that any one individual company could achieve. Otherwise, there is no rationale for collaborating.

As such, it is better to describe a collaborative development program manager's role as nurturing as opposed to controlling. "Controlling" a collaborative development program is a lot like raising a teenager. Teenagers can, and will, fend for themselves, but need support when times get hard. The program manager needs to be an effective leader, advocating an agenda and objectives common to all parties involved. The program manager needs to be able to win the confidence of every member of the Steering Group. The collaborative program manager needs to be trusted and respected by all the participants.

The program manager is responsible for:

- Making arrangements for and chairing all meetings of the program Steering Group.
- Recording minutes of program Steering Group meetings and distributing copies to all participants.
- Consolidating project performance information from all participants into a consolidated report on a quarterly basis.
- Distributing the consolidated technical reports to all participants on a quarterly basis.
- Serving as the principal representative of the consortium in all interactions with nonparticipants.
- Directing all necessary program administrative tasks, including program agreement modifications, consortium contracting and contract administration, collection of funds owed to the consortium, payment of funds owed by the consortium, and all recordkeeping related thereto in accordance with sound business practice.

Mr. William L. (Bill) Waddell of the National Center for Manufacturing Sciences was the program manager for the Rapid Response Manufacturing Program for the duration of the contracted program from 1992 to 1997. Mr. Waddell is highly regarded by all of the participants of the RRM program, and credited with making that program a successful example of collaboration. Mr. Waddell came to the program with a wealth of experience in managing advanced technology in both the aerospace and machine tool industries. Mr. Waddell's background of experience is worth reviewing, as it provided him with a valuable foundation for nurturing a large group of companies into a functioning team. In previous positions Mr. Waddell served as CEO of Lodge & Shipley, Inc., a small machine tool company (a technology supplier company), and as general manager of the Systems Division of the Acme-Cleveland Corporation. He held various manufacturing positions in the General Electric Aircraft Group (an end-user company), including managing the engine manufacturing programs for the F-4 Phantom fighter (J79) and the B-1 bomber (F101). His assignments included managing the Advanced Engine Manufacturing Operation and managing Group Manufacturing and Plant Engineering. In the latter role, Mr. Waddell organized the initial Factory Automation Group for the Aircraft Engine Group and served on the General Electric Corporate CAD/CAM Council. Mr. Waddell graduated from Michigan State University with a civil engineering degree.

While Mr. Waddell's experience made him an ideal candidate to be the RRM program manager, his relaxed leadership style enabled the RRM consortium to quickly identify common ground among the participants and establish and execute programs. Mr. Waddell understood the realities of the corporate environments of each of the RRM participants. These environments need to be recognized and understood by every collaborative program manager. This is difficult without having relevant experience. In some cases it is valuable to share these perspectives with the whole team, but in other cases it is not, as it could damage efforts in building relationships. Bill, as an exceptional program manager, had the experience and expertise to make these decisions in the best interest of the program. It is often valuable in a collaborative development program for the other participating organizations to understand and appreciate the internal relationships and sensitivities of the other participants in the program.

The PWB program manager, Ron Evans, was also a very successful program manager. He had a strong technical background in PWB manufacturing. He had a different style from Bill Waddell, but was also able to establish the relationships with the program participants needed to be successful in collaborative development. The dynamics of every group of people are different, and it is important that the program manager be able to work with the dynamics of the Steering Group. This is a major reason why the Steering Group should have some input into who will be the program manager.

Having the program manager come from a nonprofit third party, such as NCMS, is beneficial in managing a program, as the program manager is neutral relative to any company interests that might come up in the program.

Continuity of management is also very important. If at all possible, the program manager should remain in position for the duration of the program. Experience has shown that without continuity of effective program management, it is very difficult for any program to succeed, much less a program consisting of multiple companies and organizations.

Generic operating procedures for a program manager are shown in Exhibit 15.2. Again, these procedures can be modified as appropriate to meet the circumstances of specific programs.

EXHIBIT 15.2   Generic Operating Procedures for a Program Manager

---

The program manager is empowered by the Steering Group to manage the overall program. The program manager is responsible for both the technical and business success of the program including compliance with all contractual relationships. The program manager will present resource budgets and technical plans to the Steering Group for approval, and then be responsible to manage to the approved plans. The program manager will gain the approval of the Steering Group of any revision to plan. The program manager will be responsible for providing a high level of visibility of program activities to Steering Group members to enable them to fulfill their obligation to safeguard their company's investment in the program.

Specific responsibilities include:

- **Steering Group Meetings.** Members will be notified of the arrangements as far in advance as possible for each meeting, and provided a proposed agenda in advance of each meeting with a one week goal. The

(continued)

EXHIBIT 15.2 (*Continued*)

program manager will be responsible for assuring the physical arrangements for each meeting. The program manager will chair the Steering Group meetings, and will publish minutes of each meeting in a timely manner. This will be accomplished by providing a draft of the proposed minutes to each attendee. The attendees will promptly report any errors, or corrections. After reconciling suggested changes, the program manager will issue the approved minutes to key participants. Any government agency program manager responsible for government funding to the program will be invited, and encouraged to attend all Steering Group meetings.

- **Technical Management.** The program manager is responsible for management of the total technical effort. The program manager will monitor and/or attend at the program manager's discretion all technical activities to assure that the work is moving forward consistent with the schedule, content, and resources approved by the Steering Group. He will manage the teams to identify overlaps or gaps between the teams, and initiate corrective actions as necessary to achieve the program's goals.

- **Central Point of Communications for Program Coordination.** The program manager will develop and provide communication modes for participants in the program, including telephone, fax, and electronic mail. Periodic updated directories will be issued by the program manager, who will provide a library system to identify both date and content of key technical and contractual documents, and maintain a file of these documents to assure ease of availability to participants.

- **Total Program Interface to the Government Program Office.** The program manager will assure that formal and informal communication is maintained with the appropriate government program Office in accordance with the intent as well as contractual requirements of the program. This will be accomplished by using staffed resources available, program participants, as well as the program manager's own efforts. These responsibilities include the preparation of quarterly technical reports and annual oral reports.

- **Budgeting and Resource Control.** The program manager will assemble a budget for dollars, manpower, and other resources for presentation and approval by the Steering Group. The program manager will then manage the program to those approved budgets providing timely status reports to the Steering Group including identification of technical and financial risks. The program manager will be responsible for justifying to, and gaining approval of, the Steering Group of any budget revision.

EXHIBIT 15.2 (*Continued*)

- ***Publicity and Presentations.*** The program manager will prepare presentations for both internal and external use as required. In addition to making these presentations as needed, the program manager will provide materials to participants as requested. The program manager will be responsible for the protection of program proprietary information as well as information identified by participants as proprietary to their company.
- ***Third-Party Relationships.*** The program manager will be responsible for developing relationships and communications with third parties consistent with the overall objectives of the program. Third-party relationships generally fall into three categories; subcontractors, potential new program participants, and other technical programs/projects outside the program. The program manager will assure that any third party proposed as a subcontractor is identified as such in technical plans approved by the Steering Group. Third parties identified as potential new participants must be approved by the Steering Group with the recommendation of the program manager including a justification establishing that their participation will enhance program value for the current participants. The program manager is responsible for monitoring and interfacing with other research efforts that may have potential leverage for the program.
- ***Operating Procedures.*** The program manager will be responsible for maintaining the configuration of program operating procedures, and for collecting and proposing amendments as recommended by participants.

Technical Teams

The makeup of the technical teams in the Printed Wiring Board (PWB) program was essentially consistent over the five years of the program. Technical teams were established to pursue R&D efforts to improve PWB materials, to improve PWB imaging (conductive circuits are etched on a PWB in a process similar to that used in photography), to improve PWB solderability, and to improve PWB chemical processes. The PWB Chemistry Team was reconstituted in the second year of the program to consider the total PWB product. In the Rapid Response Manufacturing (RRM) program, there were a broad assortment of technical teams, none of which was in place for the entire duration of the program.

The principal difference between the RRM and PWB programs was that the PWB program focused on easily defined technology development needed to improve a product—a printed wiring board—whereas the RRM program focused on a less well-defined spectrum of technologies that could be used to improve a process—the design-manufacture process. In both cases, the technical teams were creations of the Steering Group. Generic operating procedures for technical teams are shown in Exhibit 15.3. An example of a five-block status report is shown in Exhibit 15.4, which is a report on the Analysis Advisor project in the RRM program. These reports were required every quarter for every RRM project for review by the RRM Steering Group.

EXHIBIT 15.3　Generic Operating Procedures for Technical Teams

The technical teams are empowered by the Steering Group to conduct specific portions of the work established by the program technical plan. Each technical team will develop a detailed work plan including identification of the resources required for presentation and approval by the Steering Group. The duration of a team will only be that required to accomplish the specific assigned task. It is envisioned that new teams will be empowered, and existing teams dissolved upon completion of assigned tasks, throughout the life of the program. Each technical team will work under the guidance of the program manager, and will provide quarterly written reports of its progress against work plans to the Steering Group. Direct presentations will be made to the Steering Group as scheduled by the program manager.

Specific responsibilities include:

1. *Identification of Need.* A sponsor (participating company, existing technical team, or the program manager) will identify the need for a task requiring the formation of a new technical team. The sponsor may request approval from the Steering Group to organize an application development meeting among members to validate the need, and develop common detailed requirements. The sponsor will provide the Steering Group with proposed general scope, estimate of needed resources, and expected deliverables.
2. *Recommendation to Proceed.* The sponsor will report the results of the application development meeting to the Steering Group with a recommendation as to whether to proceed. If a recommendation to pro-

EXHIBIT 15.3 *(Continued)*

ceed is approved by the Steering Group, the sponsor, working with the program manager, will organize a technical team.

3. *Technical Team Structure.* A leader will be selected and the team staffed with members from more than one participating company. The team shall be responsible for issuing minutes of its meetings on a timely basis.

4. *Work Plans.* Each technical team will develop a work plan identifying specific tasks required to achieve their technical goals. A work breakdown structure shall be developed. The tasks shall identify necessary activities and deliverables as well as the time schedule with milestones to accomplish the assigned work along with all required resources. Identification of resources should identify the man-hours and dollar contribution required by a specific company. The work plan will show dependency and time phase relationship with tasks assigned to other technical teams. Inputs required from other technical teams will be reviewed with the providing team to assure there is a "contract" in place to provide the specified input. Planned outputs will be reviewed with other technical teams to validate the need for the output, and to assure that planned outputs satisfy their input requirements.

5. *Software Application Development.* The technical teams will establish functional requirements for new, or modifications to existing, software required to meet program goals. Technical teams will assure quality documentation of any software developed.

6. *Approval.* The technical team leader will present the proposed work plan to the Steering Group for approval. Identification of other activities, problems, risks, and recommendations will be incorporated in the presentation. Modifications, and any special conditions, included by the Steering Group in its approval will be incorporated as required and the plan documented and provided to the program manager for distribution. Upon approval of the work plan, it may be necessary to revise, or complement, team membership.

7. *Reporting.* Each technical team will provide a quarterly written report to the program manager for distribution to Steering Group members. A single-page five-block format will be used to include:
   - Block 1—A brief description of the scope and deliverables of the task.
   - Block 2—Key milestones with planned completion dates with current status expressed in percent complete, or actual completion date.
   - Block 3—Significant accomplishments to date.
   - Block 4—Objectives for next reporting period.
   - Block 5—Problems and/or issues.

EXHIBIT 15.4 Quarterly Five Block Status Report for RRM Analysis Advisor Project

---

RRM
Program Review—Analysis Advisor (7.BS)
July 1, 1997

Work Scope and Deliverables

Develop a software package that will assist the casual user of analysis tools to perform first-order engineering analysis. The user would be expected to have a general knowledge of stress and strain, force equations, loads, boundary conditions, geometry, meshing, and materials. The analysis advisor will provide on-line assistance for conducting structural analysis to expand the number of engineers able to use analysis tools. This should enable analysis to be used more frequently early in the design cycle as a predictive engineering tool. Deliverables include:

- An interactive, pull-down form which shows the steps used in performing analysis.
- User query buttons corresponding to each analysis step.
- Indication of which steps have been performed, and what the next step is.
- Logic trees to query the user about the problem details and the analysis needs.
- An open logic tree software architecture to facilitate additions or changes.
- Graphics presentations showing relevant examples, possible user choices, and analysis step instructions.
- Simplification of some analysis tasks through a few built-in automation functions.

Significant Accomplishments

- Projected completed.
- Demo at MSC-Southfield.
- Proposal developed for Phase 2.

Objectives for Next 90 Days

- Finalize plan for Phase 2.

Significant Problems and/or Issues

None at this time.

Key Milestones

Event	Scheduled Date	Actual Date	% Complete
• Project start	11/01/95	12/04/95	100
• Project specification completed	12/15/95		100
• Basic advisor beta at user sites (beta)	05/01/96		100
• Additional advisor development requirements scoped	06/01/96		100
• Delivery of additional development	TBD		

Management Processes

The responsibilities and roles highlighted in the generic operating procedures shown in Exhibits 15.1 through 15.3 for the program steering group, program manager, and technical teams are summarized in Table 15.1. These collaborative management process steps are the processes that evolved through the RRM program managed by the National Center for Manufacturing Sciences (NCMS).

The main characteristic of good management in a collaborative R&D program is frequent and meaningful communication. Meaningful communications are those that convey information of value to the recipient, such as background information everyone needs to know or information on project and program status. Information is meaningful if it influences actions. Communications that do not provide meaningful data should be avoided, as they take time and establish a precedence leading to future communications being ignored.

Communications in managing a program take place through:

- Meetings
- Use of telephone
- Use of the Internet

Communications will be with the full R&D program team, some section of the program participants, such as the Steering Group or a technical team, and one-on-one between individuals. The program manager should serve as the central focal point for all communications. The program manager should be coordinating the agendas for meetings of the Steering Group and for teleconference calls. Technical team leaders will serve their technical teams in the same manner. Documentation of meetings and teleconferences should follow the day after the meeting or teleconference. The speed at which information is disseminated in a program will dictate the speed of its ability to accomplish tasks.

The organization facilitating the collaboration, whether it be a nonprofit organization or one of the participating companies, should make every effort to minimize and facilitate the overhead work (accounting, audits, rules, regulations, any task that takes away from managing or conducting R&D) for the participating parties. The managing organization

TABLE 15.1 Collaborative Management Process Steps

Process Steps	Program Manager	Steering Committee	Sponsor	Application Development Team	Technical Team	Other Technical Teams
			Participants			
Steering Committee						
1. Schedule Steering Group meetings	■■					
2. Propose agenda and logistics for meeting	■■					
3. Approve, with appropriate modifications, agenda and logistics for meeting	●	● ■				
4. Chair meeting	■■					
5. Support meeting along with alternates	■	● ■				
6. Draft minutes and open issues list, and distribute for review	●	●				
7. Approve, with appropriate modifications, meeting minutes and open issues list	●	■				
8. Distribute minutes and open issues list	■					
Technical Team						
1. Technical team process	● ■■	● ■■ ◆	● ■	■	● ■■	●
2. Technical team project management	● ■■	● ■■			● ■■	
Quarterly Resource Updates						
1. Provide projected five-year resource utilization (by company) updates to the program manager every quarter	●	■				
2. Prepare overall five-year resource utilization plan	■■					
3. Review budgets with the Steering Committee on a quarterly basis	■■	●				
Budget/Plan Changes						
1. Review all significant budget and/or plan changes with the Steering Committee to gain approval	■	■				
2. Approve, modify, or deny budget and/or plan changes presented by the program manager	●	■				
Quarterly Updates						
1. Distribute quarterly updates to the "Detailed Work Plan" document	■				●	

● Interaction
■ Main responsibility
◆ Decision

220

Configuration Management
1. Manage file of documentation, key technical and contractual document with availability to participants
2. Manage configuration management of the filed documentation
3. Maintain configuration of program operating procedures

Government Agency Interface
1. Provide general interface to government agency
2. Prepare quarterly technical reports
3. Coordinate annual oral reports
4. Present annual oral reports to NIST

Project Process
1. Identify need
2. Develop proposed general scope, estimated resources, and expected deliverables
3. Request approval for application development meeting
4. Review and modify scope, resources, and deliverables as required
5. Approve application development meeting?
6. Identify participants for meeting
7. Validate need and common detailed requirements
8. Request approval to proceed
9. Approve request to initiate technical team?
10. Identify team leader
11. Identify team members
12. Develop work plan and work breakdown structure
13. Identify resources required (manpower and dollars)
14. Establish inputs required from other technical teams
15. Establish outputs required by other technical teams
16. Establish functional requirements
17. Present workplan to steering committee
18. Review and modify workplan, etc., as required

● Interaction
■ Main responsibility
◆ Decision

TABLE 15.1 (Continued)

Process Steps	Program Manager	Steering Committee	Sponsor	Application Development Team	Technical Team	Other Technical Teams
19. Approve workplan	●	◆				
20. Distribute results	■					
21. Evaluate team membership	●	●	●		■	
22. Execute workplan and produce deliverables	■				■	●
23. Recommend disbanding technical team at appropriate time	■●	■	■●		■	●
24. Approve disbanding of technical team	●		●		●	
Monthly Reports						
1. Prepare monthly report using single-page five-block format	■	●●				
2. Distribute monthly technical team reports	●					
Presentations						
1. Schedule direct presentations to Steering Commiteee as appropriate	■	●			■	
2. Present to Steering Committee as scheduled by program manager	●					
Meeting Minutes						
1. Publish minutes of all technical team meetings	■				■	
System Engineering and Design Reviews						
1. Schedule regular system engineering and design reviews at selected milestones throughout the program	■	●				
2. Select technical reviewers	●■	●				
3. Approve technical reviewers	■	●■●				
4. Determine format for review	■●					
5. Chair system engineering and technical design review	●					
6. Support system engineering and technical design review					■	

● Interaction
■ Main responsibility
◆ Decision

222

needs to recognize the importance of minimizing overhead work; otherwise the facilitating organization can end up generating more collaborative overhead for the participating parties. Good program management recognizes the need to minimize overhead work for the participants.

MEETINGS

Meetings should be held to inform, and more importantly, to formulate a course of action. The organization, or person, calling the meeting should ensure that all of the participants are able to communicate at the same level of understanding. Most of us have been to meetings where people speak but do not communicate, or debate is generated from which nothing results. There are many subcultures within our society that become so wrapped up in their own jargon that they can not effectively communicate with anyone outside their own subculture. This is evident in academia, in the government, and in corporations.

The location of meetings is also important. It's valuable to have the meetings hosted by the different members of the consortium, and couple the meetings with tours of the host's facilities. This is valuable in establishing a better understanding of the host's business for all the participants. There is also a social side to meetings, which is valuable in getting to know and understand people. It's easier to learn another person's perspectives, incentives, and problems through a discussion in a social environment rather than at a formal meeting. People are generally more open to speaking if they view you as someone who will take action that could be of benefit to their interests. These are team-building techniques that a good program manager will use.

Meetings are most valuable for people to get to know one another. Other means of communications, such as the Internet or computer-assisted collaboration tools, are much more effective after people have met and have established respect for and understanding of their partners' perspectives (see Appendix D). Meetings should take place for a program Steering Group at least once a quarter, and more frequently if there are important decisions to be made. More meetings are likely to take place early in a program.

In the RRM program, the Steering Group conducted quarterly meetings to review the status of the program. These reviews featured selected in-depth presentations by the project working teams. These quarterly reviews were rotated between different locations, generally at participants' facilities to acquaint the members with the business environment of each participant.

TELECONFERENCES

In both the Printed Wiring Board (PWB) and Rapid Response Manufacturing (RRM) programs the Steering Groups elected to have weekly teleconferences. These teleconferences were the principal communications vehicles for managing those programs. Many of the technical teams for each of these programs also elected to conduct weekly or biweekly teleconferences.

INTERNET USE

E-mail was extensively used throughout the duration of the RRM program, particularly for distributing meeting and teleconference minutes. Fax was used as a backup for e-mail to ensure receipt of minutes, as e-mail was not always reliable due to software incompatibilities and servers not always being on-line. To ensure that important communications are received, a telephone call is appropriate. A voice mail informing the recipient of an important e-mail is a good backup if direct voice communication isn't possible.

Use of Internet collaboration tools has proven to be particularly valuable. The RRM Analysis Advisor Project was developed using the World Wide Web as discussed in Chapter 17. The Agile Infrastructure for Manufactured Systems (AIMS) program piloted Internet collaboration tools developed under the program. The AIMS Simple Low-Cost Innovative Engine (SLICE) 2 (Appendix D) pilot project demonstrated the capability to design and manufacture a rocket engine with a team which was geographically distributed around the country. The use of the Web enabled the normal six-year design time to be reduced to 10 months, and resulted in a significantly improved product. The lessons learned in the AIMS program in using the Internet for collaborative design are detailed in Appendix D.

Issues Resolution/ Avoidance

All the participants involved in a collaborative development effort need to benefit from the effort. While this might appear to be an easily obtained "statement of the obvious," benefits to one participant are not necessarily benefits to another participant. The people managing a collaborative development program need to recognize that different participants view benefits from different perspectives. Optimally, each participant will recognize how all the others view the benefits they expect from collaboration. In some cases what may be a benefit to one organization could, in actuality or perception, be a detriment to another organization involved in the program. These situations need to be avoided.

Communications, understanding, and trust are fundamental to the ability to avoid unnecessary conflict and addressing any issues that will come up over the course of a program. The ability to constructively address issues assists in making a successful program. This responsibility lies primarily with the program manager. A good program manager will avoid issues that might lead to conflict in collaboration. This is possible because there is usually such a broad area that parties are willing to collaborate on that there is no reason to focus on those areas where companies do not agree. Conflict can easily undermine collaboration. Generally, once information defining the participants' underlying positions is shared among all parties, perspectives change and common positions are adopted.

On issues that do arise, the program manager should address the issues privately with the affected parties. For issues that involve the whole collaborative team, efforts should be made to generate unanimous decisions from the Steering Group. Again, the program manager's role is more of a facilitator than someone who controls or dictates program direction. A good approach to addressing issues that might come up in a collaborative R&D program is to follow a sound engineering method in addressing them. The practice is generally accepted by people who conduct R&D, and involves:

- Defining the problem or issue.
- Identifying the resources needed to address the problem.
- Identifying options that can be followed to address the problem.
- Evaluating the pros and cons to the different options.
- Solving the problem.

Whenever possible, issues should be reduced to a physical reality, which provides a common base for defining and resolving issues.

CHAPTER 16

Project Selection and Approval

The selection of projects will determine the success of a collaborative R&D program. (A project, in this context, is a particular R&D task being pursued by a technical team or participating company.) The management of a program needs to be able to identify the most important projects that can be effectively accomplished with the resources available.

It is important that specific R&D projects are selected based on the needs of the end users in the program. Each project selected should have at least one end-user champion, and ideally champions from a number of end users from different industries. End user direction will ensure that tasks are ultimately customer- (or market-) driven. Projects that are selected in the program need to provide benefit to the participants. Participants need to be selfish in selecting projects. Projects should conclude with pilot demonstrations of the development at the end user's site.

Project Approval

Approval of projects generally requires Steering Group approval, as they are the providers of the resources needed to conduct the projects. Steering Group approval should be unanimous if at all possible. Exhibit 16.1 shows the project authorization form used in the Rapid Response Manufacturing (RRM) program to get authorization from the Steering Group to proceed with a project. The authorization form was intentionally limited to fit on two sides of one sheet of paper. This particular project authorization form was used for the first phase of the Analysis Advisor project. Details on the implementation of this project are used as an example in Chapter 17.

Pilot Demonstrations

Projects should result, if possible, in pilot demonstrations of the technology developed in the end user's manufacturing process. The benefit of piloting technology development in this manner is that the value, or lack of value, of incorporating the technology into the process is quickly made apparent. The ease, or difficulty, in integrating the technology into the process also quickly becomes apparent. A significant amount of learning takes place for all involved in piloting technology development in production processes. This includes management and workers in the production facility as well as those conducting the R&D.

The difficulty in conducting technology development pilots in production environments is that they add risk to the ability to meet production schedules and targets. This added risk is not insignificant, as the jobs of most production managers are to reduce the risks involved in meeting their objectives. External funding can sometimes be used to mitigate this risk.

EXHIBIT 16.1   Project Authorization Used for the RRM Analysis Advisor Project

---

RRM Project Authorization

Title: Analysis Advisor
Sponsors: Delphi Saginaw, Pratt & Whitney, Kodak, MSC
Key Contacts: Joe Streng, Delphi Saginaw; Rich Wells, Delphi Chassis;
                Andy Jay, P&W; Ron Auble, Kodak; Gene Allen, MSC

Objective

Develop a software package which will assist the casual user of analysis tools to perform first-order engineering analysis. The user would be expected to have a general knowledge of stress and strain, force equations, loads, boundary conditions, geometry, meshing, and materials.

Benefits

The Analysis Advisor will provide on-line assistance for conducting structural analysis to expand the number of engineers able to use analysis tools. This should enable analysis to be used more frequently early in the design cycle as a predictive engineering tool.

Approach

The advisor would provide a series of questions for the user to review which effectively walks them through the analysis. The advisor would:

1. Describe how to create an analytic model suitable for meshing from the Unigraphics (UG) model.
2. Assist the user in defining element type (rods and beams, plates and shells, solid elements).
3. Provide recommendations on how to conduct feature suppression.
4. Query the user on the type of loads and boundary conditions expected and the material characteristics such that the type of analysis can be determined.
5. Query the user as to which quantities (loads, application position, dimensions, materials) may vary from run to run in a design study to assist in organizing data.
6. Guide the user in validating mesh quality of the Finite Element Model, and material property assignments.
7. Suggest, based on the class of the model and the materials, postprocessing results displays that would be most effective.

Initial development of the Analysis Advisor will be focused on assisting a user of PATRAN in conducting structural analyses using NASTRAN for linear and ABAQUS or MARC for nonlinear analysis from imported UG models.

Deliverables

A beta working model of the basic Analysis Advisor. Some aspects of the basic Analysis Advisor would include:

(continued)

EXHIBIT 16.1 *(Continued)*

- An interactive, pull-down form which shows the steps used in performing an analysis.
- User query buttons corresponding to each analysis step.
- Indication of which steps have been performed, and what the next analysis step is.
- Logic trees to query the user about the problem details and the analysis needs.
- An open logic tree software architecture to facilitate additions or changes.
- Graphics presentations showing relevant model examples, possible user choices, and analysis step instructions.
- Simplification of some analysis tasks through a few built-in automation functions.

The basic advisor form or subforms will have provisions for action buttons that can launch future developed automation tools as they are identified and implemented according to the user community recommendations. Possible automation tools include:

- A geometry meshability checking tool.
- Automated PATRAN small feature removal of UG features.
- A run-time estimator.

Depending on the automation capabilities the participating users desire, the development and integration of automation tools into the basic analysis advisor may take an additional effort.

Milestones

Project start	11/01/95
Project specification completed	12/15/95
Basic Analysis advisor beta at user sites (beta)	05/01/96
Additional advisor development requirements scoped	06/01/96
Delivery of additional development	TBD

Risks: Risk low to moderate with ability to terminate effort after beta provided.

Metrics: Measure usage of analysis tools at user sites.

Resources:

Approvals:

Ford _____   United Technologies _____

General Motors _____   Suppliers _____

Texas Instruments _____   NCMS _____

Project Selection

Two means of project selection for a collaborative R&D program that work are:

1. Adopting a project that one of the participants has on its internal R&D path that it is willing to conduct in a collaborative manner.
2. Conducting workshops around a particular technology to identify projects.

Participating Company Internal Projects

Projects that originate from a participating company's internal R&D plan need to provide benefit for all of the other participants. A good example of this kind of project was the piloting of many of Ford's internal Direct Engineering^{SM} program projects through the RRM program. The results of these projects were then shared with the rest of the partners. The RRM partners were able to benefit from lessons learned from Ford in what worked and what did not work in capturing and reapplying knowledge. The Direct Engineering^{SM} pilots provided a valuable insight for all of the participants on Ford's development direction. Ford's interest in sharing these pilots is part of its efforts to change the corporate business culture such that technologies can be used to their full potential. Ford recognizes that these changes need to be embraced by more companies than just Ford if they are to be effective.

Projects that follow a technology supplier's internal R&D plan also have to benefit the other participants. Several projects were turned down in RRM due to being too product-specific in their development and not providing sufficient benefit to the rest of the participants. Collaborative projects that follow a technology supplier's R&D plan generally require the support of at least one end user, optimally more. An RRM project that reflected the internal R&D plan of a technology supplier was the development of an easy-to-use interface for the ICAD knowledge-based engineering software provided to the program by Concentra (now Knowledge Technology International). The ICAD tool came to be used by all of the participants in RRM, and a common need was to improve the ease of use of the software. Concentra personnel working with the RRM end users were able to develop a tool that provided them the capabilities they desired, and ensured a market for the interface after Concentra commercialized it. (RRM enabled development of the interface to be piloted, with the requirements and results shared with all of the RRM participants. The cost to Concentra, or any software company, to commercialize software from a pilot demonstration is significant. Generally, an order of magnitude more effort is needed to develop software into a commercial product beyond the effort that was needed for developing a software demonstration pilot.)

Workshop Process

Focused technology workshops are an effective means to generate agreement on the technology development direction needed to meet a program's objectives. Optimally, the workshops result in R&D projects and the formation of technical teams to pursue those projects. Numerous technology workshops were held in the RRM program, including workshops on software architectures, knowledge-based engineering, manufacturing process planning, manufacturing process control, and integrated product and process modeling, among others. These workshops were effective in providing the technology development direction in RRM. Examples of how two of these workshops generated both direction and projects in the RRM program are further described for:

• The RRM Software Interoperability Workshop held February 8–9, 1995, at Ford.

- The RRM Design to Analysis Workshop held August 19–21, 1995, at Delphi Saginaw.

Software Interoperability Workshop

This workshop was held to establish the technical direction needed to promote software interoperability for other RRM projects, and to potentially recommend new projects to provide the needed interoperability for users to better design and manufacture their products. By the end of 1994, a number of different RRM projects were in place, developing and piloting software involved in the design-manufacture process. A software interoperability matrix had been developed showing how the relevant RRM projects related to CAD-CAD, CAD-CAE, CAD-KBE, and CAD-CAM[1] interoperability.

The principal technical finding that came out of this workshop was that the workshop did not address software interoperability with PDM systems. PDM is product data management, or the software to manage all of the computer files associated with a mechanical product. This type of software is considered to provide a service to all the personnel affiliated with design and manufacture of the product—the designers, engineers, analysts, factory workers, managers, and so forth. The interoperability of these services, generally provided in a PDM system, is needed as a foundation to support the software interoperability of CAD, CAM, CAE, and KBE. As such, the workshop spawned a new technical team, called the RRM Interoperability Services Working Group (ISWG), and the following series of workshops:

---

[1]CAD is computer-aided design, or the software used to let those drafting the design of a product use a computer to assist them. CAE is computer-aided engineering, or the sofware used to help engineers analyze a product design and check the stresses and strains the product will encounter as it is built, operated, and maintained. KBE is knowledge-based engineering, or the software used to help users engineer the design of a product by using the computer to capture the reasons behind why a product is shaped as it is and performs as it does. CAM is computer-aided manufacturing, or the software used to control the machines that manufacture the products.

- Interoperability Services Workshop, Dallas, Texas, May 2–4, 1995
- Product Data Management and Product Structure Workshop, Gatlinburg, Tennessee, June 20–22, 1995
- Conceptual to Physical Schema Mapping Workshop, Arden Hills, Minnesota, September 13–15, 1995
- Milestone Review and Planning Workshop, Detroit, Michigan, May 13–15, 1996
- Object Management Group (OMG) Response Decision Workshop, Plano, Texas, August 20–21, 1996
- OMG Response Planning Workshop, Arden Hills, Minnesota, October 14, 1996
- Material Data Services Workshop, Costa Mesa, California, January 29–31, 1997

The RRM Interoperability Services Working Group (ISWG) became the RRM organization evolving the RRM software architecture that had been established early in the program. A high-level view of this architecture is shown in Figure 16.1. The architecture was evolved through implementing pilot projects established by the ISWG. EXPRESS is a software language used to describe a product. It has been chosen to be an international standard due to its ability to reduce ambiguity, ensuring as well as possible that all applications using the product date interpret the data in the same way with the same meaning. The architecture defining how software objects interrelate is being standardized by the Object Management Group (OMG) as the Common Object Request Broker Architecture (CORBA). The Interface Definition Language (IDL) provides the mechanisms to integrate with Web interfaces and legacy software that have been wrapped with object-oriented translators.

Starting in May 1995, the ISWG conducted teleconferences on a weekly basis involving participants from Ford, General Motors, Texas Instruments, MacNeal-Schwendler Corporation, Lockheed Martin, the National Institute of Standards and Technology, and Rocketdyne, eventually expanding to include Metaphase, SDRC, Object Management Group (OMG) representatives, and others as appropriate.

At the first Interoperability Services Workshop, it was discovered that Boeing, Ford, and Texas Instruments all had independently se-

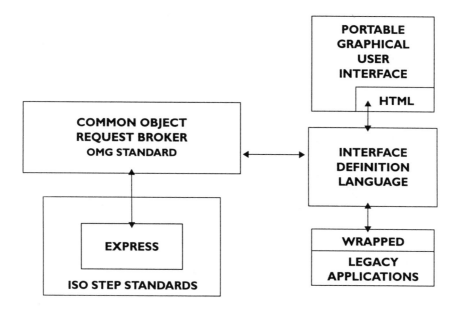

FIGURE 16.1 RRM Architecture for Interoperability

lected Metaphase as their corporate PDM system. A common concern with Metaphase was its lack of an object-oriented software interface. The lack of an object-oriented software interface was a generic problem with all commercial PDM systems available at the time. The other RRM end users also needed to have a generic, object-oriented interface to their PDM systems. As a result, the participants decided to establish a project to develop a generic object-oriented PDM interface and pilot its application with Metaphase. The RRM project spawned was named the Interoperable PDM Product Structure Services Provider. The results of this project coincided with a request from the OMG for proposals for developing an object-oriented interface to PDM systems that would become the standard. A separate RRM project was formed to integrate the results of the RRM-developed object-oriented PDM interface into a response to the OMG request. This project was named Federated PDM. In addition, the ISWG spawned RRM projects called Workflow/PDM Interoperability and Interoperable Materials Property Data Services Provider.

RRM completed and submitted its proposal to the OMG for PDM

interoperability under the Federated PDM project. The OMG received other submissions from Adra Systems, Digital Equipment Corporation, Fujitsu, IBM, the National Industrial Information Infrastructure Protocols (NIIIP) Consortium, and Sherpa. The OMG requested that RRM (Larry Johnson) coordinate the harmonization of all the PDM interoperability proposals submitted to the OMG. RRM chaired the Joint PDM Submission Team established to produce multivendor consensus in the submission of a PDM interface standard to OMG. This resulted in RRM coordinating two- to three-day workshops on a monthly basis to establish a final, harmonized, PDM interface standard. That the Joint PDM Submission Team was able to come to consensus on what the standard object-oriented interface for PDM system should be was in part due to Mr. Johnson's belief in and support for collaboration (see Chapter 12). The JPDM submission was approved by the OMG in March 1998 as the standard for exchanging systems between PDM systems, six months beyond the formal end of RRM.

ISWG Workshop Process

A two-and-a-half-day format evolved for these workshops that proved to be particularly productive. The first day was spent conducting presentations on the technology and related initiatives being pursued by the participating companies. These presentations provided a common ground for discussions, enabling the participants to effectively communicate with one another for the remainder of the workshop. Straw man objectives were defined on the second day and used to establish an agenda for the balance of the workshop. An important part of the workshops was the group going out to dinner together and getting to know one another. This was one of the best mechanisms used to establish the relationships and trust needed to ensure that the projects worked.

DESIGN TO ANALYSIS WORKSHOP

This workshop was sponsored by the Delphi Saginaw division of GM to discuss analysis tools, analysis business practices, and analysis processes.

It was championed by Gary Patelski, the Delphi executive on the RRM Steering Group. The workshop was attended by personnel from Ford, General Motors (Delphi Saginaw and Delphi Chassis), Kodak, Lockheed Martin Energy Systems (Oak Ridge), the MacNeal-Schwendler Corporation, Spatial Technologies, Texas Instruments, and United Technologies/Pratt & Whitney. Delphi Saginaw had shared its high-level requirements for integrating CAD and CAE with the RRM team prior to the workshop.

The workshop was facilitated to identify common requirements among the RRM companies. During the last day of the workshop, the users present (Delphi Chassis, Delphi Saginaw, Pratt & Whitney, and Texas Instruments) each listed their top 10 development needs. These needs emerged from the previous two days of discussion on the design to analysis process generally used in any analysis requiring meshing. Meshing is the term used to describe the division of a product model into a number of smaller discrete parts, called elements. The forces a product is expected to encounter are applied to the "meshed" product model. The impacts of the forces are analyzed by the computer on each element in the model and summed up to represent the total impact on the product model. This analysis process is referred to as finite element analysis. The process of conducting an analysis on a product model is complex and requires a great deal of expertise.

The workshop resulted in the establishment of a Design to Analysis Working Group, which conducted a series of conference calls. A consensus was reached among the working group that the best use of RRM resources in this technology area would be in the development of software that could advise users how to perform a stress analysis on a computer model of a product—an analysis advisor. The end users want to be able to conduct more analysis early in the design phase of product development. However, they are confronted with a lack of personnel with the needed expertise to be able to conduct the number of analysis runs on products they would like to conduct during product design. The Analysis Advisor project was proposed to see if it would be possible to capture the expert's knowledge on how to conduct an analysis on a particular type of problem. That captured expertise would then be provided to a novice user such that the novice could conduct the basic analysis. The individuals participating in the RRM Design to Analysis Working Group relayed these results to their respective RRM Steering Group representatives. The Analysis Advisor project was approved by the RRM Steering Group in November of 1995.

Having focused technology workshops driven by end users has been demonstrated as an effective method for project selection, particularly if the workshop is followed up with conference calls. Conducting a follow-on workshop to formulate the project scope is a proven means for identifying market requirements to focus the development project.

CHAPTER 17

Project Implementation

The ability to implement projects and get results is the core purpose of conducting R&D. Results are information on a technology area. The information may show that the technology can improve a process or product, or it may show that the technology can not provide improvements. In either event, the information resulting from R&D projects is used by companies to determine their future direction. Therefore, it is just as important to know what technology does not work as to know what technology can be applied in a company.

Getting results from a collaborative R&D project can be more difficult that getting results from an internally conducted R&D project. Technical experts are not necessarily good at working with others. It is important that a good collaborative working environment be established if the execution of the project is to be effective in leveraging a group of experts. The collaborative working environment has to be, both in fact and in perception, more beneficial for the participating developers than their normal working environment.

The personnel managing a collaborative R&D project are responsible for establishing the collaborative working environment. They need to establish good and frequent communications practices, ensuring that the appropriate information is provided at the right level of detail for the right people in the project and the program. A good way to start a project is to have a kickoff meeting to develop the detailed research and development plan for the project. This enables all the participants to share their perspectives and start from a common base. After the initial kickoff meeting, a regular communications process should be established among the participants on the technical team.

The RRM Analysis Advisor project is shown as an example of successful execution of a collaborative development project. This project was selected and approved as a result of the RRM Design to Analysis technology workshop described in Chapter 16. The following sections provide overviews of:

- The project scoping kickoff meeting
- Project working environment and communications procedures
- Project demonstration
- Project product development

Project and program managers in collaborative development need to recognize that different practices work for different groups of people. Managers need to be flexible in trying different processes to ensure that a good working environment is established. Managers and participants also need to be persistent in ensuring that project R&D objectives are met according to the agreed-upon schedule and with the resources available.

Project Scoping

Project approval should require a general scope for a project with an estimate of the level of effort needed from personnel, usually in man-months; other resources needed, such as software, computation, or fabrication hardware; and a schedule. Once a project is approved, it's a good idea to hold a project kickoff meeting to develop a detailed scope for the project. A project kickoff meeting was held for this reason to initiate the RRM Analysis Advisor project. The agenda for that meeting is shown in Exhibit 17.1, with the minutes from the meeting in Exhibit 17.2, and the results of the scoping effort in Exhibit 17.3. The levels of effort identified in these Exhibits were not included for publication, nor are any of the referenced handouts included.

EXHIBIT 17.1   RRM Analysis Advisor Kickoff Meeting Agenda

RRM Analysis Advisor Meeting Agenda
December 4–5, 1995, MSC, Costa Mesa, California

Meeting Objective

Establish the detailed development specification for the RRM Analysis Advisor. The development specification will identify what will be expected in the Analysis Advisor at the end of the project, and what will be in the beta analysis advisor after six months. The project is to be conducted within the scope identified in the RRM project authorization.

Agenda

December 4, 1995

8:00	Welcome and introductions
8:15	Review scope and resources available

Scope—Establish an advisor to assist the casual user to conduct linear analysis using MSC/NASTRAN and nonlinear analysis using ABAQUS or MARC on a Unigraphics model pre- and postprocessed using MSC/PA-TRAN. The advisor is to be architected such that advice can be extended to other analysis packages with minimal development.

User Expectations

Each user will present what that user would like to have (within proposed scope) by presenting an example product which would be analyzed by a casual user using the Analysis Advisor.

8:30	Delphi Chassis expectations
9:30	Kodak expectations
10:30	Delphi Saginaw expectations
11:30	Pratt & Whitney expectations
12:30	Lunch

MSC Capabilities

MSC will present projects which have been used to develop the background technology that will be used in the Analysis Advisor.

1:30	Analytical design package—a CAE tool developed for aircraft transparency design for the U.S. Air Force
2:30	Advanced composites repair analysis tool—a CAE tool developed for the U.S. Air Force to assist in composite repair of aircraft
3:30	Initial MSC vision of the Analysis Advisor
4:30	Review of day's discussion and tomorrow's agenda
5:00	Adjourn
6:30	Group dinner

December 5, 1995

8:00	Identification of end-of-project Analysis Advisor requirements
9:30	Discussion of Analysis Advisor architecture
10:30	Establish acceptance testing requirements
11:30	Identification of requirements for beta
12:30	Lunch
1:30	Identification of how work is to be accomplished—who is to do what by when, how work will be validated at user sites; establish means for communicating
3:30	Address contract/administrative issues
4:30	Adjourn

(continued)

EXHIBIT 17.2   RRM Analysis Advisor Kickoff Meeting Minutes

RRM Analysis Advisor Meeting Minutes
December 4–5, 1995, MSC, Costa Mesa, California

Meeting Objective

Establish the detailed development specification for the RRM Analysis Advisor. The development specification will identify what will be expected in the Analysis Advisor at the end of the project, and what will be in the beta Analysis Advisor after six months. The project is to be conducted within the scope identified in the RRM project authorization.

Attendees

Design analysis experts from GM Delphi Saginaw, GM Delphi Chassis, Pratt & Whitney, Kodak, and MSC.

Scope

Establish an advisor to assist the casual user to conduct linear analysis using MSC/NASTRAN and nonlinear analysis using ABAQUS or MARC on a Unigraphics (UG) model pre- and postprocessed using MSC/PATRAN. The Advisor is to be architected such that advice can be extended to other analysis packages with minimal development.

Day 1
User Expectations of the Analysis Advisor

Delphi Chassis

Example part selection (see handout):
- J-car park brake lever
- Torque strut bracket
- Ball screw gear
- Suspension link
- Strut top plate

1. Automate internally developed "Finite Element Analysis Job Simulation" workbook.
2. Would like to handle assemblies connected with joints (i.e., bolted joints).
3. Finite Element Analysis engineering fundamentals advice/help.
4. Allow user to build loading/boundary condition "library" for typical parts modeled in organization; plug in "plate with a hole" model from Delphi Chassis training course.
5. Provide training tutorials on generic problems (i.e., plate w/hole in tension). Provide step-by-step (mouse picks) instructions on how to run through the analysis. Focus on issues such as:
- Stress concentration effects
- St. Venant's Principle

EXHIBIT 17.2 (*Continued*)

6. Provide example of how MPCs are used. Advisor should perform an input deck check for basic things such as load and displacement cases, node and element definition and so on.

Engineer Profile: Design engineer who knows basic engineering and physical theories. This person may be of two types:

1. Just wants to get through an analysis as fast as possible and get usable results.
2. Inquisitive person who wants to learn more about FEA modeling.

This person will most likely start with a rough linear analysis to gain more understanding of where the hot spots are (i.e., high stress and temperature gradients). Next, the engineer may desire a detailed analysis requiring more sophisticated modeling techniques. The analysis may be handed to a full-time analyst or, with the aid of an advisor, be performed by the same design engineer.

The engineers who would potentially use the Analysis Advisor are in two groups at Delphi Chassis: product development engineers for whom structural analysis is becoming more and more a driver in product development, and design engineers who understand FEA engineering fundamentals and want to ask a question and receive a first-order answer through FEA.

Kodak

(See handout.)

1. Focus advisor on design engineers.
2. Initial focus.
3. Analysis process.
4. Ease-of-use: Guide through PATRAN techniques for common modeling practices.
5. Focus on design engineer for first phase of project, and automation for the analyst requirements for later development.
6. Suggest prep of UG geometry needed in order to create mapped solid or surface meshes in PATRAN.
7. Provide advice on necessary detail of mesh.
8. Example part selection:
   • Sheet metal spring with large displacement.
   • Camera shutter switch needing stiffness evaluated.
   • Optomechanical device with stress induced from a rotational velocity.

P&W

1. Support metal forming—contact.
2. Super-elements.

(continued)

EXHIBIT 17.2 (*Continued*)

3. Transient dynamics.
4. Capture analyst expertise.
5. Help for analysis/analysts.
6. WIZARD concept is good model.
7. Would like MACRO abilities to automate repetitive tasks such as producing identical post processing output results.
8. Has built internal rules–based analysis advisor for MARC (prototype only)
9. Intended to capture expertise.
10. Features context-sensitive help abilities (considers this to be extremely helpful).
11. Part selection to be drawn from investment casting consortia parts of which MSC has models.

Delphi Saginaw

Several parts were reviewed, including the shaft. The Advanced Product Engineering group are the envisioned users of the Analysis Advisor vice production engineering.
Complexity level—assemblies.
Provide the ability to communicate to the user when they will be getting in trouble.

Developer Expectations of the Analysts Advisor

MSC (see handout)

1. Assist the user in performing first-order engineering analysis.
2. Live on-line assistance.
3. Expand the number of engineers able to perform analysis.
4. Eventual commercial MSC/PATRAN product.
5. Not intended to replace existing on-line help—intended to complement it.
6. Provide hypertext links between on-line help and Analysis Advisor.
7. Avoid producing automated analysis tool to perform analysis on two or three specific Finite Element problems. Keep as generic as possible.
8. Possibly review project progress using file transfer protocol (FTP) on the World Wide Web.

Architecture

- Go with option #1 from handout.
- Separate "Initial Query" from the analysis window.
- Map screen space reserved for analysis windows.
- Auto resizing analysis window not to cover critical windows.
- Add "successful completion" indicator next to each analysis step where applicable.

EXHIBIT 17.2 (*Continued*)

- Each "description" under Analysis Steps could be a clickable button such as used in the "advice" area.
- Advice page-scan should not cover up the graphics viewport.
- Help pages may cover up graphics viewport.

Day 2

MSC

Covered development schedule (see handout).

Approach is to present advice in a nontextbook manner.

Literature search is complete with the efforts we have expended in this workshop.

Delphi Chassis's workbook offered as a source for advice material.

Delphi Saginaw to will provide UG models to MSC by Monday, December 11.

Initial advisor window will offer the following selections:

- Tutorial Exercise
- Query to Categorize Model
- Jump to Main Form

First conference call on Tuesday, December 12.

Beta 2 will involve:

- Automating hooks to PATRAN
- "Do It" in PCL
- Focus on "Do Its" for the Delphi Saginaw shaft problem in MARC and ABAQUS
- Automated checks

Action Items	Target Dates
1. Circulate meeting minutes	12/9/95
2. Obtain model tape from Kodak	12/8/95
3. Obtain Pratt & Whitney turbine model	12/5/95
4. Obtain Delphi-Saginaw shaft model	12/11/95
5. Select advisor team communication process	
	Decision by 12/12/95
6. First weekly conference call	12/12/95
7. Write lead-in documentation to advisor tutorial	12/11/95
8. Pratt & Whitney commitment decision	
9. Establish contact names from each sponsor	12/5/95
10. Draft "Report Card" Acceptance Test evaluation forms	12/12/95

(Names of individuals responsible for actions were deleted.)

(*continued*)

EXHIBIT 17.3 RRM Analysis Advisor Statement of Work

RRM Analysis Advisor
Phase 1 Statement of Work

MSC is to work with GM/Delphi Saginaw, GM/Delphi Chassis, Eastman Kodak, and United Technologies/Pratt & Whitney to deliver to the RRM participating companies a beta working model of the basic Analysis Advisor. The basic Analysis Advisor will be a software package which will assist the casual user to perform first-order linear analysis using MSC/NASTRAN on a Unigraphics model of a product pre- and postprocessed using MSC/PATRAN. The user would be expected to have a general knowledge of stress and strain, force equations, loads, boundary conditions, geometry, meshing, and materials. The user will be given generic advice to help on philosophies and guidelines. The advisor is to be architected such that advice can be extended to other analysis packages with minimal development.

Some aspects of the basic advisor would include:

1. An interactive, pull-down form which shows the steps used in performing an analysis.
2. User query buttons corresponding to each analysis step.
3. Indication of which steps have been performed, and what the next step is.
4. Logic trees to query the user about the problem details and the analysis needs.
5. An open logic tree software architecture to facilitate additions, or changes.
6. Graphics presentations showing relevant model examples, possible user choices, and analysis step instructions.

The basic advisor form, or subforms, will have provisions for action buttons that can launch future developed automation tools as they are identified and implemented according to the recommendations of the participating users.

The Phase I Deliverable will be a complete Analysis Advisor application, narrowly focused on providing advice to perform linear structural analysis on one application model. If possible, advice to perform linear structural analysis on other models will be provided. The advisor would provide a series of questions for the user to review relating to the model, effectively walking the user through a linear analysis of the model.

Project Working Environment and Communications Procedures

The way in which a project team works together shows how effective it is in achieving technical milestones. Frequent communications among team members collaborating in a development project are a good indication that they are making progress. A manager should assist in establishing a good working environment with agreed-on communications practices at the start of a project.

The working environment and communication procedures used in the RRM Analysis Advisor project were as valuable as the final software product, as it was one of the first experiences the participating companies had with working over the Internet. The process used in jointly developing the Analysis Advisor requirements and monitoring its development is likely to replicate the product design process expected to be used in the future.

As shown in the action items from the initial meeting in Exhibit 17.2, the project decided to use weekly teleconferences to coordinate development efforts. MSC established a protected Web site that could be accessed by the participants. The Analysis Advisor was developed by MSC on this Web site. During one of the early teleconferences, the development team agreed that the general development process for the Analysis Advisor would be as follows:

1. The Analysis Advisor Web site will be updated by Dave Bremmer (the MSC project manager and lead developer) every Friday.
2. Team members will review the Web site every Monday in preparation for a Tuesday conference call.

The Analysis Advisor development team held weekly, or at times biweekly, teleconference calls. Minutes of the conference calls were distributed within a day or two to keep anyone on the development team who was not available for the call informed on the progress of development. Access to the MSC Web site enabled the software architecture design and the detailed descriptions of the various program modules to be reviewed by all participants as they were being developed. The robustness of this development environment was evident with the success of the final testing.

The use of other Internet tools promises to be particularly valuable in collaborative development programs. The Agile Infrastructure for Manufactured Systems (AIMS) tools discussed in Chapter 15 and detailed in Appendix D show one example of the potential of productivity improvements generated from computer-assisted collaboration tools.

Project Demonstration

Project demonstrations are important to show a proof of concept and to validate what a development team has been discussing. In a collaborative development project it is important that the end-user sponsors see and understand the technology and have the opportunity to provide feedback. End-user feedback is an important source of information for directing future commercialization development. The RRM Analysis Advisor project highlights the benefit of conducting a demonstration of the technology developed with the end users.

The first phase of development of the RRM Analysis Advisor was successfully completed with the delivery of beta software to the RRM sponsor companies on May 30, 1996. (Beta software is the common term in the software industry for preproduction software.) The project was on schedule and within budget. The Phase I development concentrated on producing advice that bridged the gap between knowledge of classical mechanics (strength of materials) and the specialized practice of finite element analysis. The sponsor companies had 10 novice users conduct all-day testing of the beta software. Detailed, written evaluations of the software were provided back to MSC from the testers.

These evaluations indicated acceptance of the expert advice provided in the software.

Recommendations for the next development phase for the Analysis Advisor were presented at a management review of the Analysis project at MSC's Southfield, Michigan, office on May 31, 1996. The Phase II development built upon all of the advice generated during the Phase I effort. The Phase I testing with novice users highlighted the need for assistance with MSC/PATRAN modeling operations to achieve the Analysis Advisor goals. A second phase for Analysis Advisor development was agreed upon by all RRM sponsor companies, and a follow-on RRM project was presented to the RRM Steering Group to address this need. The fundamental goal of the second phase of Analysis Advisor development was to make MSC/PATRAN usable by the occasional or inexperienced user of finite element analysis software.

The objective of the second phase of the Analysis Advisor was to build on the Phase I Analysis Advisor to achieve a 100 percent success rate for novice users to perform the analysis task for an example brake lever problem supplied by GM Delphi Chassis. Specifically, the development created a newly architectured software platform that provided assistance to make MSC/PATRAN usable by the occasional or inexperienced finite element analyst.

The second phase of the Analysis Advisor project resulted in successful proof-of-concept testing at MSC's Southfield, Michigan, office on April 2, 1997, with participants from Delphi Saginaw, Delphi Chassis, Eastman Kodak, and United Technologies/Pratt & Whitney. Achievement of the development effort's fundamental goal was demonstrated with 100 percent success with eight novice user testers from the participating companies. The software was distributed to the participating companies at the meeting. The Analysis Advisor software delivered to the RRM sponsor companies was able to be built upon, extended, and customized such that the sponsoring companies could meet their industry-specific analysis needs and objectives.

The Analysis Advisor provides on-line assistance for conducting structural analysis to expand the number of engineers able to use analysis tools. It is intended to enable analysis to be used more frequently early in the design cycle as a predictive engineering tool.

Project Product Development

MSC evaluated the commercial potential of the Analysis Advisor. The MSC program manager for developing the Analysis Advisor, David Bremmer, championed the commercialization of the development internally in MSC with strong support from his manager, Ray Amador. The level of development needed to get the Analysis Advisor software into a commercially marketable package was approximately the same as that needed to complete the first two phases of development.

The additional funding needed to develop and commercialize the Analysis Advisor was provided through Sekisui Chemical, a Japanese company that produces sewage piping systems made of PVC. The 1994 Kobe earthquake prompted the Japanese government to demand earthquake-proof construction. A major problem in the Kobe earthquake had been the rupture of underground gas, water, and sewage lines. The failure of gas lines contributed to numerous fires with the failure of water lines impeding the ability to control the fires. The failure of sewage lines caused large-scale health problems.

As a result, a Japanese institute developed an earthquake simulation code that could be used to analyze sewer system piping. The only problem for Sekisui was that the earthquake simulation model was too complex for designers to use. It took an expert analyst 40 days to run the code on one sewage piping model. With a catalog of different pipes, pipe joints, and configuration options, Sekusui could not meet customers' needs in a timely manner if it had to ensure earthquake-proof construction.

Sekisui learned of MSC's Analysis Advisor development through MSC's Tokyo office, and contracted for the development of a tool to enable novices to run the earthquake simulation analysis. On October 5, 1998, MSC announced the release of a new business offering, MSC/Acumen, the productization of the Analysis Advisor. In prototyping MSC/Acumen at Sekisui, the product enabled a novice user to run the earthquake simulation on one of their products in one day. MSC/ Acumen provides a new process for capturing the knowledge of experts and providing that knowledge to novices in a way they can understand and use. The RRM Analysis Advisor project represents an ideal collaborative development process in which end users define a market-driven need and support development by a company that will commercialize the technology.

CHAPTER 18

Administration

A number of administrative actions involving reports and audits accompany collaborative development. These tasks need to be accomplished to keep the organization legally and financially accountable. While the overhead effort (the amount of time personnel expend in administration) involved in performing these tasks should be minimized, these tasks need to be accomplished in a professional manner. Administrative tasks can be characterized as:

- Contractual
- Financial
- Management support

Third-party organizations such as the National Center for Manufacturing Sciences (NCMS), or the Consortium for Advanced Manufacturing—International (CAM-I), can provide a valuable benefit to a group of companies collaborating on R&D by providing these services.

Contractual

A requirement for all collaborative development programs conducted in the United States is an antitrust filing. To ensure that the consortium is not in violation of U.S. antitrust acts, the consortium must file an antitrust report to the U.S. Department of Justice as required under the National Cooperative Research Act of 1984 (amended in 1993). This simple filing should be done while establishing any contract vehicle among companies to conduct collaborative R&D.

The contracts that generally are used to form a collaborative R&D program involve a partnership agreement, and a funding contract with a government agency if any government funding is being provided. These contractual agreements are addressed in Chapter 14.

A third-party organization such as NCMS or CAM-I can be used to:

- Provide contracting services.
- Assist in resolving contractual issues and problems.
- Provide an interface to U.S. government agencies.
- Assist in closing a program on completion.

Financial

Financial procedures and conditions exist as a result of contractual obligations, and must be adhered to by the participating companies. Some of the administrative functions associated with these procedures include:

- Maintaining financial records.
- Invoicing to a government agency if the agency is providing a cost share.
- Preparing cost share reports for a government agency if there is a cost share.

- Preparing financial reports for the program Steering Group and program manager.
- Preparing final program reports.
- Providing auditing assistance.

As referenced earlier, collaborative R&D programs often involve a government providing a minority portion of the funding. U.S. federal agency programs that provide matching funds to a program require invoicing procedures to be established and followed by the participating companies. Government funds in these programs are provided through a cooperative agreement on a cost reimbursement basis. As most collaborative R&D programs with the government involve cooperative agreements, an overview of the financial administration needed to support cost share from a government agency is provided.

U.S. government cooperative agreements generally work in the following manner:

1. The private sector companies conducting the R&D expend the full amount on the R&D over a particular period of time, usually three months.
2. The companies prepare an invoice for the full amount of the cost of their R&D effort and submit a request for reimbursement, as well as a financial status report, to the government agency.
3. The invoices have to contain certain types of cost categories. The cost categories vary from agency to agency, depending on the federal regulation used in the contract.
   - Costs are usually divided into direct and indirect costs.
   - Indirect costs require that a government agency has reviewed the indirect cost rate calculations.
4. If equipment is purchased as part of the R&D effort, a copy of the invoice for equipment purchases must be attached to the participant's invoice. The invoice, or other supporting documentation, for equipment purchases must have a brief description of the equipment, model number, and serial number. At the end of the project, the government agency can claim the equipment if government money was used, even in part, to buy the equipment.

5. The government agency reimburses the companies for a percentage of the invoice submitted (50 percent or less depending on what was proposed to the government and accepted in the contract).

The requirement to have a government-accepted overhead rate has caused problems with some companies in getting reimbursement in past collaborative development programs. In the Printed Wiring Board (PWB) program, Digital Equipment Corporation (DEC) never received government funds because it did not have a government-approved overhead rate. The process for DEC to get a government-approved overhead rate and change its internal accounting systems to support the PWB program could not be internally justified. DEC continued to participate in the PWB program without government reimbursement until DEC sold its PWB business, at which time it left the PWB program.

AUDITS

Commercial companies must save financial records to support government audits of collaborative development R&D programs which receive federal funds. Records must generally be retained for a period of three years unless otherwise stated by the government. Audits require copies of source data that must identify the program at the component level. Personnel costs must be supported by time sheets and payroll records. Original invoices are required to support costs for travel, supplies, subcontract, or other materials.

Third parties, such as NCMS, can provide some assistance to the participating companies to help prepare for audits, but the government will audit each participating company directly. NCMS was able to provide value to the participants in the RRM program, when government auditors unilaterally determined that software that had been used as a match for the program had no value. NCMS provided a common legal base for challenging the audit findings on behalf of all of the industry partners.

Grants and contracts are governed by different regulations. Government funding is provided directly if the funding vehicle is a grant, and after specific deliverables have been met in the event of a contract. Cooperative agreements with the government require less administration than contracts with the government.

Management Support

The administration support needed to manage a collaborative R&D program has been stated in the generic operating procedures contained in Chapter 15. The administrative tasks can be summarized as:

- Support for the quarterly program team meetings, including planning and organizing the meetings, preparing and issuing meeting invitations and agendas, and preparing and circulating minutes of the meetings with action items and a schedule of follow-up activities.
- Support for program communications, including scheduling and facilitating conference calls, circulation of conference call minutes with action items and schedules of follow-up activities, maintaining central program files, and managing the production and distribution of progress reports and the program final report.
- Support for technical management, including statements of work for subcontracts, evaluating subcontractor proposals, preparing level of effort assessments, preparing sole source justifications (needed when government funds are involved), preparing and maintaining the program plan, evaluating deliverables, managing intellectual property as required, facilitating technical reviews and meetings, maintaining related activity awareness, conducting technology searches when appropriate, and preparing project reports.

Unless a company has the infrastructure in place to deal with a government agency and is willing to coordinate the administration for the rest of the partner companies in a collaborative R&D program, it is beneficial for a team of companies to use a third party to provide administrative support for a collaborative development program.

PART VI

Tomorrow's Business Culture— Collaboration

Global markets and competition will continue to dramatically expand and intensify. Success in this new global economy will require surviving companies to continuously improve their efficiency in producing products. The advantage of a competency in collaboration will be in having a significant asset that will enable businesses to reduce the risk of R&D for the products and processes which must generate innovative products in shorter cycle times than ever. The overwhelming need for new technology and the process knowledge that enables its deployment and fuels this economic engine has become so complex and expensive that collaborative alliances are now, or soon will be, essential.

Companies are adopting multiple approaches to bolster and leverage in-house research. One of these techniques is to establish strategic relationships with other organizations to gain access to useful technologies or knowledge that has been or will be developed. Partnerships also may be formed to shorten product development cycles in other ways. "The currency of a partnership may be exchanges of ideas. This type of an association is typical when none of the partners is sure about how to best use a technology."[1] The value of this currency can be pegged to the complimentary nature and transferability of the process, technology, knowledge or skills brought into the relationship.

In this new business environment, companies must reach out at an ever-increasing rate for new sources of innovation and technology. These sources will almost surely come from outside the traditional core competencies and internal enterprise structures of these companies. Business managers are viewing solely homegrown technologies from inside R&D departments as an increasingly risky investment and practice. Companies can not afford the risk that their product or process will be a stand-alone, without the critical ties to the mass market that are being provided through the ever more integrated information technology infrastructure. Bennett Harrison stated, "Simply put, investments in production technologies cannot achieve their potential without a number of concurrent developments. These might include the introduction of more flexible workplace organizations, the delegation of greater responsibility to nonmanagerial labor, the enhancements of skills among both managers and their employees, and the installation of new infrastructure, ranging from Internet connections to new-fashioned airports to 'smart,' energy-efficient buildings."[2] New products or processes need to be able to be integrated to take advantage of emerging and converging technologies being provided by others.

These managers are increasingly making decisions on return on assets and capital. Agility and flexibility are now weighted higher in business planning models than the potential technological breakthroughs which may or may not happen. Collaboration in R&D is becoming the preferred practice for technology development because it has demonstrated this capability at an increasing rate. However, as we have stated, collaboration is hard, and while we have described numerous successful collaborations, many corporate efforts in this area have failed. A recent McKinsey report suggests that more than 50 percent of all the joint ventures and collaborative alliances proposed fail or never get off the

---

[1]Joseph Longo, vice president and general manager, Rockwell Science Center, basic research white paper, "Defining Our Path to the Future," R&D magazine, 1997.
[2]Bennett Harrison, Technology Review. October, 1996.

ground. The challenge is how to execute these newfound skills in a way that delivers value by today's metrics on a consistent basis. We believe that the methods shared and described in this book will provide a viable track for the execution of this process.

Summarizing, the requirements needed for success in collaboration include:

- Correct identification and involvement of the user community.
- Identified, agreed-on benefits for all participants.
- Existing processes to integrate the technology development into.
- Commitments to provide the resources needed.
- Accurate scoping of projects.
- Sufficient maturity of the hardware and software technologies (infrastructure) needed to support the planned technology development.

One of the characteristics of the new economy is that fewer people are actually involved in the physical processes of making or fixing things. Instead, more and more of us make our living by interacting with others, planning strategies, striking deals, solving problems, managing people, and analyzing information. One reason is that we became efficient producing things and it takes fewer people to do it. McKinsey & Company calculates that 60 percent of all labor costs consist of interactions between people, while 40 percent are in manufacturing. McKinsey argues that over the next decade, thanks largely to dramatic decreases in the cost of computing and data transmission, that interaction costs will be reduced by 50 to 65 percent.[3] Collaboration will also be a big benefactor in the evolution of these new, less costly tools. We must be ready.

Collaboration promises to become a dominate characteristic of the business culture of the 21st century. Given the continuing advances in communication and information technologies, businesspeople will be able to tap a broad range of information and expertise prior to making the decisions. This information and expertise will extend over multiple competencies, representing all of the parties in the extended enterprise,

---

[3]McKinsey analyst A. Hanna, analysis of U.S. Census Bureau and Bureau of Labor Statistics data published in the *Washington Post*, April 21, 1997, "Finding Grist for Investment from Management Gurus," by staff writer Steven Pearlstein.

including customers. Collaboration is a key to acquiring collective knowledge. Collaboration provides the ability to tap the collective knowledge available across the extended enterprise to make better business decisions than any one individual can make in isolation. Those companies that make the best decisions will be rewarded with a competitive advantage.

The benefits of getting better business decisions as a result of collaboration do not come without a cost. The effort it takes to effectively collaborate—the time spent in meetings and phone calls to collaborate and exchange ideas with others with whom you would not normally work—is the overhead cost delta for collaboration. The benefit of having a better result from a task or decision due to prior collaboration has to be worth more than the overhead cost of the collaboration. Collaboration provides decision makers with a broader background of knowledge from which to make decisions. As a result, those involved in collaboration will make better decisions. The value in making better decisions needs to exceed the overhead cost delta for collaboration.

Business success in the near future is likely to be judged not only by financial returns or return on physical assets, but also by knowledge or human capital. These assets will need to be assessed, valued, and managed. Ways to do this will be viewed differently from the standards used today, but very much the same as one might assess a collaboration opportunity:

- Is the knowledge complementary to other known parts of the problem?
- Is there a network for this knowledge to thrive and coexist in?
- Is there leverage in this network which is identifiable to *my problem?*
- Does my enterprise have the competency needed to manage and extract this knowledge in order to fit an identifiable goal that has a quantifiable value?

Brian Arthur[4] stated that a new business model of "increasing returns economics" is emerging as knowledge-based companies become

---

[4]"Increasing Returns and the New World of Businesses," *Harvard Business Review*, August 1996.

more common. These new returns opportunities are characterized by relatively low up-front costs (e.g., software versus the physical assets of heavy industry) and network effects (products compatible with a network of users and other products). Collaboration and the diversity of intellectual property plays to this advantage, especially in dealing with manufacturing processes that have to integrate tool designs and products into their processes.

While many research and development issues justify collaboration costs, collaboration is likely to expand into a tool for decisions in other areas of business. The case for using collaboration as a tool boils down to those cases in which the benefits of collaboration outweigh the costs. Changes in the following are impacting the collaboration cost-benefit equation (collaboration benefit is more than the collaboration cost to justify collaboration) that drives the decision to collaborate:

- Technology infrastructure
- Culture
- Business environment
- Funding
- Ability to conduct collaboration
- Measurement of results
- Potential legal risks

Looking at each of these shows why collaboration will be a major business characteristic of successful firms.

Technology Infrastructure

A major emphasis in this book has been the impact improvements in communications and information technologies are having on business. The world of the late 1990s is witnessing an ever more rapid adoption of technology. This can be shown by the amount of time it took to get 50 million users of the following new technologies from the time of their

262 ■ TOMORROW'S CULTURE—COLLABORATION

first commercial product availability: radio took 30 years, television took 13 years, and the World Wide Web took 4 years.[5]

Those companies and corporations that change their business environments to take advantage of the improvements in communications and information technologies will gain a competitive edge. The ability to effectively collaborate to get the knowledge needed to make better decisions faster is one of these changes.

As faster, easier-to-use information technologies become more readily available, the cost of collaboration will drop. When the Printed Wiring Board (PWB) program was put together in 1990, the broadcast fax was the primary means of keeping the team informed. Today, that role has been replaced by e-mail, which is both more cost- and time efficient than broadcast fax.

Culture

In the United States, one of the largest barriers to collaboration is the individualism of U.S. culture. The drive to be the best, stemming from the emphasis on individual competitiveness that is part of growing up in the United States, has been a strength of U.S. culture. The inclination of an individual to share one's talents for the good of the group is not usually an individual's first thought.

But another characteristic of U.S. culture is the high degree of trust relative to other societies. It's easier to establish trusting relationships in our culture, as the first inclination in dealing with others in the United States is to trust them until they demonstrate a reason why they can't be trusted. This higher threshold of trust makes it easier to collaborate in the United States.

Coupling the "individualism" and the "trust" characteristics of U.S. culture will provide for a richer collaboration in which more perspectives will be provided to address issues. Multiple inputs lead to better solu-

---

[5]Daniel Burrus, *Technotrends*, HarperBusiness, 1993.

tions. Therefore, as collaboration becomes more accepted, the benefits of collaboration will be stronger as resulting decisions will be based on the convergence of a more diverse input.

Business Environment

Today's industrial environment has many regulatory requirements, suffers periodic energy shortages, experiences continuous cost pressures, must accommodate fast-moving new technologies, and enjoys relaxed antitrust laws allowing precompetitive collaboration. These factors were identified by Bill Powers,[6] vice president of research at Ford Motor Company, as the principal differences between today and the business environment of the early 1970s. In addition, the need to collaborate is drive by:

- Little customer differentiation.
- R&D that is required for societal good.
- Large original equipment manufacturers having common suppliers that are critical to each company's success.
- The need to implement lean manufacturing[7] to stay competitive.

Dr. Powers defined tomorrow's business world as one of "coopetition," meaning:

1. Working, especially developing, together.
2. An industry consciousness centering on market-driven organization.
3. A party, or parties, with whom one has "coopetition."

---

[6]Address at the University of Michigan Automotive Management Briefing Seminar, August 6, 1998.

[7]The principles of lean production include teamwork, communication, efficient use of resources, the elimination of waste, and continuous improvement as described in *The Machine That Changed the World*, by James P. Womack, Daniel T. Jones, and Daniel Roos, Rawson Associates, 1990.

He sees the following events driving the evolution of "coopetition":

1. Transnational relationships that respond to global markets.
2. Enhanced global OEM-supplier relationships.
3. Linkage to partner systems.

He then emphasized the importance of information technology as the exchange medium for "coopetition" with computers as the exchange medium for information. He concluded by indicating that simulation will become increasingly vital for developing both product and business models.

Collaboration is needed to ensure that the continuously changing, geographically variant market is provided with desired products at the most cost-effective prices, at assumed high-level quality, and at an as-needed, or expected, timeliness.

In this business environment, the competitive advantage gained through the better decisions that result from collaboration will force companies to collaborate or risk losing business. The benefit side of the collaboration cost-benefit equation is certainly higher in today's business environment than it was in the business environment of the 1970s. All indications are that the trend in the world's business environment will continue toward a more favorable environment for collaboration, potentially to the point of collaboration becoming a necessary business competency.

Funding

External funding is needed at present in most collaborative R&D programs to:

1. Offset the overhead cost of collaboration (described earlier in this section (Part VI) and in Chapter 6).
2. Reduce the risk involved with piloting new technologies in a production environment.

The costs of piloting emerging technology in a production environment may be the main challenge to establishing effective collaborative R&D programs. These pilots demonstrate the actual capabilities of today's technology, and provide road maps as to where the technology gaps are in getting emerging technologies deployed. Production pilots of emerging technology are the principal means of reducing the Technology Development Process.

The cost of these pilots to end users and parts suppliers is the risk involved in disrupting their production processes and/or distracting their production personnel from meeting the company's production schedules. External funding has been able to be used to offset the risk of technology pilots involving production resources in successful collaborative R&D programs.

Another cost of these pilots is the need to provide incentives to technology suppliers to work together to produce generic solutions to address technology interoperability and ease of use as well as functionality. Technology suppliers will expend resources toward developing their next products so they can stay, and ideally grow, in business. While technology suppliers would like to be able to work with their markets to develop generic solutions, these take more resources than are needed to develop proprietary solutions. As technology suppliers are often smaller firms, they need incentives to be able to cover the costs involved in developing generic solutions. Cash flow is often a real concern for smaller companies, which external funding addresses. Other incentives may be in the form of assured markets.

SOURCES OF EXTERNAL FUNDS

As previously addressed, the source of external funds for most of the collaborative R&D programs the authors have experience with has been U.S. federal government agencies. The effort to obtain government funds raises the collaborative overhead cost side of the collaborative cost-benefit equation by a substantial amount. The overhead cost of the Technologies for Enterprise-Wide Engineering (TEWE) proposal to the NIST ATP easily ran over a thousand worker-days from December 1997 to October 1998 with no resulting funding. The time and effort needed to get external matching funds from the government for the Robust Design

Computational System is documented in Chapters 3 and 12. While the intentions of the U.S. government are in the best interests of society, the cost of their assistance to commercial industry can be prohibitive.

While the return on funding collaborative R&D is a most promising investment, the availability of private sources of funds for supporting collaborative R&D has not yet materialized. Certainly, the availability of private funds for collaborative R&D would reduce the overhead cost. The government could potentially provide more of a stimulus for collaboration in the United States by providing some incentive for private capital investment in collaborative R&D.

Ability to Conduct Collaboration

An improved ability in society to develop teams that can effectively work together to make collaboration work will go a long way toward establishing collaboration as a core business competence. The purpose of this book is to share with readers experiences of what has and has not worked in establishing and managing collaborative development efforts, and pass on this experience in a way that will assist others in pursuing collaboration.

A key point is the need to be proactive in networking ideas, introducing people to others with new ideas, and attempting to improve the economic climate, even if you may not know what opportunity may result. As events unfold, new opportunities will emerge to a point where a person or company needs to be selective in the opportunities pursued.

Promoting better understanding among industry, government, and educational institutions as to their roles in the Technology Development Process is important. Many people in government and academia do not recognize the importance of industry's leadership in dealing in an open market world.

As the ability to conduct collaboration becomes a recognized and rewarded business competency, more personnel will seek to acquire the skills and expertise needed to be effective in collaboration. This will in effect lower the overhead cost and raise the benefits in the collaboration cost-benefit equation.

Measurement of Results

An underdeveloped aspect of collaboration involves the metrics that could be used to measure the benefit of collaboration. The improvement in being able to make the right decisions as a result of collaboration and the estimate of the overhead cost of collaboration which have been described are informal rules of thumb that have come from discussions with senior industry officials.

Dr. Rebecca Henderson of the MIT Sloan School has worked with companies to measure the productivity of their research, and to help them make decisions on where they should invest in technology development. She relayed from her experience that the determining factors regarding what technology development a company invests in are luck, personnel, strategy (project portfolio management), and organization (the way research is managed). What she found was that a company's technology strategy is evolved through a constant cast of characters who accumulate experience together, characterized by local learning in a complex, multidimensional environment.[8]

The author's experiences in industry validate Dr. Henderson's observations with the possible exception that the degree of luck needed is more a function of how much corporate management fully understands the technology behind the company's products and processes. Much of the research focus direction selected by a company boils down to personal relationships, trust, and track record. Given that the participation of one or more major end users are needed to have successful collaborative development, the following statements outline the metrics a senior manager at a manufacturing company might apply in making a decision to commit to collaborate with other companies in development:

---

[8]June 15, 1998, luncheon address at the International Conference on the Economic Impact of Technological Change sponsored by the National Institute of Standards and Technology Advanced Technology Program at Georgtown University.

- The manager knows what the organization wants to achieve as a company. It has a technology development objective, with a commitment from one of its product centers providing focus.
- The company does not have all of the resources needed to achieve what it wants.
- The personnel within the company are receptive to collaboration.
- The manager has confidence that collaborating will work to achieve what is wanted.
- There is an internal company champion providing the personal commitment and impassioned leadership for the program.

Some of the metrics different companies use before making an R&D investments include:

- Net present value/internal rate of return
- Risk versus return
- Building capability and strategic projects, which is evolving to real options theory

Others have developed processes that are being used to try to direct and control R&D efforts. Some of these include:

- The "stage gate" process in which there are staged reviews of an R&D program which it has to pass to continue being funded.
- Project portfolio management, which seeks to establish a balance of R&D characterized by risk level and time frame to getting into product.

There are also various metrics for monitoring the return on investment in R&D, such as:

- Patents and papers produced
- New products produced per year
- Performance of R&D versus R&D budget
- Time to market for technology being developed

- Time to break even for cost of technology investment
- Share of revenue for new products

Other metrics that are used, but are not reliable, include:

- Corporate history (we've always spent 5 percent of sales on R&D).
- Stories of past experience (the company wouldn't be here except for the XYZ company experience of investing in ABC technology).
- Stopping the R&D effort and seeing what happens.

Some metrics the authors use to measure their success in establishing and managing collaborative development programs include:

- Improved products or processes resulting from the application of technology developed under a collaborative development program.
- Sharing the results of successful and unsuccessful proof-of-concept technology pilots among the participants in a collaborative program.
- Funding, or some other form of subsidization, to companies and organizations to conduct research.
- Unanticipated program expansion as evidenced when the participating companies provided more resources than they originally commit, and other companies join a program without requesting funding (as was the case in both the Rapid Response Manufacturing and Printed Wiring Board programs).
- Establishment of a program. Some organizations measure the fact that a program is in place or receives a funding award as a metric. This metric is often used by the government and government contractors. The capability of the program to execute the expected development is often not measured, and in some cases does not exist.
- The confidence that other individuals and companies have in the ability of an organization or person to establish and manage collaborative development programs.

Much of the rest of the conference at which Dr. Henderson spoke dealt with the difficulty of measuring productivity, featuring some of the leading economists in the world who are the experts on the topic. The conclusion reached is that if society cannot measure productivity, it will be impossible to measure productivity resulting from collaboration. As such, the core evaluation criteria relating to the benefits and costs of collaborating will most likely continue to lie with the business instincts and acumen of the senior management of the involved company or organization. Establishing metrics for the benefits and costs of collaboration will be an academic exercise for the foreseeable future.

Potential Legal Risks

While the legal environment in the United States is favorable toward promoting collaboration, the explosion in information technology has raised several new legal issues regarding the access, exchange, and use the information that is now readily available to everyone through the Internet. Many in the legal community do not know how to protect, or even define, what is proprietary knowledge.

Progressive companies recognize that in sharing information, others need to apply resources to understand the information sufficiently to be able to use it. During the time it takes for a company to understand the information it receives from another company, the company that provided the information will be developing additional new technology. From this perspective, the sharing of information is not a concern, and certainly not a concern worth spending legal resources on.

While it is not expected that the future legal environment will be a detriment to collaboration, and it is anticipated that collaboration will continue to be permitted, societies and governments around the world change depending on their perception of world events. It wasn't that long ago that books were burned in Germany. If it is perceived that the free flow of information is detrimental to society, then governments will take actions to impede or stop information flow. The net effect is that the future legal environment is uncertain, but is assumed to be compatible with promoting collaboration. All that personnel collaborating can do is to monitor the progress of legal changes in society. The success of collaboration will influence legal changes in the environment.

The Future of Collaboration

At present, collaboration is a tool most comfortable for those who are not afraid to share information even if it's counter to their business culture; those who can quickly learn and grasp new concepts; those who can visualize the application of technology and the type of business it can generate.

However, collaboration will not be limited to this set of people. The ability will soon exist to extend the collaborative process beyond being a tool for just research and development to crossing business cultures and engaging people of varying education levels. Advancements in information technology will not be complete until sufficient complexity is removed from the collaboration process to enable all of society to participate. The Internet is providing access to information for individuals around the world. The ability to integrate this information into knowledge is at present left to individuals, but learning tools are being developed to improve getting information into knowledge. These tools will enable all people to live to their potential, more accurately value their contributions, and improve their quality of life.

We're all individuals with our own thoughts, understanding, and beliefs. It's the ability for us to all work together, to collaborate, that will determine how we live and what our future will be. Collaboration will likely be the foundation for the governments of the future, as it has been for the United States since 1789.

Our objective has to be to expand the amount of collaborative opportunity to people of all levels worldwide, to give them an easy means to learn, to escape the shackles of their culture, their nationalism, prejudice, and interface with the world as members of the human race. This can give them a positive appreciation for the culture and nation they belong to, yet foster better understanding as to how the world is integrated into one vast socioeconomic-political system. They can better understand their role in the world and how they can play a constructive part in ensuring that the future is better for their families.

APPENDIXES

APPENDIX A

Printed Wiring Board (PWB) Program

Description

The PWB program was a very successful five-year, $31.76 million collaborative development effort which ended in 1996. The purpose of this collaborative development effort was to develop technologies to improve the performance per unit cost and manufacturability of printed wiring boards. Each of the eight companies and organizations participating in PWB realized benefits. Participants included original equipment manufacturers (OEM) production centers at AT&T, Digital Equipment Corporation, Texas Instruments, and Hamilton Standard Interconnect, Inc., Allied Signal, Hughes Electronics, and IBM. Each of the OEMs also had internal R&D centers conducting development. Allied Signal primarily participated as a PWB materials supplier. Government entities participation consisted of an agency, the National Institute for Standards and Technology, and a national lab, Sandia National Laboratories. The National Center for Manufacturing Sciences (NCMS) facilitated the program development and managed the effort. The program received $12.86 million from the NIST Advanced Technology Program (ATP). The U.S. Department of Energy provided $5.2 million to Sandia for its participation.

Results

A case study of the PWB program was commissioned by the ATP to economist Albert N. Link. His report was released by NIST on December 8, 1997, and relayed the following information on the PWB program. Major technical accomplishments of the project included:

- Practical technology for making high-quality PWBs from single-ply laminates, a cost-saving technique previously frustrated by manufacturing problems.
- Development of a new, dimensionally stable, thin-film material that outperforms any other material used in the industry.
- Improved test methods and data that led to commercialization of a superior surface treatment for PWBs.
- Improved imaging technology to produce PWBs with 3 mil line features, increasing the standard yield from 30 percent at the start of the project to better than 98 percent.
- Development of a new photolithography tool for noncontact printing of high-resolution PWBs.
- Development of a revolutionary new interconnect structure for multilayer PWBs.

Several significant improvements in test methods, processes, and manufacturing techniques were developed during the project, according to Link, and already have resulted in productivity gains worth millions of dollars to the industry annually.

A very significant benefit was the exposure R&D center personnel got to others outside their corporate culture. Once the development personnel from AT&T, DEC, Hamilton Standard, and Texas Instruments realized that their processes were fundamentally the same, and they started sharing experiences, new development ideas resulted from their sharing of information. These new ideas included development of alternative surface PWB finishes, evaluation data for projection imaging, new test vehicle designs, process monitoring equipment, modeling software, and other advances that would not have been attempted without the program.

The following benefits were identified in the case study:

1. The 32 research tasks in the project that participants felt they would have undertaken even without the ATP were accelerated by at least a year (in an industry where timing is critical), and the research savings engendered by the joint venture through sharing information and avoiding duplication of effort amounted to about $35.5 million.

2. The 30 research tasks that would not have been attempted without ATP support provided a whole set of technical capabilities that the industry otherwise would not have had. These included the development of alternative surface finishes, evaluation data for projection imaging, new test vehicle designs, process monitoring equipment, modeling software, and other advances.

3. Transfer of technology from the project participants to the PWB industry as a whole has happened rapidly, spurred in part from 214 research papers presented by project members, two of which received best paper of conference awards.

4. Early spin-offs of the project's work incorporated into commercial production lines already have realized significant savings for the industry. These include:
   - The technology for reducing PWB ply count, which has saved one firm alone more than $3 million per year.
   - Reduced scrap due to a new model for predicting PWB layer shrinkage, which has saved one firm alone more than $1.4 million per year.
   - Reduced solder defects due to improved coating and soldering techniques, which one firm reported as halving the number of defects per board.

5. In addition to strengthening the competitiveness of U.S. producers and increasing their share in world markets, aggregate long-term benefits of the PWB project will come through the incorporation of lower cost and improved printed wiring boards in a myriad of electronics products, providing benefits to consumers.

The Link study concentrated on early benefits, including research efficiencies, produced by the ATP project, which was completed in mid-1996. Longer-term economic benefits for the industry as a whole are expected in future years as the results of the project are disseminated more widely and incorporated into production facilities.

Members of the ATP project now say that as a result of the work, their companies—and the U.S. PWB industry as a whole—have improved their competitive positions in the world market. In 1997, the NCMS gave the project its Collaborative Project Excellence award and NCMS president John Decaire said the project "quite literally saved" the roughly $7-billion U.S. PWB industry, with its approximately 200,000 jobs.

Rapid Response Manufacturing (RRM) Program

Description

The RRM program was a very successful collaborative development program that ended in 1997 after having expended over $65 million. The goal of the program was to develop engineering tools to reduce the product to market time by 50 percent through the application of advanced computer technology to leverage concurrent engineering methodology. The program was established as a five-year collaboration involving four manufacturing companies—Ford Motor Company, General Motors, Raytheon Systems Company (formerly Texas Instruments Defense Systems Group), and United Technologies Corporation/Pratt & Whitney—and six software development companies—the MacNeal-Schwendler Corporation (Aries Technology was the initial participant and acquired by MSC in 1993), Cimplex, Concentra (previously ICAD and now Knowledge Technology International), Spatial Technology, Teknowledge (previously Cimflex Teknowledge), and Parametric Technology Corporation (PTC dropped out of the program after it was awarded but prior to contract signature). Over the course of the program, Structural Dynamics Research Corporation (SDRC) took the position left by PTC. The total in-kind effort committed by the partners was originally set at $45.8 million. The National Institute of Standards and Technology (NIST), through the Advanced Technology Program (ATP), reimbursed the partners for approximately 40 percent of their committed costs, a total of $19.8 million. Eastman Kodak and the Rocketdyne division of Boeing also participated in specific projects without receiving NIST matching funds. Lockheed Martin Energy Systems (Oak Ridge Y-12) participated through a cooperative research and development agreement (CRADA) between the U.S. Department of Energy (DOE) and the RRM program. DOE provided approximately $4.5 million for the Oak Ridge work. NIST funded an internal Factory Automation System Division RRM to complement the industrial RRM program. The National Center for Manufacturing Sciences (NCMS) facilitated the program development and manage the effort. The partners exceeded their committed in-kind effort by a conservative estimate of $3 million per year. An average equivalent of 100 people worked full time on RRM across the partners.

The RRM program objective was to shorten time-to-market, improve quality-to-cost, and enhance product reliability in order to provide the U.S. manufacturing infrastructure competitive advantage in a variety of global market sectors. Efforts to accomplish this objective focused on coordinating and extending the application of feature-based solids modeling, knowledge-based systems, integrated data management, and direct manufacturing technologies in a cooperative computing environment.

The intent in RRM was to implement available technology by achieving interoperability between existing commercial software applications and across the existing legacy systems used by the partners through the use of open architecture. The program was directed through practical application and integration of existing commercial software through enhancements. Development efforts focused on interoperability and ease of use.

Each of the manufacturing partners selected a specific product and an operating organization to participate in the program. Ford Motor initially selected its Powertrain Group and increased their participation through the addition of their Climate Control Group. Delphi Saginaw Steering and their Powertrain Group were selected by General Motors. United Technologies had initially selected Sikorsky, but ended up utilizing Pratt & Whitney for their implementation. Texas Instruments focused on their Defense Systems Electronics Group.

The work was accomplished through 97 individual projects chartered by the Steering Group. The direct involvement of operating people in these projects assured practicality with ownership by the end users. RRM-evolved technology has been implemented in many of the operations of the partners. The technology providers have commercialized software in new products or enhanced existing products.

Results

The overall RRM effort was divided into six broad categories:

1. **Direct Manufacturing.** Projects and tools that directly interfaced with fabrication of products such as process planning, generative numerical control, and rapid prototyping.
2. **Engineering Data Management.** Projects and tools built around the use, formation, and management of engineering databases.
3. **Advanced Computer Tools.** Knowledge-based interfaces to, and between, application software.
4. **Knowledge-Based Engineering.** Projects piloting knowledge-based applications in the performance of engineering tasks.
5. **Engineering Environment.** Projects which included test beds and efforts establishing the environment in which individual engineers perform their work.
6. **Data Exchange.** Projects dealing with the exchange of engineering data, including direct translation as well as standards-based exchange.

Some of the accomplishments in each of these categories were:

Direct Manufacturing

- Piloted a capability to rapidly produce the tooling needed in product production using selective laser sintering.
- Integrated the stereolithography software format (STL) used to run many free-form fabrication processes into the international standard for product data exchange (STEP).

- Piloted the use of an STL file in driving the conventional numerical control (NC) used to run machine tools. The software that normally produces NC is referred to as computer-aided manufacturing (CAM).
- Piloted the ability to automatically generate NC for turned parts from a computer-aided design (CAD) file.
- Piloted the capability of emerging three-dimensional printers to "fax" product representations.
- Piloted development of knowledge-based engineering applications for the design of composite fan exit guide vanes for the Pratt & Whitney engine made for the Boeing 777.

Engineering Data Management

- Piloted emerging product data management (PDM) software systems and built prototype interfaces needed to integrate these systems into a company's established information technology environment. The effort helped influence the acceptance of PDM software by the RRM end users.
- Piloted the application of workflow software for the product design process.
- Developed a standards-compliant, object software–based "Archive for Software Reuse" which Raytheon continued to develop through 1998.
- Mapped PDM software to the Express software modeling language and developed software objects that can interface to international software object standards being defined by the Object Management Group (OMG). This effort led to the establishment of an OMG standard for the object-oriented software interface for PDM systems, which is being adopted by many PDM vendors.
- Improved the capability to access data describing material properties through PDM systems using the object-oriented interfaces.

Advanced Computer Tools

- Developed the ability to integrate ICAD knowledge-based engineering software with the ACIS geometric modeling software kernel.
- Integrated a user-controlled parametric sketcher into ICAD knowledge-based engineering software.

- Developed a user interface for ICAD knowledge-based engineering software that enables the user to understand the actions that take place in the software.
- Piloted design visualization technology which influenced the acceptance of this technology among design engineers.
- Developed an Analysis Advisor to assist the novice or casual user in conducting first-order stress and strain analysis on a CAD product model.
- Developed enhancements to improve the flow of data back and forth between CAD and analysis functions to be integrated into MSC's PATRAN software.

Knowledge-Based Engineering

- Collected and submitted a major OEM's drawing requirements to the International Standards Organization's software standard for product data exchange (STEP) in an effort to replace drawings with CAD models.
- Integrated ICAD knowledge-based engineering software with Unigraphics CAD software and CIMPLEX generative NC software and evaluated the ability to drive Unigraphics CAM automatically.
- Developed a knowledge-based engineering tool kit to provide substantial assistance to engineers in developing knowledge-based engineering applications to improve engineering design activities.
- Piloted the use of knowledge-based engineering in variant design.
- Developed and piloted a knowledge-based engineering application for developing the packaging needed for material handling of a crankshaft in the engine assembly process.
- Developed a knowledge-based process planning tool to efficiently provide the planners of manufacturing processes the knowledge of manufacturability, costs, machine tooling, routings, and material removal volumes.
- Developed an automated process planning system for the creation of aircraft engine tubing work instructions for use on the shop floor.
- Developed a capability to generate production gauges for tube bending operations using geometric associativity, free-form fabrication, and knowledge-based engineering. This development was piloted in a production environment for an air-conditioning hose

assembly and reduced a five-day operation needed to produce gauging to 18 hours.

- Initiated development of a software system to provide manufacturing cost visibility and cost reduction opportunities during the design process. This development continued after the RRM program ended.
- Established generic and company-specific requirements for knowledge-based process planning. Software tools that could potentially meet these requirements were identified and evaluated.
- Evaluated and piloted the ability to automate process planning through the use of three-dimensional simulations of manufacturing work cells. (A work cell is a group of machine tools in a factory used to perform manufacturing operations on a common group of products.)
- Developed and piloted a software application to generate modular fixtures needed to make tubes for aircraft engines.

Engineering Environment

- Developed a test bed at Oak Ridge for rapid implementation, testing, and validation of the software specifications and requirements generated in RRM.
- Piloted the ability to rapidly distribute technical information (drawings and specifications), which led to the elimination of aperture cards in a division of a major automotive company worldwide.
- Investigated alternatives for providing manufacturing engineers with affordable, single-point-of-access tools to leverage math data needed for manufacturing, including the creation of process sheets, assembly documentation, process planning activities, NC programming, and feedback to product design.
- Prototyped a Direct Engineering[SM] environment with limited product and process data models, knowledge-based engineering applications, solids-based modeling, associativity for limited numbers of components, and historic data on former designs.
- Piloted the use of a blackboard-based software application framework to integrate 13 software systems involved in the design, analysis, and manufacture of a crankshaft.
- Piloted the international use of desktop videoconferencing.
- Evaluated the emerging computing environment for engineers, defining an environment that allows multiple hardware (PCs and

workstations)/software (Windows NT and UNIX operating systems) platforms to exist and defining single desktop solutions.

- Developed a knowledge-based engineering applications for Direct Engineering^{SM} of throttle bodies.

Data Exchange

- Developed and piloted an ability to progressively stack the tolerances of parts in a three-dimensional computer model of a product assembly, a capability that was later commercialized into Unigraphics CAD software.
- Developed software to tie geometric dimensions and tolerances to the part features on a computer model of a part and provided requirements to the International Standards Organization for the software standard for product data exchange (STEP).
- Developed part features requirements, which were provided in the STEP development process.
- Developed a software reference architecture and an Integrator's Handbook.
- Developed STEP interfaces to ICAD and MSC/Aries software.
- Demonstrated the use of STEP in exchanging product definition between Ford and its Delphi supplier.
- Implemented STEP in a test bed at Ford to exchange, store, and navigate product data.
- Identified the data exchange requirements for sharing total product model knowledge and rules.
- Established a STEP Translation Center at GM to validate the maturity and robustness of commercially available software.
- Developed an interface between ICAD knowledge-based engineering software and SDRC's I-DEAS Master Series™ CAD system.
- Developed a STEP-enabled die processor advisor software system which continued after the RRM program ended.

A primary benefit to the partners of the RRM companies came from the results of both planned and incidental collaborative activities. The above results were planned. Equally valuable were the instances of unplanned collaborative benefit that occurred only because of the close intercompany working relationships that were made possible through mutual commitment to and participation in the RRM program. Examples included:

- Texas Instruments discovered that Ford, Pratt & Whitney, and GM had a depth of experience in the use of ICAD for knowledge-based systems development. Raytheon Systems is now incorporating a proven knowledge-based systems development technique based on GM/EDS providing training for five of their engineers in their "automated concurrent engineering" development methodology.
- Through incidental observation, Pratt & Whitney discovered how to solve its problems in the creation of large SLA prototype parts based on lessons learned in observing Ford's methodologies developed in their free-form fabrication laboratory.

The constant underlying motivation for this collaborative effort was the belief that the technology development and application in RRM was one of the critical elements needed to establish the cooperative agile company environments required to meet customer demands for product performance at a competitive price within a very challenging global marketplace. The effectiveness of the collaborative development working environment established under RRM was demonstrated with the participants providing over $3 million per year in resources over their commitment to the program. While Ford had a contractual commitment of seven people per year on the program, at one point it had over 100 people committed to RRM projects.

Technologies for Enterprise-Wide Engineering (TEWE) Initiative

Description

The TEWE program was proposed in 1998 to be a five-year, $62.39 million collaborative development effort. The purpose of this effort was to establish generic, interactive knowledge-base engineering (IKBE) technologies. A generic, broad-based, and consistent approach to interactive knowledge-base technology will enable a company to work with its suppliers and partners to efficiently capture, create, manage, and reuse knowledge. The IKBE technologies will allow manufacturers to readily conduct engineering over the extended enterprise through use of the Internet. An extended enterprise is an original equipment manufacturer (OEM) and its supply chain, subsidiaries, and partners affiliated with the life cycle of a particular family of products. Boeing, Eastman Kodak, Ford, and General Motors proposed to work with their supply base and technology development companies to develop a capability to conduct engineering over their respective extended enterprises. Supply base companies committed to the program included Key Plastics, Standard Products, and Tower Automotive representing Ford's supply base; Harbec Plastics and Liberty Precision Industries representing Kodak's supply base; and Howmet representing Boeing's supply base. Technology suppliers committed to the program included the knowledge-base engineering (KBE) companies Cognition, Engineous, and Knowledge Technology International (previously Concentra); the enterprise-wide product visualization company Engineering Animation, Inc.; the mechanical computer-aided engineering (MCAE) company MacNeal-Schwendler Corporation; Web-based collaboration companies Nexprise and WebEnable; the National Industrial Information Infrastructure Protocols (NIIIP) Consortium led by IBM; and the product data management (PDM) and computer-aided design (CAD) company SDRC. The team was to be coordinated and managed through the National Center for Manufacturing Sciences.

The key to being able to conduct engineering over the extended enterprise is dependent on being able to communicate the rationale behind decisions made in the design and manufacturing of a product—the fundamental knowledge that defines what a product is and does. Although demonstrated in specific applications, a generic ability to electronically capture, express, and exchange knowledge in a meaningful way does not exist. A metric in realizing this goal is the ability to provide the right information to the right person at the right time—integrating people, processes, and organizations.

The technical challenges that need to be addressed to establish IKBE technologies include:

- Identifying a comprehensive source for knowledge.
- Establishing a capability to capture knowledge and make it accessible such that it can be intuitively and unambiguously understood from many different user perspectives.
- Establishing the ability to understand and define the key characteristics underlying a product's form and function.

A necessary precondition for IKBE is general enterprise interoperability. While substantial advances have been made in integrating information technology, significant barriers continue to confront IT's integration, particularly at the levels of detail needed to efficiently conduct engineering. Key technical challenges to interoperability improvement include:

- Ensuring the ability to maintain secure, competition-sensitive information while sharing the information needed to conduct engineering with suppliers and partners.

- The ability to conduct real-time collaboration by exchanging massive amounts of information over varying hardware and network configurations.
- The ability to provide real-time access to databases distributed worldwide.

This team proposed to develop an Internet-based information infrastructure through conducting demonstration pilots in the extended enterprises of Boeing, Ford, GM, and Kodak that would have supported an integrated enterprise model to enable efficient engineering among all participants in the extended enterprise. The program was to pilot enterprise engineering using IKBE technologies to improve product design, manufacture, maintenance and support, modification and upgrade, and disposal. The composition of the team, with research being focused through real-world extended enterprise pilots, provided a pragmatic development environment for innovative IKBE technology solutions needed to enable enterprise-wide engineering.

In addition to the use of technology demonstration pilot projects to focus and apply enterprise-wide engineering development, the other principal feature of the proposed technical plan is the use of workshops to focus development. The experience of most of the TEWE participating companies in past collaborative development programs has shown the use of focused workshops as the most effective means of allocating development resources in a rapidly evolving technology society. Planning by the team has identified 12 technology development objectives, separated into three broad areas: knowledge acquisition, knowledge accessibility, and enterprise engineering.

The benefits of the use of generic, interactive knowledge bases that can be broadly accessed, used, and evolved will be to provide any individual who can add value through providing a product or service in conjunction with a larger enterprise with the ability to access and contribute to the extended enterprise. Establishing the ability to integrate the extended enterprise with a usable capability to readily capture and reuse knowledge will lead to higher-quality products and services—products and service better suited to performing the functions people really desire of them. The products and services will be able to be cost-effectively developed fast enough to meet and influence market demand as a result of having integrated enterprises and interactive knowledge bases.

Comment

The TEWE initiative was proposed as a program submitted to the National Institute of Standards and Technology (NIST) Advanced Technology Program (ATP) in 1998. A $23.95 million reimbursement was requested from the government to get the participating companies to work together to leverage $62.39 million of their internal efforts. The government funding was primarily needed to support the development of technology pilots in the OEM extended enterprise. This would have resulted in getting the OEMs to work, both together and with the technology suppliers, in common efforts to develop standard IKBE technology solutions that would be quickly validated.

While the proposal was favorably reviewed, with the TEWE management team invited to NIST to provide an oral review of the effort, the proposal was not funded.

Status

At the end of 1998, the future of the TEWE initiative is undetermined. The separate OEMs will continue to pursue their efforts to streamline their extended enterprises independently, investing with technology providers to provide custom solutions for their applications. The technology suppliers will focus on evolving their products to meet the needs of their major customers. Without external funds, justification to establish production pilots to test new development, or for the OEMs to expend the overhead effort needed to work together on technology development will be more difficult. The largest loss is in the ability to come to consensus on standard means for defining and exchanging knowledge.

The TEWE initiative may be able to find other external sources of funding, may be able to stay in place as an informal entity to serve as a means for sharing information among the participating companies, or may dissipate. As long as the benefits from working together are greater than the overhead involved in collaborating, the group will continue to interact. The relationships established among the participants may result in future formal collaborations.

Lesson

The principal lesson from the TEWE experience is that it demonstrated the difficulty, risk, and uncertainty involved for companies serving commercial markets in working with the U.S. government. A significant amount of collaborative overhead is expended in efforts to get government funds, and is a primary reason for the chasm that separates commercial and government businesses. Companies that depend on government funding as their principal source of revenue know they need to develop relationships with government agencies and understand their direction and interests, as the government is their customer. The TEWE participants expended this effort before they started working on the proposal, in attending workshops at NIST and working with NIST to further their efforts to work with industry.

The NIST ATP has been the subject of a significant amount of political debate from 1993 to 1998. The political debate focuses on the role of government with industry. The decision not to fund the TEWE initiative was a political decision, taken in a politically unstable environment. The segment of industry represented in TEWE had an understanding of the NIST ATP objectives that was close, but ultimately off-base. In future years, industry will determine if the overhead costs of working with the NIST ATP are worth the potential benefits. Certainly the government funds spent by the ATP on the Printed Wiring Board and Rapid Response Manufacturing programs were some of the best-spent taxpayer funds, given the objective of improving the welfare of the populace.

Agile Infrastructure for Manufactured Systems (AIMS) Simple Low-Cost Innovative Engine (SLICE) 2 Project

Description

The AIMS program was a three-year, $16 million collaborative development effort which ended in 1997. The purpose of AIMS was to develop technologies to enable geographically dispersed businesses to rapidly enter into, conduct, and exit business relationships by using the Internet. Participants included OEM R&D centers at Boeing-Rocketdyne, Lockheed Martin, and Texas Instruments. The program received $8 million from the Department of Defense Advanced Research Projects Agency (DARPA), with the other $8 million coming from the participating companies.

The AIMS program ended in 1997 with the Simple Low-Cost Innovative Engine (SLICE) 2 Project, which demonstrated a 10-month virtual enterprise. A virtual enterprise is a group of geographically dispersed real companies that work together for a specific period of time to make a particular product or perform a particular function. The companies go their own ways after the particular work or functions have been completed. SLICE 2 demonstrated the use of collaborative technologies in the concept definition phase of design engineering across multiple, geographically dispersed companies.

The SLICE 2 project was driven by a real business need at Boeing-Rocketdyne. The major manufacturer of liquid fueled rocket engines in the United States is facing new competition in an expanding market driven by the need for commercial launches of communications satellites. The competition is from warehoused liquid fuel rocket engines in the former Soviet Union available at bargain prices. Rocketdyne's business objective in the SLICE 2 project was to be able to drive the cost of a rocket engine down by 100, be able to get the engine to the market 10 times faster than it had been able to for the Space Shuttle main engine, and increase the useful life of a rocket engine by a factor of three.

The participants in the SLICE 2 demo were Boeing-Rocketdyne, Raytheon, and the MacNeal-Schwendler Corporation. The Multimedia Environment for Collaborative Engineering (MECE) developed under the AIMS program was used as the communications vehicle for the team to meet the business objective in 10 months. The spin-off company from Lockheed Martin which had developed MECE, ComerceNet (now NexPrise), supported the SLICE 2 effort.

Results

The end result of the SLICE 2 demo was a polyurethane prototype new rocket engine made of 6 parts instead of the normal 450, with a quality level of 9 sigma (meaning less than 1 failure out of 10 billion). The normal development cost of $4.5 million was reduced to $47,000. Manufacturing costs were reduced from $20 million to $1.5 million. The full design effort took 10 months as compared to the 6 years needed to do a comparable design-manufacture effort for a comparable rocket engine in the past.

One of the major successes Boeing-Rocketdyne got out of designing a new rocket engine as part of the AIMS program was incorporating new ideas generated by involving people who had no background on rocket engine design or manufacturing. These people asked good questions about why parts were designed the way they were.

The SLICE 2 project demonstrated how a virtual Integrated Product and Process Development (IPPD) team can actually work. A unique aspect of AIMS was the cultural monitoring conducted as part of the program. Dr. Ann Majchrzak, of the University of Southern California Marshall School of Business, documented the use of collaborative technologies in the SLICE 2 pilot. The use of computer-mediated collaborative tools was monitored as a mode for an individual to work in. Other individual work modes are working by yourself, having discussions with others in person, and having discussions with others over a phone. The following is an overview of Dr. Majchrzak's report:

REPORT OF THE SLICE 2 DEMONSTRATION PROJECT

Executive Summary

The SLICE 2 demonstration clearly indicates that virtual design enterprises are not only possible but highly productive. Some of the accomplishments observed included:

- Assembling and maintaining a team of part-time experts distributed across space, time, and company.
- The collaborative cross-company creation and monitoring of project management documents.
- Seamless electronic transfers of engineering drawings across companies.
- Realization of an innovative product concept that met design objectives.
- Extensive use of a collaborative tool, including extensive documentation of design process and decisions.
- Advances in concurrent engineering, including concurrent analysis with design, integration of suppliers into the design process, and in-

tegration of producibility at the concept definition phase of the design process.

- Engineering labor savings over traditional design projects.
- Creation of a team esprit des corps among coworkers with no shared history, little shared knowledge, and no physical cues.

In addition, the demonstration resulted useful lessons, which included:

- The use of new collaborative tools was identified by facilitating a design team to fundamentally improve design concepts virtually (instead of doing this in traditional collocated meetings).
- Use of the collaborative tool during design created more equal participation among team members during the engineering design process than the traditional hierarchical design process; while such equality of participation had benefits for the team, it created management challenges as well.
- Collaborative tools have limited utility in the interactive creation phase used to generate an initial design, as well as for resolving conflicts of interests and facilitating external reviews of designs.
- Teams will not enter all design-related information into the electronic notebook because information published in the notebook is "public" (even if just to the team), open to misinterpretation and (even inadvertent) misuse, and involves engineering time to enter. Thus, at the outset, a team should develop its own standards concerning the information that must be shared.
- Reuse of knowledge in the notebook is a critical problem for team members, external reviewers, and future teams. One possible solution is the establishment of a person who has the role of a knowledge broker role for the team.
- Virtual teams create new management challenges for team leaders such as maintaining focus of team members on project objectives and buffering the team from management redirections.
- Kickoff meetings for virtual teams are essential and should include such innovations as sharing of best practices across the company representatives in the team, team members agreeing on standards for work and communication, and training in common software.

- Information technology support is essential throughout the life of the project, not just at the inception, and should include not just technical support but also the facilitation and maintenance of a co-ordination protocol.

Project Description

A complex problem was posed to the team to design a new product for an unknown customer for which there was no precedent within any of the companies involved, using many team members without past experience in injector design, merging team members with different corporate cultures with regard to concept development, using a collaborative technology that was at best useful and at its worse inhibiting, and limiting travel to only two relatively brief occasions. Despite these complexities, the team still managed to exceed its main objective: develop a new rocket engine that meets performance and cost goals while demonstrating the use of a collaborative technology.

The team consisted of sixteen people with seven considered core team members, dispersed across three companies (Rocketdyne, Raytheon, and MacNeal-Schwendler) and five geographical areas. The core team included specialists in modeling, combustion design, combustion analysis, producibility, stress, and thermal analysis. The team kicked off June 3, 1997, after several months of planning to ensure that every member would have the proper technology and a set of standards (called the coordination protocol) to facilitate the proper integration of the tool within the design team environment. A major objective of the team involved not just developing an innovative new product, but also demonstrating virtual integrated product development across companies. While all members were highly regarded specialists in their own area (thermal, stress, combustion, producibility, modeling), several had relatively little experience designing injectors. All team members were part-time (ranging from 5 percent to 50 percent, with project team leader less than 20 percent time).

While the team was presented with an initial design concept, the team actually reevaluated and generated up to 10 different concepts during the life of the project, submitting several detailed analyses. The team was reinventing and modifying the design in critical ways up until the very end of the project. The final resulting design (and physical stereolithography model) was a synthesis among a number of competing concepts, rather than the result of a formal downselect among competing designs.

Nature of the Collaborative Tool

To help manage the distributed team, a collaborative technology was put into use. The technology was called the Internet Notebook. The Internet Notebook has an HTML (HyperText Markup Language) browser interface that allows members of the virtual collocated IPT (integrated product team) access to the project notebook over AIMSNet via a Web browser. IPT members recorded information and activities in a logical format through entries into the notebook.

Accomplishment Details

Making the Team Possible At All All of the engineers involved were highly respected in their organizations and were desired on many other projects. For many, the only way that their management would consent to involvement in this project was to keep their time to a minimum, preserving them for other projects. Moreover, there was talent in the three companies that would have been difficult to tap if mechanisms for allowing their involvement without substantial time weren't found. Thus, the team could not have functioned if extensive travel and time commitment were needed. This imposed a major constraint since it meant that the distributed team could not meet for long periods of time to work through the difficult early concept origination phase of the development process. Thus, most are convinced that without the Internet Notebook (combined with team members outfitted with headsets calling into a 800 conference line), this team wouldn't have happened at all.

In addition, most examples of virtual teaming are where the initial concept design is done by a collocated team, and where the team only becomes distributed once a design is selected for detailed design and production. This is one of the first examples demonstrated in which the team was able to develop an innovative concept entirely in a distributed fashion.

Collaborative Working Agreements across Companies A major accomplishment of the demonstration was the speed with which a purchase order was created due to the existence of a continuous ordering agreement (COA) between the two major companies on the team. A COA is similar to a blanket order agreement, but even more open. Essentially it means there does not need to be any purchasing negotiation between the two companies. Based on discussions between the companies, one company writes a proposal and it is accepted by the other. This implies a high degree of trust in that one company trusts the other to manufacture and participate with it at a fair price. The basis of this trust is that both companies are committed to helping each other get new business, and price their work accordingly. Because of the COA being in place, the actual elapsed time to create a statement of work (SOW) agreed to by all parties (time in days from kickoff meeting to completed and approved work breakdown structure (WBS) and SOW) was significantly reduced.

During the demonstration, the involved companies were able to produce several collaborative documents including a SOW, two quarterly budgets, the initial budget, a continuously updated financial statement, a task order, a coordination protocol, and a final design. All of these were distributed and commented upon using the collaborative tool, with most entered into the document vault to maintain configuration control.

Seamless File Transfers All members of the team were up and functioning on the collaborative tool. This meant that *all* information could be distributed to all members (including suppliers such as Howmet) within minutes, instead of by fax or mail. The team was able to work out protocols for sharing detailed drawings and initial graphics exchange standard (IGES) data, in which Rocketdyne created the initial 2-D drawing, Raytheon created the 3-D PRO-E drawing and IGES file, and MSC used the IGES file to do its stress analysis results and created a mesh that was then used by Rocketdyne to do its thermal analysis. The flow and interdependency of data among the three companies was virtually seamless.

Extensive Use of Collaborative Technology   The team "met," using the Internet Notebook and teleconference capabilities, 96 times. In total, 16 team members were supported on the Internet Notebook including the seven core team members directly responsible for the design. All electronic information was transmitted over the Internet Notebook with no need for other mechanisms. During the course of the project, almost 1000 entries were published in the Internet Notebook containing administrative as well as design data. Initially, the project leader was the only one putting in entries. Over time, more team members became accustomed to putting in entries themselves (with, on the average, 2 to 12 entries created per person per week). Despite the increase in use, team members continued to actively use in-person and phone-based communication, in addition to computer-mediated communication. Thus, this suggests that design work can never be entirely, nor even primarily, computer-mediated.

Concurrent Analysis and Design During Meetings   An advantage of a distributed team is that team members can have access to their personal desktop analytic tools while simultaneously being in a design meeting with others. Thus, tabling decisions until analyses are performed off-line outside the meeting is no longer necessary. This means that the speed with which the design can be reviewed, problems identified, solutions identified, and new analyses conducted can be greatly enhanced. We found that for some functions, such as combustion, stress, and thermal analysis, analysis did not occur concurrently with the generation of design ideas during design meetings. However, for other functions, such as producibility and layout (or detailed drawing), some real-time analysis could occur.

Team Group Process   Team members felt it was a significant accomplishment that they were able to develop a productive working relationship with new coworkers they never saw, who worked at companies about which they knew so little. They were impressed at how open and supportive everyone was on the team. A real esprit de corps had developed for the virtual team.

   In addition, team members felt that, because of the virtual environment, they were more likely to speak their minds and equally participate in the design process. They contrasted this to conventional design where informal face-to-face design discussions often preclude information-sharing and obtaining input from others.

A final accomplishment in the team's group process was the use of the Internet Notebook to document the team's work. Several members felt that the notebook encouraged a much-needed discipline in documenting analysis results and design conclusions for the team to review. The use of the minutes posted in the notebook for each of the 96 computer-mediated teleconferences helped individuals to become quickly updated on missed meetings. Finally, the ability to post entries for members to examine on their own time allowed members to contribute even without attending meetings or in-person discussions.

Lesson Details

Need for Face-to-Face Meetings   The experiment began believing that the entire design process could be done virtually, with the intention to have only one face-to-face meeting: the kickoff meeting. As a result, everything was tried from brainstorming sessions to formal management design reviews to frequent technical meetings—all virtually. As time progressed, it was discovered that many individuals were having face-to-face and telephone conversations and not documenting the results in the notebook. Later, after a design review, it was felt that the team needed to get together in a face-to-face meeting. In addition, the team got together at the end to celebrate and review our lessons learned. The team's desire to have face-to-face meetings provided a valuable lesson about the limits of virtual work. In particular, there are at least three aspects of the concept design process that are best done with people collocated, either as part of their work environment or at a meeting:

1. The interactive creation of new concepts.
2. The resolution of conflicts of interest and opinions which cannot be resolved using data.
3. Conducting an external review of the team's work.

Making Information Public   At the outset, it had been envisioned that all information would be put into the central repository of the electronic notebook. As more experience was gained, a phenomenon of central repositories was recognized: By creating an entry, information takes on more formality and broader distribution than simply oral communication. Because the information is written down and made available to anyone with log-in identification, team members appeared to become quite conscious of what information would be put into the notebook. This consciousness manifested itself by members filtering what they decided to write and members censoring or critiquing what others had written.

Knowledge Management for Knowledge Reuse   The introduction of the Group Communication Support Technology created the paradox of knowledge management: Individual team members could now easily share all information needed; however, the amount of information provided quickly became overwhelming. The information that quickly amassed during the course of the project became overwhelming (almost 1000 entries). This meant that information retrieval became increasingly difficult, particularly in the latter stages of the design process, when hundreds of entries needed to be searched.

Role of Information Technology Support   An information technology support person should help the team by facilitating the development and maintenance of:

- What information should be put into the notebook.
- What identifiers should be attached to published entries.
- How keywords are to be used.
- How to avoid overpublishing someone else's work during a meeting.
- The use of templates for minutes, action items, and decisions.

Kickoff Meeting   Every team, virtual or not, should be exposed to a kickoff meeting. Typically for concept design, at such a meeting team members are introduced, the project objectives are explained, issues of resource availability are discussed, and occasionally technical concerns are raised. Because the team crossed companies and we had learned from our previous pilot that the companies followed different design processes, we particularly felt a need to have the different best-practice design processes shared among the team members and decisions made about what the design process should be for this team.

Several important decisions and information-sharing instances occurred at that meeting.

A learning from this process then was that kickoff meetings for virtual teams may necessitate additional activities and more time than typical kickoff meetings. Using the meeting to have team members describe the various design processes (not just milestones), design assumptions (e.g., use of reference models), design analysis styles (e.g., intuitive versus analytic), design knowledge bases, and standards for file exchange, version control, file viewing, and file manipulation, and then forcing agreement toward one process is needed. Finally, members should use the kickoff meeting to receive training in any software and standards identified.

Managing Cross-Company Virtual Design Teams Managing a cross-company virtual design team demands the same excellent leadership and project management skills as any team needs. These include strong meeting management skills, motivation, and ability to buffer the team from external pressures. In addition, there are new demands placed on virtual team leaders, as managing a team in a virtual environment is more complex than when the team is collocated.

Robust Design Computational System (RDCS) Program

Description

The RDCS program was a three-year, $6.5 million collaborative development effort which started in 1996. The program's purpose was to develop software to enable engineers to effectively complete a complex product design at significantly lower cost. The companies participating in RDCS are Boeing-Rocketdyne, Boeing–St. Louis, Ford, and the MacNeal-Schwendler Corporation. The Defense Advanced Research Projects Agency (DARPA) funded $3.07 million.

The RDCS software developed enables an engineer to:

- Fully explore design options.
- Account for variabilities in materials, processes, and operations in the design of a product.
- Quantify design risks and sensitivities.

Results

The RDCS program is leading to the adoption of 12 years of research and development Boeing-Rocketdyne personnel have conducted in improving the ability to engineer product designs. The program is developing the capability to identify and understand the key parameters that drive a new aerospace or automotive program's cost, performance, support, and schedule. Processes can then be put in place to minimize the effects that changes or uncertainties in these key parameters, such as manufacturing capabilities or the temperature and pressure environment during operation, have on the product. This will lower product costs.

Rocketdyne piloted an application of RDCS with its production engineers working on the X-33 (next-generation Space Shuttle) in 1997. With an engineering analysis of a flange joint that previously had taken two weeks to perform, several hundred analyses of the problem were able to be conducted overnight. This resulted in better understanding and engineering of the flange joint. Ford and Boeing–St. Louis (McDonnell Douglas) are prototyping additional applications and the MacNeal-Schwendler Corporation is evaluating commercialization potential.

The RDCS program is an example of a collaborative program helping a research and development center to sufficiently develop a product to the point that is can be provided to a technology supplier to commercialize and market. Another benefit RDCS has provided the Rocketdyne research and development center is recognition from the production center on the value their new computational tools provide. The resulting credibility and relationship mean closer collaboration between the production and R&D center in future efforts, improving the likelihood of future success.

PDES, Inc.

Description

PDES, Inc., is a private and publicly funded nonprofit consortium of over 20 U.S. and European companies and U.S. government agencies dedicated to the development and implementation of the STEP (Standard for the Exchange of Product Model Data) software interoperability standard. Major end users in most major industries are driving the development, and demanding the adoption of STEP to provide them with a "plug and play" capability among their CAD/CAM/CAE/PDM systems. STEP provides an unambiguous, computer-sensible description of the physical and functional characteristics of a product throughout its life cycle. STEP is the software interoperability standard being evolved through the International Standards Organization (ISO).

Results

Boeing–St. Louis (previously McDonnell Douglas) developed electronic data exchange capabilities between their C-17 facilities in Long Beach,

California, and St. Louis, Missouri, using STEP as the neutral exchange mechanism. Boeing–St. Louis is now using STEP in production to exchange C-17 configuration management data on a daily basis, having reduced the information exchange process from 2 to 10 weeks to overnight.

General Motors' STEP Translation Center is enabling GM divisions, their customers, and suppliers to cooperate more closely on new designs and move them into production in less time and at reduced cost. Solid models of product designs are currently being exchanged.

Lockheed Martin is implementing STEP within engineering design applications for their F-16, F-22, Joint Strike Fighter, F-2, and KTX-2 tactical aircraft. Initial pilot programs have shown a 10 percent improvement in reliability of data exchange, 10 percent process savings for noncomposite parts, and a 50 percent process savings for composites.

Delphi Delco is using STEP in support in providing climate control systems for two major automotive manufacturers who use CAD systems different from Delphi's. This has resulted in a reduction in the time needed to make the needed CAD translations from 24 to 32 hours per part to an average of 30 minutes per part.

Boeing has agreed with United Technologies Corporation/Pratt & Whitney, Rolls-Royce, and GE to use STEP as the production data exchange process to support the 777 and 767-400 extended range aircraft programs. Boeing and the engine companies exchange product data in support of the digital preassembly process, which verifies the form and fit of the parts to integrate the engine and the airplane.

Comments

Interoperability standards are key to society being able to effectively take advantage of the improvements in information and computational technology. The instructions written to use computers (software) are in almost as many different languages as there are career fields. As society and understanding progress, we are learning that people in different career fields need to be able to effectively communicate. This communication includes exchanging information on computers as well as person-to-person communication. Research in establishing standards for computer software interoperability has been ongoing for over a decade.

Hundreds of millions of dollars are spent by industry every year in translating or re-creating software used to design and manufacture products. Progress toward establishing standards and improving the interoperability between different software systems is difficult, and the payback is long-term. However, the payoff for having software interoperability standards that are easy to use will be so large as to be difficult to measure.

Compressing Integrated Product Engineering (CIPE) Using Massively Parallel Processing (MPP) Initiative

Description

The CIPE initiative was a three-year, $48.36 million collaborative development program proposed in 1993 to develop software to take advantage of the improved computational capabilities of the massively parallel supercomputers that had been recently developed. The companies involved were end users and software developers at Ford and Rockwell-Rocketdyne, supercomputer manufacturers Cray and Convex, and software developer and supplier companies Aries Technology and Comco. The National Center for Manufacturing Sciences facilitated the program development. A proposal was submitted to the Defense Advanced Research Projects Agency for $24.18 million in response to Broad Area Announcement (BAA) 93-11. The objective of the proposed research project was to develop computational algorithms that would take advantage of the then emerging high-performance massively parallel processing (MPP) supercomputer architectures.

Comment

Billions of dollars were been spent by the U.S. government to create MPP supercomputers. However, little commercial software was ever written to be able to effectively run on these computational platforms. This contributed to slow market adoption of MPP computational hardware. The emergence of more powerful workstations and personal computers has also limited the market for supercomputers; however, the market for information and computation technologies has yet to be worked out.

APPENDIX H

Computational Aeroacoustics Analysis System (CAAS) Program

Description

The CAAS program was a three-year, $4.1 million collaborative development program that ended in 1998. Boeing-Rocketdyne led the program, which involved Ford as the other end user, the MacNeal-Schwendler Corporation as a software developer and commercialization path, and NASA Marshall, NASA Langley, Stanford University and the University of Southern California as research participants. The program received $1.92 million in cofunding from NASA's Aerospace Industry Technology Program. The CAAS objective was to develop and commercialize software code to model acoustic fields. Acoustic vibration has been the cause of many test failures in the aerospace industry. Car noise is a key design feature in the automotive industry.

Result

While a commercial product did not result from this development effort, a significant amount of development advanced the state of the art in modeling acoustics.

Direct Metal Deposition (DMD) Initiative

Description

The DMD initiative was an effort that existed in 1993 and 1994 to investigate the feasibility of using lasers to manufacture parts by fusing powdered metals. The participants involved in the initiative included end users Hasbro, Ford, Rockwell-Rocketdyne, Baxter Health Care, and Laserfare; hardware technology provider Hobart; materials supplier Crucible; software technology provider MacNeal-Schwendler Corporation; research labs at Los Alamos and the University of Illinois; a testing center at the National Center for Tooling and Precision Components; and organizational support from the National Center for Manufacturing Sciences.

The goal of the initiative was to develop, design, and build a prototype laser/machining cell. Tasks would have included research and development of:

- Optical tooling for delivering laser beams and feeding metallic powder or wire.
- The method of fitting optical tooling into a direct numerical control (DNC) machining center.

- Establishment of communication and central control of the laser/machining cell including the DNC machine.
- The laser unit and the optical tooling.
- In-processing sensing.
- Inert gas supply, vacuum cleaning, oxidation protection, and air/vacuum jets for removing loose metal powder.

An objective was to enable the U.S. machine tool industry to supply the user industry with a machine capable of producing finished metal prototype parts, molds, and dies in one step from a CAD design. It was hoped that this would provide a productivity improvement for users of at least two over conventional practice, with the potential of having a factor of ten improvement in productivity.

Comments

While the DMD team expended a good amount of effort in scoping the R&D that would be needed in software integration, machine control, hardware and process development, sensor development and application, and materials, the team was not able to stay together long enough to pursue any external funding options. There were no known external funding opportunities from the federal government for this type of development during the time period the participants met.

APPENDIX J

Open Supplier Integration Center (OSIC) Initiative

Kodak started championing the OSIC initiative in late 1996 as an effort to establish an integrated, geographically distributed, tool-independent supply chain capable of producing 6 sigma (3.4 defects per million) quality products. This initiative requires that the supplier companies who produce mechanical parts become more closely involved with their major customers in the design of their final products.

The major customer companies supporting the OSIC are Boeing, Ford, Kodak, and Raytheon. Kodak is leading the initiative following a mandate from their president and CEO, George Fisher, to improve the quality of Kodak's products. Active involvement of product parts suppliers in the product design process is required to cost-effectively get to internationally competitive quality levels of less than one defect per million products.

Major customer designers need to work with their parts suppliers to integrate the suppliers' process capabilities into the design process. The integration of process capabilities into the design process requires a sound understanding of the key characteristics driving the product's desired functionality. Once the product's key characteristics are understood, the relevant variables in the suppliers' manufacturing processes can be identified. Process monitoring and refinement methods can then be established to ensure the desired quality.

The challenges involved in integrating supplier inputs into a major customer's design process are considerable. A few of these challenges include:

- New design tools and methods need to be developed and adopted.
- Personnel in design, manufacturing, contracts, accounting, and legal need to think and act outside their present corporate process and culture.
- New ways of measuring personnel performance need to be established.

The OSIC is establishing pilot projects to demonstrate a particular technology, method, or process that can be used in integrating suppliers into their customer's design process. Pilots are sponsored by the major customer companies with the results of the pilots being shared among the OSIC participants. The intent of conducting pilot projects is to address the challenges in small, focused efforts that can demonstrate benefits of using a particular technology or method.

As of 1998, the OSIC is involving the National Tooling and Machining Association, Harbec Plastics and Liberty Tool (two Rochester, New York, area suppliers) and Michigan Spring Company to pilot projects tying suppliers into the design process. The Center for Integrated Manufacturing Studies at the Rochester Institute of Technology is being used as a training site for suppliers and design methodologies, as well as a central repository for OSIC information.

An electronic design environment is being piloted which will allow suppliers and customers to work collaboratively on a design regardless of their geographic location. Pilot projects are using the Agile Information Manufacturing Network to initially provide this environment.

The following functional supplier activities have been identified as those that are necessary to develop and produce the mechanical portion of a new product.

- **Component Supplier.** An organization that has production capability, skills, and knowledge to produce a specific class of component (e.g., sheet-metal, plastic injection molded, cast, machined, etc.).
- **Tooling Supplier.** An organization that has the processes, skills, and knowledge to deliver the physical tools and fixtures required to pro-

duce the product and its components (e.g., epoxy resin molds and dies, conventional molds and dies, etc.).

- **Model Supplier.** An organization that has the processes, skills, and knowledge to convert ideas or concepts into physical entities that can be used for evaluation, demonstration, or manufacturing purposed (e.g., stereolithography, selective laser sintering, conventional machining, etc.).
- **Metrology Supplier.** An organization that has the capability, skills, and knowledge to assess the variability of an "as produced" product or component against the "as specified" intention (e.g., CMM, on-machine probing, process characterization, acceptance testing, etc.). This includes the reverse, an ability to define the specification from an available model or prototype (e.g., laser digitizer).
- **Assembly Supplier.** An organization with capabilities, skills, and knowledge about what is needed to cost-effectively assemble a product or subsystem (e.g., flexible assembly, hand assembly, component handling, etc.).
- **Simulation Supplier.** An organization that has the capabilities, skills, and knowledge to apply basic engineering principles to predict how a component, product, or system will respond to a certain set of stimuli (e.g., stress analysis, tolerance analysis, mold filling, sheet metal forming, work cell function, factory floor work flow, etc.).

It's Kodak's intent to build a capability that will demonstrate how a real product development team, using existing tools, technology, standards, and processes, can rapidly engage these functional suppliers to cost-effectively produce 6 sigma quality products. This demonstration facility will also be used to train interested suppliers to utilize this capability in a way that fits their businesses' needs. It will also offer a platform at which new or emerging capabilities can be evaluated. Because Kodak's needs in this area are not unique, Kodak is working with other companies that have similar needs and/or functional expertise to realize this capability.

APPENDIX K

Examples of Mr. Allen's Networks with Major End Users

Texas Instruments

Gene Allen's first encounter with employees of Texas Instruments (TI) was in the summer of 1990 when he was working as a consultant to the National Center for Manufacturing Sciences (NCMS). NCMS had asked him to help them put together a proposal for a new program that the federal government was starting, the National Institute of Standards and Technology (NIST) Advanced Technology Program (ATP).

TI was a strong, proactive champion for NCMS with the TI vice president for defense electronics, Jimmy Houlditch, also being the chairman of the NCMS board of directors. Senior NCMS management had met with TI senior management earlier in the year to determine if there wasn't a better way to leverage R&D efforts through NCMS. Prior to this period, most of the member companies of NCMS separated their internal R&D into technology development that was critical to the company's future and could not be shared, and technology development that was of less importance that they were comfortable in collaborating on. It was at this meeting that TI decided that it needed to identify some of its key technology development concerns to NCMS to see if it could leverage the technology development it needed. Part of this decision came from TI's realization that it did not have all the resources needed to conduct the needed research itself. Printed Wiring Board (PWB) technology was one of the needed technology development areas TI identified. TI had contacted individuals at Digital Equipment Corporation (DEC), while NCMS had received indications of interest from AT&T, Hamilton Standard division of United Technologies, and Sandia National Laboratories.

NCMS asked Mr. Allen to attend and help coordinate the first meeting, which was held at DEC's Advanced PBW Fabrication Facility in Greenville, South Carolina, in August 1990. Mr. Allen had outlined what needed to be written in the proposal, and was very impressed with the team that had been put together. The individuals at the meeting were some of the best experts in the country on manufacturing PWBs. They knew the business and its problems. Kurt Watchler of TI was the program champion who provided Mr. Allen with most of the technical input for the program proposal, the drafting of which he coordinated. Mr. Watchler and Mr. Allen established a strong working relationship in establishing the PWB program. The collaborative processes developed to manage that program provided the basis for future collaborative development programs Mr. Allen would be involved with. Working with Mr. Watchler and the other end-user champions, most notably, Ted Polakowski of AT&T, they established a program management organization that enabled collaborative research projects to be created and managed in a manner that would meet the program's objectives.

Others from TI who were also fully committed and participating in the effort were Kurt's boss, Phil Gray; TI's chief PWB technologist, Foster Gray; and his deputy, Rick Ricketson. During this time Mr. Allen was the NCMS program manager of the PWB program. His working relations with TI became so close that he felt he was a TI employee.

Phil Gray was instrumental in working with NCMS to identify other potential collaborative development program areas. Phil was to later set up a meeting with Mr. Allen and Peter Lillianthal at AT&T's Bell Laboratories, which served as the foundation for another ATP program focused on developing optoelectronic assembly machines. Phil retired from TI shortly after the PWB program was awarded, being replaced by Allan Hrncir.

In early July 1991, Ed Miller, the president of NCMS, asked Mr.

Allen to attend a meeting of a proposed Feature Based Manufacturing program, which was being hosted by Ford to evaluate the program as a prospect for a proposal to the NIST ATP. Feature Based Manufacturing was a program that had been in formation at NCMS for the previous eight months. The focus was to develop a means to define and exchange software used to describe the features of a physical product, like holes, corners, and edges. Mr. Allen had attended a previous Feature Based Manufacturing program meeting at Pratt & Whitney in December 1990. The presentations at the Ford meeting appeared to be more synergistic than those given a the first PWB meeting.

Those presentations provided the common vision that evolved into the Rapid Response Manufacturing (RRM) program that summer. TI's John Richardson was the principal supplier of the technical content for the RRM proposal, which Gene Allen was again responsible for creating and coordinating. John received a lot of support from Mike Kennedy, who was a key player in TI's Integrated Product and Process Deployment (IPPD) effort. John worked for Allan Hrncir, with whom Mr. Allen was able to establish a good working relationship as well.

Neither the PWB program nor the RRM program would have been established without the proactive support of the TI program champions.

Ford

Mr. Allen's relationship with Ford started at the Feature Based Manufacturing program meeting at the Dearborn Marriott in early July 1991. Larry McArthur, the president and CEO of Aries Technology, had encouraged Ford to get involved in the proposed Feature Based Manufacturing program. Mr. McArthur, a proactive member of the NCMS board of directors, was a strong supporter of collaborative development and wanted to get Aries involved in a program like the PWB program. Mr. McArthur and Mr. Allen had established a good relationship after Mr. Allen visited Aries Technology in the fall of 1990. Aries Technology produced software used to create three-dimensional solid models on a computer that could be analyzed using other software to simulate physics. Ford was the largest customer of Aries, and a partial owner of the company.

Pete Sferro, a senior manager at Ford's Alpha Simultaneous Engineering Center, hosted the Feature Based Manufacturing meeting. Mr. Sferro became the Ford champion for the Rapid Response Manufacturing (RRM) program that evolved out of the Feature Based Manufacturing initiative. Mr. Sferro was a primary driver in the RRM program. He was instrumental in piloting Direct Engineering^{SM} pilot projects in RRM. Direct Engineering^{SM} was a concept originated by Fred Bowling, the director of the Alpha Simultaneous Engineering Center. Direct Engineering^{SM} is a Ford in-house effort to dramatically improve product quality, decrease time to production, and reduce cost. Direct Engineering^{SM} is a methodology that gives the engineer all the applicable design rules, manufacturing rules, system constraints, and best practices during the initial phase of product design. This approach significantly reduces the product redesign that typically occurs because manufacturing or system constraints were not considered early in the design phase. All these rules and best practices are approved and kept up to date by a cross-functional Knowledge Management Organization, composed of subject matter experts from product design, manufacturing, plant layout, production, shipping, and service. The information is delivered to the engineer when it is needed by knowledge-based engineering software tools.

Mr. Sferro and Mr. Allen shared a strong common bond in ensuring that the RRM program was successful. Mr. Allen found that Ford had one of the most progressive corporate cultures in industry. This culture traced its roots to a relationship that had been established between Ford president and CEO Donald Peterson and Edwards Demming, the quality champion largely credited for the improvements in manufacturing quality demonstrated by the Japanese in the 1970s and 1980s.

Larry McArthur arranged for Mr. Allen to meet with Dr. Howard Crabb of Ford during the summer of 1992, and George Joseph in 1993. As manager of CAE functions at Ford's Alpha Simultaneous Engineering Center, Dr. Crabb was largely responsible for acquiring and integrating computational hardware, as well as software, into Ford's design processes. George Joseph worked in Ford headquarters for Dr. John McTague, vice president for corporate research. Mr. Allen worked closely with Dr. Crabb and Mr. Joseph in attempting to establish the CIPE program, and with Dr. Crabb in establishing the CAAS and RDCS programs.

While Mr. Allen came to know a large number of individuals at Ford, it was the relationships with Pete Sferro and Howard Crabb that were key to establishing collaborative programs with Ford. Mr. Allen's introduction to both of these men was through Larry McArthur, who later hired him to work at the MacNeal-Schwendler Corporation (MSC) to do the same thing he was doing at NCMS—put together collaborative development programs. Larry had become president of MSC after MSC merged with Aries Technology in the summer of 1993.

Rocketdyne

As a result of establishing the Rapid Response Manufacturing (RRM) program, Mr. Allen received a call from Steve Babcock in late 1992, to see if he could meet with him and his associate Dr. Bob Carman. Mr. Babcock was from the Rocketdyne division of Rockwell, now Boeing (the leading manufacturer of liquid fueled rocket engines in the United States).

Mr. Babcock coordinated collaborative development programs for Rocketdyne to leverage the internal development efforts of Rocketdyne's group of rocket scientists. Dr. Carman, an energetic and brilliant individual with a PhD in physics from Harvard and extensive experience at Los Alamos and Lawrence Livermore, has a broad perspective and understanding of many of the developments being pursued at Rocketdyne. Dr. Carman has been the program manager for many of Rocketdyne's contractually committed collaborations.

Mr. Babcock had been informed of RRM by Len Allgaier of General Motors (GM) on a visit to the GM Tech Center. Mr. Allgaier told Mr. Babcock that Bob Early was the main person from GM involved in the program and that he might be interested in talking about it. Steve Babcock had worked with both of them earlier in his career when he was at GM. He saw Mr. Early at the next NCMS annual meeting and learned that the project was still being planned, and that they really were struggling to become a team. Mr. Early, therefore, was not willing at that time to discuss details, although he supplied an overview of

RRM and a list of participants and their phone numbers. Mr. Allen was one of those names.

Steve Babcock and Bob Carman flew from California to meet with Mr. Allen in northern Virginia in an effort to help get them involved in collaborative development programs with other NCMS member companies. This meeting started a strong business relationship between Mr. Allen and a number of Rocketdyne individuals over several programs. They exchanged perspectives on the future of manufacturing technology development. The following actions resulted from this meeting:

- A commitment to pursue concurrent engineering with Ford.
- An invitation to Mr. Allen to visit Rocketdyne's facilities in Canoga Park, California.
- Rocketdyne participation in RRM.

CONCURRENT ENGINEERING

Concurrent engineering is the process of integrating all aspects of the product life cycle that require engineering into the initial design process. This is done by developing computer software which facilitates the exchange and modification of product design information that interfaces with all aspects of the product life cycle taken into consideration. It is now sometimes referred to as integrated product and process development, but essentially boils down to pragmatic development and application of computer-based information tools to the design process.

Dr. Carman is a champion of applying a number of different technologies to a variety of applications. His interest in meeting with Mr. Allen was to see if he was aware of the potential of concurrent engineering, and find out if any other major companies were internally investing in concurrent engineering. Mr. Allen had championed the same vision in 1987 while serving as the Economic Development Assistant to Senator Robert Byrd. This vision had been relayed to him in a briefing to Senator Byrd from Dr. Clint Kelly of DARPA. The RRM program was in essence an extension of that vision. The visions Dr. Carman and Mr. Allen had of the potential for concurrent engineering were identical, and independently derived.

Dr. Carman and Mr. Babcock then asked what other companies

could be potential collaborators with Rocketdyne to conduct design-centric R&D. From the companies Mr. Allen was familiar with, Ford had the most progressive design development program. At the end of the meeting, Mr. Allen called Dr. Howard Crabb, who was the director of CAE applications at Ford. Dr. Crabb invited the Rocketdyne personnel to visit Ford, and a meeting was set up for January 1993. This trip coincided with a broad area announcement (BAA) from DARPA to fund the development of multidisciplinary analysis software. This BAA was the precipitating event that brought Ford and Rocketdyne together to develop a collaborative development program to integrate and leverage common design technology development efforts. The meeting at Ford initiated a long-term relationship between Mr. Allen and personnel at Ford and Rocketdyne, which has resulted in several collaborative development programs.

The timing of the meeting and BAA resulted in developing a proposal to DARPA for the cofunding of an effort they called the Compressing Integrated Product Engineering (CIPE) using Massively Parallel Processing (MPP) program. The companies participating in CIPE were Ford, Rockwell-Rocketdyne, Aries, Comco, Convex, Cray, and NCMS. After the CIPE proposal was initially submitted to DARPA in March 1993, the DARPA program manager invited the team in for discussions. It was relayed to them that DARPA had been looking for a proposal like CIPE for two years. Unfortunately, the DARPA budget was redirected the week of the meeting and there were no longer any funds available for the program. It was recommended that the team resubmit the proposal later under the Technology Reinvestment Program (TRP), a multiagency group managed by DARPA. The program was not selected for funding under the TRP. While the CIPE proposal was competitive, it requested a significant amount of federal funding at $22.9 million in a $47.3 million program, and much of the in-kind ($10 million) was in the form of supercomputer time—a lower-quality match than personnel or cash. The cost-effectiveness of computer processing using MPP was starting to be challenged by distributed parallel processing of clusters of workstations, which made additional government investment in MPP less attractive.

After Mr. Allen left NCMS for the MacNeal-Schwendler Corporation (MSC), Rocketdyne approached MSC and Ford to submit three proposals to NASA under the Aerospace Industry Technology Program (AITP), a NASA program paralleling the NIST ATP. These proposals were subsets of what had been proposed in CIPE. The collaborative development proposals submitted to NASA were:

- The Robust Design Computational System (RDCS) program was proposed to develop and commercialize software codes to replace discrete values for product properties and process characteristics with probabilistic functions for those characteristics. This would yield designs that better reflect reality, leading to reductions in the number of prototypes needed and increased operational flexibility of final products.
- The Optimization-Based Aerodynamic Design System program was proposed to develop and commercialize a generic analysis optimization software module. While the program would validate the optimization module to run on a CFD aerodynamics code, it was intended to be structured to tie in to other analysis codes, enabling multidisciplinary optimization.
- The Computational Aeroacoustics Analysis System (CAAS) program was proposed to develop and commercialize software code to model acoustic fields. Acoustic vibration has been the cause of many test failures in the aerospace industry. Car noise is a key design feature in the automotive industry.

Of these, only the CAAS program was selected for funding. The RDCS program was the program Rocketdyne was most interested in. NASA had previously funded about $10 million to develop many of the underlying technologies that provided a foundation for RDCS. The RDCS proposal was resubmitted to DARPA, and this time the program was accepted and placed under contract to receive matching funds in July 1996. Rocketdyne managed both the CAAS and RDCS programs. RDCS has a Steering Group that oversees the program, modeled on the RRM program model. The government contracts are with Rocketdyne, but Ford and MSC provide commercial funding to the efforts through program agreements. MSC's role in these programs is to assist in development and provide a commercialization path for any promising results.

Another action that resulted from Mr. Allen's 1992 meeting with Steve Babcock and Bob Carman was Mr. Allen's visit to Rocketdyne's facilities in Canoga Park, California. At that meeting, Mr. Allen was introduced to a group of 25 senior program managers by Dave Mitchell, a Rockwell vice president. Mr. Mitchell emphasized the need to leverage their internal efforts through collaboration and encouraged them to contact Mr. Allen. In addition to Steve Babcock and Bob Carman, several additional Rocketdyne collaborative development champions were introduced to Mr. Allen, including Dr. Gene Jackson, Dr. Glenn Havskjold, and Mr. Lyle Spiegel. This group of individuals are not only proactive champions for collaboration, but they also have been able to get significant in-kind resource commitments for collaborative programs.

As a result of this meeting, Mr. Allen became a program champion for the Direct Metal Deposition (DMD) initiative. He actively networked the Rocketdyne vision of using a laser to fuse powered metals into a desired shape with the desired properties. The results of this networking were discussed in Chapter 8.

The final action that came from the 1992 meeting Mr. Allen had with Steve Babcock and Bob Carman was an effort to get Rocketdyne involved in the Rapid Response Manufacturing (RRM) program. Interest in RRM was the primary reason they had come from California to northern Virginia to meet Mr. Allen. Actions from this meeting led to a RRM Steering Group meeting at Rocketdyne's Canoga Park facility in 1994. It had become evident even before that meeting that Rocketdyne and the rest of the RRM team shared a similar vision. While Rocketdyne did not become a full official member of RRM, they were invited by Bill Waddell, the NCMS program manager, to attend meetings and participate on specific projects if they wished. Many Rocketdyne contacts and meetings resulted from its RRM collaboration. Some of these led to specific benefits for Rocketdyne, one of which was the software from Cimplex for Generative NC Programming. A user license was obtained to use that product in production. A major initiative that was revealed to Rocketdyne through working with RRM was the Ford Direct Engineering^{SM} initiative. Many of the thoughts and ideas found in Direct Engineering^{SM} had been considered in Rocketdyne's initiative called Rocketdyne Advanced Process Integration and Development (RAPID).

List of Acronyms

AIMS	Agile Infrastructure for Manufactured Systems (program)
AMT	Advanced Manufacturing Technology (organization)
ASME	American Society of Mechanical Engineers
ATP	Advanced Technology Program
BAA	broad agency announcement
CAAS	Computational Aeroacoustics Analysis System
CAD	computer-aided design (software)
CAE	computer-aided engineering (software)
CALS	Continuous Acquisition and Life-Cycle Support (program)
CAM	computer-aided manufacturing (software)
CAM-I	Consortium for Advanced Manufacturing—International
CBD	*Commerce Business Daily* (periodical)
CEO	chief executive officer
CIPE	Compressing Integrated Product Engineering (program)
COA	continuous ordering agreement
CORBA	Common Object Request Broker Architecture
CRADA	cooperative research and development agreement
DARPA	Defense Advanced Research Projects Agency
DMD	direct metal deposition
DNC	direct numerical control
DOD	Department of Defense

DOE	Department of Energy
ECO	engineering change order
ECU	European currency unit
EDM	electronic discharge machine
EU	European Union
FAR	Federal Acquisition Regulation
FTP	file transfer protocol
GUI	graphical user interface
HTML	HyperText Markup Language
IEEE	Institute of Electrical and Electronics Engineers, Inc.
IGES	initial graphics exchange standard
INEEL	Idaho National Engineering and Environmental Laboratory
IP	intellectual property
IPPD	integrated product and process development/deployment
IPR	intellectual property rights
IPT	integrated product team
ISWG	interoperability services working group
IT	information technology
JESSI	Joint European Submicron Silicon Initiative (program)
KBE	knowledge-based engineering (software)
MADE	Manufacturing Automation and Design Exploration (program)
MIT	Massachusetts Institute of Technology
MSC	MacNeal-Schwendler Corporation
NASA	National Aeronautics and Space Administration
NC	numerical control
NCMS	National Center for Manufacturing Sciences
NIFM	National Institute for Flexible Manufacturing
NIIIP	National Industrial Information Infrastructure Protocol
NIST	National Institute of Standards and Technology
NMTA	National Machining and Tooling Association
OEM	original equipment manufacturer
OMB	Office of Management and Budget
OMG	Object Management Group
OSIC	Open Supplier Integration Center
PDM	product data management (software)
PWB	printed wiring board
R&D	research and development

RaDEO	Rapid Design Evaluation and Optimization (program)
RAPID	Rocketdyne Advanced Process Integration and Development (program)
RDCS	Robust Design Computational System (program)
RFP	request for proposal
RRM	Rapid Response Manufacturing (program)
RTD	research and technical development
SBA	Small Business Administration
SBIR	small business innovative research
SLICE	Simple Low-Cost Innovative Engine
SME	Society for Mechanical Engineers
SOW	statement of work
STEP	Standard for the Exchange of Product model data
TEIN	Technical Entrepreneurs and Intrapreneurs Network (organization)
TEWE	Technologies for Enterprise-Wide Engineering (program)
TRC	Technologies Research Corporation
TRP	Technologies Reinvestment Project
VRML	Virtual Reality Modeling Language
WBS	work breakdown structure

Index